WILLIAM PENN

William Penn

A RADICAL, CONSERVATIVE QUAKER

J. WILLIAM FROST

THE PENNSYLVANIA STATE UNIVERSITY PRESS
UNIVERSITY PARK, PENNSYLVANIA

Library of Congress Cataloging-in-Publication Data

Names: Frost, J. William (Jerry William), author.
Title: William Penn : a radical, conservative Quaker / J. William Frost.
Description: University Park, Pennsylvania : The Pennsylvania State University Press, [2024] | Includes bibliographical references and index.
Summary: "Investigates the religious life of William Penn, and his importance to the history of Quakers and early Pennsylvania"—Provided by publisher.
Identifiers: LCCN 2024035999 | ISBN 9780271097770 (hardback)
Subjects: LCSH: Penn, William, 1644–1718—Religion. | Quakers—Pennsylvania—Biography.
 | Quakers—Pennsylvania—History—17th century. | Quakers—Pennsylvania—History—18th century. | LCGFT: Biographies.
Classification: LCC F152.2 .F94 2024 | DDC 974.802092 [B]—dc23/eng/20240814
LC record available at https://lccn.loc.gov/2024035999

Copyright © 2024 J. William Frost
All rights reserved
Printed in the United States of America
Published by
The Pennsylvania State University Press,
University Park, PA 16802–1003

The Pennsylvania State University Press is a member of the Association of University Presses.

It is the policy of The Pennsylvania State University Press to use acid-free paper. Publications on uncoated stock satisfy the minimum requirements of American National Standard for Information Sciences—Permanence of Paper for Printed Library Material, ANSI Z39.48–1992.

*To Maxine and Jon,
who exemplify the best of friendship
and scholarship*

CONTENTS

List of Illustrations | viii
Preface | ix
Acknowledgments | xviii
List of Abbreviations | xix

1 Introducing William Penn | 1
2 Convinced | 34
3 The Dissident Quakers | 49
4 The Business of Quaker Meeting | 64
5 The Quaker Quest for Religious Liberty | 82
6 Moralist | 106
7 Preacher | 132
8 William Penn in Myth and History | 148
9 Afterthoughts: The Enigmatic Mr. Penn | 175

Additional Reading | 183
Appendix: Penn and the Bible | 185
Notes | 192
Index | 226

ILLUSTRATIONS

1. Francis Place, *Portrait of William Penn*, n.d. | xi
2. *The Quakers Synod*. From Francis Bugg, *The Pilgrim's Progress from Quakerism to Christianity* (1698) | 100
3. *William Penn's Treaty with the Indians*. Engraving by David Hall from the painting by Benjamin West, 1775 | 154
4. Edward Hicks, *The Peaceable Kingdom*, ca. 1827–35 | 160

PREFACE

William Penn is the best known and yet the least understood of all the founding fathers of seventeenth-century America. To those who live in the Philadelphia area, his image is omnipresent. All thirty-seven feet and fifty-three thousand pounds of his statue look down from Philadelphia's City Hall, but whether he approves or disdains what we do is unclear. He extends one hand toward Shackamaxon Creek, where he signed a peace treaty with the Lenape, although there is no documentary evidence of this event. He represents respect for Native Americans and peace, both important in early Pennsylvania history and prominent elements in his Quaker faith. In the other hand he holds the 1701 Frame of Government, which symbolizes his commitment to religious liberty and respect for elected representatives. Of course, this part of the statue oversimplifies Penn by ignoring his support for monarchy and his unhappiness with what he saw as the Pennsylvania Assembly's power grab and the weakening of proprietary power in this new constitution.

A video made in 2015 confirmed that today some Philadelphians think the statue atop City Hall depicts Benjamin Franklin.[1] They should read the introductory chapter summarizing Penn's life and times. My ideal reader is a person who knows a little about Penn and wants to understand why he became a Quaker, how that decision shaped his later life, and when he became significant in the history of Quakers and early Pennsylvania.

Since he disapproved of painted images glorifying any man, Penn would have been troubled both by his monument and by the Second French Empire building that it graces. A further incongruity is his wearing a beaver hat and an elaborate coat with many extra buttons and lace sleeves—very fashionable in the seventeenth century. Quakers wanted simplified dress they called "plain style." Plain the hat, coat, and lace are not.[2] There are many images of him, but we don't know whether Penn was actually the subject in any of the frequently reproduced paintings and drawings of him (fig. 1).[3] A false picture of Penn does no harm and fulfills our desire to see how he could have looked. Because Penn, in life and reputation, presented a vision of a benevolent governor creating a tolerant, prosperous, and moral society, he reminds Pennsylvanians, on the rare occasions on which they think of him, that they would do well to live up to his ideals.

Many residents of Pennsylvania believe that the state is named after him, although in actuality King Charles II bestowed that honor on his father, the naval hero Admiral William Penn. The colony owes its existence not to the peaceful son William but to the debt owed to his warrior father for feeding British sailors in the wars with Holland.[4] Still, the belief is essentially correct, because there would have been no Pennsylvania without the court connections, lobbying, and skill with which the Quaker son approached the king. Charles II owed many debts that he neglected to pay, and although historians have offered various reasons why the monarch granted this land, all are speculative, because he never said. There is good written evidence, however, of what the younger William Penn wanted for his new colony.

Penn is often conflated with the religious group that he joined as a young man, the Religious Society of Friends, or Quakers. Unlike other churches, Quakers are identified with a particular American state. There is no such entity as a Methodist or Roman Catholic state (Puritan Massachusetts and Morman Utah come closest), but the Commonwealth of Pennsylvania is "the Quaker state"—an odd juxtaposition because the Quakers were a minority within a few years of Pennsylvania's founding and today represent less than 1 percent of its population. Whatever legitimacy comes from the name, members of the Society of Friends controlled the Pennsylvania General Assembly (as the state legislature is called) for the first ninety years of its existence, and there are Quaker meeting houses (other denominations call such structures "churches") throughout the Commonwealth, though they are concentrated in the eastern part of the state.[5]

In addition, though they have no connection to the religious group, there is Quaker State Motor Oil, a Quaker moving company, a Quaker real estate firm, the Quaker Oats Company, and dozens of other businesses that use "Quaker" in their names. Sometimes the name is used ironically; during Prohibition, the largest producer of illegal booze in Philadelphia was the Quaker Brewing Company. Wm Penn Perfecto cigars, manufactured in Pennsylvania and advertised as the "mildest cigar ever made," sold for five cents, although the retailer could sell them for no less than four and no more than six cents apiece. (There is no evidence that Penn smoked, but if he had, he would

FIG. 1 | Francis Place, *Portrait of William Penn*, n.d. The family that owned this portrait for many years thought it was Penn, but modern examination has proved this unlikely. © Britain Yearly Meeting of the Religious Society of Friends (Quakers). Courtesy of the Historical Society of Pennsylvania.

have smoked a pipe.) Sometimes the images conflate Penn and Quakers; the generic benevolent man supposedly dressed like Penn on the Quaker Oats label is supposed to convey the high quality of the oats, not any religious significance. Strawbridge and Clothier, formerly a leading department store in Philadelphia, used a model of Penn shaking hands with a Native American. The Quaker-style clothing in both images is based on Benjamin West's 1771 painting *William Penn's Treaty with the Indians* (see fig. 3) rather than on seventeenth-century garb. Sometimes Penn stands alone, as in the logo of the Colonial Penn Insurance Company, whose building towers over and provides spectacular views of Independence Hall, surrounding colonial-era buildings, and the Liberty Bell, the biblical inscription on which proclaims "liberty throughout the land and to all the inhabitants thereof," celebrating Penn's 1701 Frame of Government, though there is only a later oral tradition linking it with the Liberty Bell.

Preface | xi

Penn's policies still affect daily life in Philadelphia. His plan for the city named streets going east-west for trees and assigned numbers to streets going north-south, establishing a grid pattern that became normative for many American cities. The four squares he envisioned still endure as parks, now named Franklin, Logan, Washington, and Rittenhouse; there is also a central square that replaced a reservoir. The area on the bank of the Delaware River where he first came ashore is now named Penn's Landing. The site of his house is a park filled with plaques recording his sayings. In New England, the town is the basic local unit of government, but in Pennsylvania it is the county, as Penn intended, and people lived on their farms rather than in villages clustered around a green. At some point in virtually all television coverage of Philadelphia sports events, the announcers will refer to Philadelphia as the city of "brotherly love"—assuming that Penn intended the Greek meaning. The term can also be used as a sarcastic reference to the failure of the city's residents to live up to Penn's high expectations.

Penn would have approved of his identification with religious liberty. From the day he became a Quaker until his incapacitating stroke in 1712, he consistently advocated freedom of worship. In England, where the only legal worship was in a state church supported by tithes, he desired liberty of belief and worship, though he did not seek to end other privileges of the Church of England. In West Jersey and Pennsylvania, he wanted no established church, no tithe, and either no militia or no one forced to serve in it. Freedom of belief and worship were inalienable rights, but Penn also thought that government should enforce clear moral standards that were learned through Bible study, reasonable thought, and religious experience. He feared anarchy, desired deference and order, saw strict morality as necessary for any society, and advocated laws to prohibit all licentious behavior. A major goal in all of Penn's writings and political activities was the creation of a civil polity that would promote internal and external harmony. As an observer of violence within and outside the state, he advocated policies designed not just to prevent war but to foster peace, and he was thus the first exponent of what would become the Quaker peace testimony in the twentieth century. He was also an English imperialist and saw no contradictions among colonization, empire, and harmony among states and with Native Americans.

William Penn remains the most comprehensively studied seventeenth-century Friend, a prominence that is well deserved. Through his writings, debates, political agitation, and statesmanship, he made significant contributions to Quaker, English, and American life as a theologian, political theorist, courtier to three kings and two queens, founder and lawgiver of Pennsylvania, and Philadelphia city planner. Penn wrote two classic works on the moral life—one based on religious discipline and the other on rational prudence. As a pacifist, he advocated a parliament of European kingdoms and a union of British North American colonies so as to avoid war. Penn converted to Quakerism around 1667, and for the next forty-five years he preached, lobbied, traveled, and wrote on behalf of his fellow believers. He published more pages than any other Friend except George Fox. His willingness publicly to espouse controversial positions landed him in prison, made him enemies, and earned him respect. Historians, journalists, antiquarians, and many Friends have sought to understand this complicated man—a fascinating but also an elusive person. He was a rebel who supported authority, an aristocratic plain Quaker.

The primary sources on Penn are massive and include Joseph Besse's two-volume *Collection of the Works of William Penn* (1726, 1,800 pages) and Richard S. Dunn and Mary Maples Dunn's five-volume *Papers of William Penn*, which comprise four volumes numbering three thousand pages, plus an additional volume of bibliography, edited by Edwin Bronner and David Fraser, covering all the early editions of Penn's published writings.[6] The Historical Society of Pennsylvania's microfilm edition of Penn's correspondence comprises fourteen reels. It is not difficult to learn what Penn wanted us to understand about his life and thought.

Although we know more about Penn than about any other seventeenth-century Quaker, and even given the voluminous primary and secondary sources, significant gaps in our knowledge remain. Some of these lacunae may have been caused by Penn's attempts to protect himself after the Glorious Revolution in 1688 and the deposition of James II, with whom he had been closely associated. There are no surviving letters from Penn to his first wife, Gulielma, from his first visit to Pennsylvania, although she mentions having received several.[7] His second wife, Hannah, her sons, or later descendants may have discarded papers for various reasons, including fear that his support for King James II could be used to blacken his reputation, Hannah's possible jealousy of Gulielma, or perhaps just a desire for privacy.

Although Penn wrote accounts as a traveling minister on the Continent and in Ireland and left a fragmentary story of his life in one short period, nothing comparable to Fox's or other Quakers' journals has survived.[8] Even if, like many other prominent Friends, Penn had kept a diary, I doubt that it would have shed much light on what we would like to know. What was his mother like? What were his attitudes toward his brother, his sister, his daughter

Letitia? Who were his friends, if any, and how well did he get along with non-elite Quakers? Did he recognize his evolution from Christian humanist to apocalyptic radical, and then to orthodox authoritarian? Penn would have insisted that we can know him as a man who experienced the Inward Christ and attempted to follow its guidance in daily life. All our other questions, he believed, were irrelevant.

There are many modern biographies of Penn. The best older ones, William I. Hull's *William Penn: A Topical Biography* (1937) and Catherine Owens Peare's *William Penn: A Biography* (1956), are based on extensive reading in original sources, but both reflect a liberal or modernist understanding of Quakerism that has been significantly revised in recent years. Two-thirds of the footnotes in the Wikipedia entry on Penn cite Bonamy Dobrée's *William Penn, Quaker and Pioneer* (1932) or Hans Fantel's *William Penn: Apostle of Dissent* (1971), but the entry ignores Harry Emerson Wildes's *William Penn* (1973). All of these works contain dubious assertions and repeat stories for which there are no primary sources. The extensive documentation in the Dunns' *Papers of William Penn* required a rethinking of all earlier biographies. Mary Geiter's *William Penn* (2000) is a study of Penn in power and a corrective to earlier laudatory accounts, and instead stresses his political skills and business acumen. John Moretta's *William Penn and the Quaker Legacy* (2006) is a readable popular version designed for undergraduates, but it lacks adequate documentation. Andrew Murphy's *William Penn: A Life* (2019) makes excellent use of Penn's papers and of Murphy's own research on political theory, and it deserves to become the standard scholarly biography of Penn.[9]

Although I have learned much from these books, they were not very helpful on the topics that most interest me as a scholar of American religions who specializes in Quaker history. For example, all of them ignore Penn's few published sermons, even though preaching was a major activity for most of his adult life. None deals with Quaker writings on religious liberty before Penn's conversion. To cite the most recent example, Murphy spends more time on a libelous account of Penn's alleged romantic involvement in Ireland than on the contents of the two editions of *No Cross, No Crown*, nor does he discuss the differences between the two editions or why the second has remained in print for more than three hundred years.[10]

The three major influences on Penn's life were seventeenth-century political events, his social status, and his Quakerism. This is not a book for those interested only in Penn's theology, politics, business, theories of government, or contributions to the shaping of Pennsylvania. There are good books and articles on each of these subjects, but even professional scholars rarely have the time (or patience) to read them all. (See the "Additional Reading" section at the end of the book.)

The focus of this book is Penn's religious faith and his roles within the Society of Friends. Each of the first eight chapters is designed to stand alone, even at the risk of minor duplication. Chapter 1 provides an overview of Stuart England, the evolution of the Society of Friends, an account of Penn's parents, and a summary of his life. Penn's writings show evolving interests, partially because he adjusted to the major changes in England and the Quaker faith between 1660 and 1712. Penn's conversion around 1667 changed the trajectory of his life; instead of a would-be courtier, he became a leading advocate for the Quaker form of Christianity. Chapter 2 utilizes all of the extant documents on Penn's conversion to show why it occurred and what it meant to him. Chapters 3 and 4 deal with Penn's roles within the Society of Friends. He had greater wealth, better education, and higher social status than virtually all other Friends, but Quakers considered such metrics of little religious significance. How did Penn fit his strong personality into the organizational framework being established by English Friends? Chapter 3 shows that Penn combined his subjective religious experience with a demand that Quakers who publicly dissented must submit to the guidance of the leaders of London Yearly Meeting. Beginning in the 1670s and for the next thirty years, Penn sought to define and enforce Quaker unity. Diversity was allowed, but questioning the authority of ministers, including Penn, was not. Chapter 4 examines Penn's importance in shaping Quaker policies during the reign of James II, throughout the Keithian schism of the 1690s, in the debate over whether the English government's form of affirmation was really an oath, and in the context of the increasing conservatism of early eighteenth-century Quakers. For Friends, the essence of the Quaker religion was an encounter with the divine in the meeting for worship. Penn's leadership rested upon his ability as a preacher. For years he "traveled in the ministry" in England, the Low Countries, and America. An outsider took down in shorthand twelve of his sermons in various meetings in London in 1693–94. These sermons show what Penn considered to be the essence of religion and are addressed in chapter 7 and the appendix.

Chapters 5 and 6 deal with Penn's writings on religious liberty and morality that were ostensibly addressed to outsiders but were read and approved by Friends. On the issue of religious liberty, Penn followed a policy of "walk when we must, run when we can," with walking appropriate to England and running to Pennsylvania. Penn's advocacy of freedom of conscience echoed ideas he encountered in France that were discussed during the Commonwealth period and expressed by early Quakers. In many treatises, Penn employed scripture, church history, reason, English history, and pragmatism, and he changed his arguments depending on his audience. At first he advocated only freedom to worship and an end to persecution of dissenters, but he soon extended such protections to Roman Catholics. Although he insisted that the privileges of the Church of England would not be compromised by these protections, Penn did not specify what this meant. In Pennsylvania, by contrast, there would be no tithes, no oaths, and no militia, and all Christians (including Roman Catholics) could serve in any political office. (After 1705, in response to demands from the Crown, Pennsylvania would deny Catholics naturalization and political office, but open worship continued.) His Quaker contemporaries appreciated Penn as a moralist, and his major treatises on ethics—*No Cross, No Crown* (1669; 2nd ed., 1682) and *Some Fruits of Solitude in Reflections and Maxims* (1693; he published a sequel in 1702)—are analyzed in chapter 6. As late as 1679, his *Address to Protestants* could threaten hellfire, invoke scriptural literalism, stress personal piety, cite natural law, and rely on reason to reduce Christianity to its essence. In 1693 and 1702, reflecting the changing times, Penn's moral advice relied on reason and advocated adjusting to society rather than mortification and salvation. Soon after his death, Penn became a hero to Quakers in Pennsylvania and England, and then a symbol of religious liberty in America. In order to separate legend and fact, chapter 8 examines four myths or legends about Penn: the story of when he gave up his sword, the circumstances of his alleged treaty with the Native Americans, the meaning of his "holy experiment," and the features of his evolving posthumous reputation. The brief final chapter, "Afterthoughts," addresses Penn's accomplishments and weaknesses and the difficulty of understanding his complex character.

Readers should keep in mind that focusing on Penn's religion risks oversimplifying his larger significance. Such a focus neglects his role as a member of the upper class with properties in Ireland and England and ignores his skill in dealing with the Crown and Parliament as he obtained and developed in Pennsylvania an enormous tract of land and substantial powers of government. Biographers grapple with understanding modern men and women whose families and friends they can interview. Although I began reading about Penn in the 1960s, taught about him for many years in history and religion classes, and have written and edited articles and books on him and related subjects, William Penn remains to me a man of contradictions, an enigmatic Quaker founding father. He was a radical when converting to an outlawed sect, enduring prison, advocating religious liberty, reforming criminal justice, seeking a moral transformation in England, and attempting to create a Christian utopia in Pennsylvania. As a conservative, he never questioned the existence of the monarchy and supported Charles II and James II, enjoyed the support of the nobility, disapproved of revolution, opposed so-called schismatics within the Society of Friends, and demanded deference from the settlers in Pennsylvania.

ACKNOWLEDGMENTS

Brian Drayton, Stephen W. Angell, H. Larry Ingle, members of Henniker Friends Meeting (Bob and Connie Brooks, Marion Baker, and Ann Luder), John Pirris, and Sandi Lawrence read individual chapters or, in some cases, the complete manuscript at various stages. Two outside reviewers for Penn State Press provided valuable suggestions. Penn State provided an excellent (and therefore demanding) editor in Suzanne Wolk. Special thanks go to Jordan Landes, a knowledgeable historian of seventeenth-century England and a careful reader. I owe a special debt to the staff of the Friends Historical Library, Swarthmore College, particularly Pat O'Donnell, Celia Caust-Ellenbogen, and Susanna Morikawa, for researching and answering dozens of queries, sending articles, suggesting sources, editing chapters, and listening to me for many years drone on about Penn.

The original minutes of the London Yearly Meeting, Meeting for Sufferings, and Second Day Morning Meeting of Ministers are at the Library of the Religious Society of Friends in London and are also available on microfilm there. I am grateful to the library for allowing me to purchase copies, which are deposited at the Friends Historical Library at Swarthmore College and are available to scholars via interlibrary loan. My citations of these minutes are to the microfilm copies in London. The dates of LYM, MFS, and MMM minutes use the Friends' dating system, that is, English Old Style, which followed the Julian calendar, the new year beginning in March. Thus 23/3/1702 refers to May 23, 1702. This dating style was in effect until 1752, when it was replaced by the Gregorian calendar, with the new year beginning on January 1. For meetings held in January, February, and March, clerks occasionally give a double year—e.g., 1701/2 (a practice followed by some modern historians); to confuse matters further, one MFS clerk gave the date in the order year, month, day. I have followed the original spelling and punctuation in quotations from these minutes but have removed italics.

ABBREVIATIONS

DSP   *Diary of Samuel Pepys*, edited by Robert Latham and William Matthews, 11 vols. (Berkeley: University of California Press, 1970–83)

FOS   *Some Fruits of Solitude in Reflections and Maxims* (London: Thomas Northcott, 1693)

LYM   London Yearly Meeting

MFS   London Meeting for Sufferings

MMM   Second Day Morning Meeting of Ministers, London

MPWP   Microfilm Papers of William Penn, 14 reels, Historical Society of Pennsylvania, Philadelphia

NCNC   *No Cross, No Crown, or several Sober Reasons against Hat-Honour, Tituler-Respects, You to a single Person, with the Apparel and Recreations of the Times* [. . .] (London: Andrew Sowle, 1669; 2nd ed., London: Benjamin Clark, 1682)

PWP   *The Papers of William Penn*, vols. 1–4, edited by Richard S. Dunn, Mary Maples Dunn, et al. (Philadelphia: University of Pennsylvania Press, 1981–87); vol. 5, edited by Edwin B. Bronner and David Fraser (Philadelphia: University of Pennsylvania Press, 1986)

WWP   *A Collection of the Works of William Penn*, edited by Joseph Besse, 2 vols. (London: J. Sowle, 1726)

Chapter 1

INTRODUCING WILLIAM PENN

To understand William Penn, it is necessary to take him down from the tower and put him in historical context, or what is often termed "the life and times," although context comes first here. This biography looks at seventeenth-century England, the Quakers, Penn's family, and the major events in Penn's career.

PENN'S CONTEMPORARIES

If the reign of Elizabeth I was England's golden age, the period of Penn's life (1644–1718) is a silver age marked by major accomplishments in science, literature, and architecture. In science, Isaac Newton was at Cambridge University at the same time Penn was at Oxford. Newton's *Principia Mathematica* (1684) sought to understand through mathematics the physical world and the laws of motion and gravity. Penn socialized with Robert Boyle's family, prominent Irish landowners, and many of us learned of Boyle's law on the diffusion of gases in physics class. King Charles II was a patron of the Royal Society of London for Improving Natural Knowledge and is the only English monarch who had his own laboratory. Penn was not a practicing scientist, but he was a member of the Royal Society, sent back specimens from America, and sought to practice scientific agriculture.[1]

In literature, John Bunyan's *Pilgrim's Progress* was a basic text for evangelical Protestants for two hundred years.[2] Penn probably never met John Milton, whose essays and poems, including *Paradise Lost*, are monumental achievements, but he was a close friend of Milton's secretary, Thomas Ellwood, and lived nearby. Penn praised the writings of John Donne, and it would have been hard to escape the poetry of other metaphysical poets, such as Andrew Marvell, or the epics and satires of John Dryden.[3] Penn condemned the reading of popular romances, but he sought to ease the punishment of Daniel Defoe for writing a satire of high church Anglicans.[4] Defoe's *Robinson Crusoe* is considered the first English novel and is a fascinating mélange of Christian conversion, travel narrative, and justification of imperialism and slavery. As a satirist, Defoe was less accomplished than Jonathan Swift, whose *Gulliver's Travels* exposed the absurdities of English class society.[5] Swift knew Penn well enough to praise his conversation and disagree with Bishop of Salisbury Gilbert Burnet's negative view. Penn and the philosopher and political theorist John Locke shared Whig principles and knew of each other's writings; both men advocated religious toleration, but only Penn advocated giving Catholics freedom to worship and never supported revolution.[6]

In the aftermath of the Great Fire of London in 1666, Christopher Wren rebuilt St. Paul's Cathedral, fifty-three London parish churches, and the Royal Naval College in Greenwich.[7] Penn would design Philadelphia as a "greene country town" to avoid fire and plague, and Wren's principles would be exemplified in many of its brick buildings, including Independence Hall.

The cultural achievements of Stuart England are more impressive when one considers that 75 percent of women and 50 percent of men were illiterate.[8] (Scholars estimate literacy by counting signatures on documents. By today's standards, even a second-grader would qualify as literate.) Craig Muldrew, in 2012, concluded that "the middling sort of life was intensely financially insecure" and that "the poor formed at least 50 percent of consumers in society." A second estimate is that 50 percent of the population experienced poverty at some time during their lives.[9] Penn hoped to improve the life of the poor by curtailing the ostentatious consumption of the rich and ending the persecution of dissenters.

The seventeenth century is now labeled "a little ice age" because of the unusually cold weather, which resulted in bad harvests. In the 1690s there were five such harvests and Scotland and France suffered famine.[10] Malnutrition and disease combined to increase susceptibility to the plague, which remained a constant reality. Penn advised living in the country, though he grew up near London and often kept lodgings there. London's population grew steadily through rural migration, reaching four hundred thousand by 1700, but its death rate always exceeded its birth rate.[11] In 1664 the Penn family fled the bubonic plague by moving to the country. Approximately a hundred thousand Londoners died; in 1666 the Great Fire destroyed one-third of the city, leaving eighty thousand people homeless. (Fearing the fire, Penn's father buried his wine and Samuel Pepys's parmesan cheese in the backyard.)[12] And although insurance was available for shipping, coverage for homeowners did not exist. One effect of the fire was to kill the rats whose fleas spread the plague, potentially reducing transmission and expediting the end of London's last outbreak.

William Penn lived through three revolutions, three wars with Holland, two wars with Spain, and two with France.[13] He was born in the midst of a civil war often called the Puritan Revolution, though modern scholars call it the Wars of the Three Kingdoms because battles were fought among the English and with the Scots and the Irish. The war led to the execution of Charles I and the creation of the Protectorate or Commonwealth under Oliver Cromwell, which lasted until 1660, when Parliament restored Charles II to the throne.[14] A second revolution, against the Roman Catholic James II in 1688, was relatively peaceful in England but resulted in major battles against the Scots and Irish. The wars against the Dutch were not ideological but stemmed from commercial rivalry and a desire to monopolize the slave trade. The Dutch traded with the English colonies in the New World and supplied the Caribbean sugar islands with slaves. Penn's father became a naval hero in England's victories in the first two Dutch wars and a scapegoat for its defeat in the third. Admiral Penn owned a slave and his son owned, bought, and sold men, never expressing misgivings about the slave trade or slavery.[15]

All English governments in Penn's lifetime experienced major rebellions. Because he grew up on Tower Hill in London, the young Penn could have seen the heads of rebels prominently displayed on the Tower walls. In addition, Penn heard stories of violence. His mother's first husband died in the Irish uprising of 1641 and lost his lands; his father's brother was a merchant in Spain and had married there. The Inquisition arrested and tortured this brother, confiscated his estate, and made his wife marry a Roman Catholic. A lawyer whom Penn employed, a Catholic, though innocent of plotting, was arrested and executed in the Titus Oates anti-Catholic hysteria of 1679. Algernon Sidney, the candidate Penn supported for the Exclusion Parliament in 1679, was arrested and executed for treason in 1682. When Penn was accused of treason in 1692, he wisely went into hiding until he could clear his name.

Success at court in seventeenth-century England required finesse or adaptability in dealing with the power of Oliver Cromwell, the immorality of Charles II, the stubborn Catholicism of James II, the military stoicism of William III, and the pro-Anglican virtues of Queens Mary and Anne. Penn knew, advised, lobbied, and remained loyal to each monarch, but he was influential only during the brief reign of James II, whom he later called a friend.[16] In retrospect, historians see this government instability as a consequence of the ill-defined relationship between the power of Parliament and that of the monarchy over taxation, foreign policy, and religion. Not until the reign of George I and the failure of the 1715 rebellion for the young Pretender, the son of James II, would England enjoy a secure establishment of church, king, and Parliament.

After spending eleven years in exile, Charles II (r. 1660–85) wanted to keep his throne, guarantee the legitimacy of succession to his brother, and enjoy life. He had at least ten mistresses and fourteen illegitimate children, and he provided well for his ladies and his offspring.[17] The duplicity of the monarch, the extravagant lifestyle and corruption of the court and aristocracy, and the constant changes in advisers and policies made relations with a strongly royalist Parliament difficult and contributed to a constitutional crisis over the succession in 1679–81. After 1660, the experiment in limited religious toleration, initiated by necessity by Cromwell, came to an end, not because the new king wished it but owing to the insistence of Cavalier Parliaments that weakness in the Church of England and the challenges caused by Presbyterians and Independents had contributed to the late revolution and might lead to another. Allegedly, the unity of the realm had suffered because of the proliferation of sects during and after the fighting; as a result, Baptists, Quakers, Muggletonians, and the more respectable dissenting churches could not engage in public worship and had to pay tithes to the established Church of England. Between 1662 and 1665, Parliament passed the Act of Uniformity, the Five Mile Act, and the Conventicle Act (passed again in 1670), making only Anglican worship lawful and forbidding public worship by dissenters within five miles of town; the king suspended these laws in 1672, but Parliament forced him to back down the following year.[18] The English government's persecution of dissenters was erratic, depending upon the fears of local magistrates and Parliament's desire to eradicate religious dissent through fines and imprisonment. By the late 1670s, the Commons could pass bills granting some form of toleration, but the Lords refused to agree. Fear of Holland and sectarians subsided in the face of threats caused by the claim of the Roman Catholic James, Duke of York, to the throne and the French king Louis XIV's expansionist foreign policy.[19] The emergent Whig faction sought to create a common Protestant alliance against Catholics, James, and France by advocating religious toleration. After 1680, Charles II ruled without Parliament and persecution was as rigorous as it had been in the early 1660s. Louis XIV's revocation in 1685 of the Edict of Nantes, which had granted toleration to Calvinists in certain areas, and the rising power of France contributed to paranoia about the influence of Roman Catholics in Britain. Paradoxically, at just the moment when Charles II's financial problems were easing thanks to a secret alliance with and subsidy from France, he suspended Parliament, allowed (or at least did nothing to hinder) persecution, and granted Penn a colony in the New World. That decision is the more puzzling because Penn had been an advocate of the Whig opposition, a supporter of Parliament, and a prominent defender of religious toleration.[20]

In 1685, the Roman Catholic James II became king, released Friends from prison, suspended the most onerous laws against Catholics and dissenters, and attempted to pack Parliament with supporters of toleration. James easily suppressed a rebellion led by Charles's illegitimate son, the Duke of Monmouth, but he frightened the governing class of Anglicans, and many Presbyterians and Independents, by bringing Catholics into the government, creating a standing army in Ireland led by Catholic officers, centralizing power, and—perhaps most important—having a son in 1688, which meant that the monarchy would not pass to his Protestant daughter, Mary, the wife of William of Orange. The result was the so-called Glorious Revolution, in which James fled and Parliament recognized William and Mary as reigning monarchs.[21] Parliament soon passed a toleration act allowing Protestants, but not Catholics, to worship but restricted high government offices and membership in Parliament to members of the Church of England. Penn, as a supporter of James and thus under suspicion, played no role in achieving toleration, but he went into hiding and the Crown seized control of Pennsylvania. While in forced seclusion, Penn wrote the first history of Friends, classic defenses of Quaker beliefs, a proposal for means to avoid war, and maxims on moderate conduct. In 1694 King William restored the colony to Penn, but on the condition that he provide for its defense and return to Pennsylvania to reform the government. Penn was initially welcomed on his return to the colony in 1699–1701, but disputes over land and the power of the Pennsylvania General Assembly meant that the 1701 Frame of Government brought no harmony and no solution to his chronic indebtedness.

Under the reigns of William and Mary and Queen Anne, Penn spent his time on the defensive, trying to preserve his colony from being taken over by the Crown and to defend his prerogatives from the Board of Trade, restive Pennsylvania Quaker politicians, and unhappy Anglican settlers.[22] Although he attempted to preserve Pennsylvania's distinctive freedoms in negotiations with the Crown, in 1702 Penn offered to sell the power of government of the colony, a sign of his desperate need to pay his debts and an acknowledgment that his utopian hope that Pennsylvania might become a new Jerusalem, a Christian utopia, had failed.[23] Badgered by demands for money from the family of his deceased steward, Philip Ford, Penn spent time in debtors' prison until the courts adjudicated what he owed and Quaker friends paid that amount, taking a mortgage on Pennsylvania as security. That England was at war with France almost constantly, with only five years of peace between 1689 and 1713, made pacifist Pennsylvania an anomaly in the emerging British Empire. Although Penn continued to be active in Quaker affairs, he published little after 1700, and his most important efforts involved persuading members of Parliament not to make Pennsylvania a royal colony like New Jersey and the Carolinas.[24]

ADMIRAL PENN AND HIS SON

William Penn Sr. (1621–1670), a naval officer, married the widow Margaret Jasper in 1643 (d. 1681/82) and they had three children: William (1644–1718), Margaret (d. 1718), and Richard (d. 1673). About the mother we have only scattered information.[25] Margaret had primary responsibility for raising the three children, because William Sr. was absent at sea for long periods. She later gave money to her son William when he was disowned, and though she did not become a Quaker herself, she wrote a letter urging the king to let George Fox out of prison. Samuel Pepys, who was a neighbor, described her in 1664 as a "well-looked, fat, short old Dutch woman, but one that hath been heretofore pretty, and is now discreet, and I believe hath more wit than her husband." Pepys recounted dancing, dinners, and parties at the Penns' and, in company, romping and laughing on the bed with "my lady Penn" and other ladies.[26] A conversation with Lady Penn while her husband was dying, recorded by a visiting Friend, indicates that she never approved of her son's Quakerism and his repudiation of courtly manners. Although no letters from his mother to her son survive, William endured a period of depression after her death.[27] The Penn family seems to have been conventionally Anglican, and none of them became Quakers.[28]

The son owed his career to the accomplishments of his father, who became Vice Admiral Sir William Penn, a member of Parliament under Cromwell and Charles II and Commissioner of the Navy. As noted above, Penn Sr. became a naval hero in the first Dutch war, and Cromwell rewarded him with lands in Ireland, command of a castle, and troops needed to ensure English control of that restive island. In 1655 Cromwell made him the naval commander of the fleet, with an army under a separate general, in a major expedition to take Hispaniola. The expedition failed because Santo Domingo was heavily fortified and the English soldiers succumbed to disease, probably malaria or yellow fever. On the way home, the British took Jamaica as a consolation prize. Either because of the defeat or because Admiral Penn was suspected of disloyalty, Cromwell had him imprisoned in the Tower of London for a few months and then released.[29] In 1656 the admiral took his family to Macroom Castle in Ireland. While there, he invited the Quaker traveling minister Thomas Loe to speak to his household. As far as we know, there was no other personal contact between the twelve- or thirteen-year-old son and Quakers for the next ten years.

In 1660 Admiral Penn helped deliver the navy to King Charles, was present on the ship that brought the king from Holland to England, and served in the Convention Parliament. After the coronation, the admiral and his son watched from a balcony as the royal procession passed by and enjoyed being acknowledged by the king. Charles knighted the admiral and appointed him a commissioner of the navy, where he, along with Samuel Pepys, was responsible for maintaining the ships, paying sailors, and selecting officers. (Pepys lived next door to the Penns and his diary is the best source of personal information about the Penn family, even though he came to detest the admiral, probably because of rivalry over perquisites of office.)[30] In the second Dutch war, the admiral served as second in command to James, Duke of York, and was again praised for what the English rather misleadingly called a victory. The navy, under Charles, was always short of funds, with the result that the Dutch won major victories in the third war (1665–67), but Penn had retired from going to sea by then. Opponents of the king in Parliament still tried to make Penn Sr. a scapegoat, but he retained the confidence of Charles and James.

As a commissioner, Penn allegedly paid a substantial sum from his own pocket to feed the sailors, so the Crown was indebted to him. William Jr. would defend his father's reputation against charges made in Parliament of pocketing money while the men went hungry.[31] It should be remembered that making money from holding office in Restoration England was normal practice. For example, Pepys estimated his worth in 1660 at £600; after ten years as a commissioner, he valued his assets at £6,000 and calculated that he was owed at his death £28,000.³² The Crown never paid that debt. Pepys wrote that the admiral was a proud man, liked to enjoy life, and was sometimes drunk, and that when they walked in London, he insisted that outsiders give him the right of way.³³ After he captured a boat carrying a Spanish diplomat, Penn Sr. tortured the diplomat as recompense for what the Inquisition had done to his brother George. Although the Penn family's social position was not comparable to that of the English nobility, the admiral's wealth placed him among the wealthy members of the House of Commons.³⁴ Young Williams's social status, his contacts with royalty, his ease among aristocrats, and his ultimate triumph in being given Pennsylvania depended upon his father's accomplishments. From a young age, Penn enjoyed being recognized as a person of "quality."

A YOUNG MAN IN OXFORD, FRANCE, AND IRELAND

In 1660 the admiral sent his sixteen-year-old son to Christ College, Oxford, at that time a center of strong royalist and Anglican sentiment.³⁵ The boy, studious, bright, and morally sensitive, was so unhappy at Oxford that his father debated sending him to Cambridge. After two years Penn was, in his own words, "banished" from Oxford. There are alternative accounts as to why, but the only documentary evidence suggests that he was meeting with John Owen, a leading Puritan clergyman and former vice chancellor of the university. Penn could have been participating in illegal worship or studying religion with Owen and perhaps skipping chapel.³⁶ At any rate, he later claimed that he was "persecuted" at Oxford and beaten—probably by his father, who as a navy commander was used to having miscreants whipped. Expulsion for being too religious was not good preparation for the life of a courtier, but a grand tour of France and Italy was another form of education. William, now age eighteen, went to France, where he was presented to Louis XIV, but instead of continuing his travels he journeyed to Saumur, a town in the Loire Valley, where he would spend the next years studying in the leading French Calvinist academy. He read theology in one of the few towns where Protestants and Catholics could live together in the toleration guaranteed by the Edict of Nantes. There, Penn encountered a humanism emphasizing ethics, the reasonableness of Christianity, and the responsibility of the state to foster morality but not to coerce belief.³⁷

Called home because of an impending war with Holland, young William was on his father's ship as it prepared for battle, but the admiral sent his son to Charles II with dispatches—a clever means of getting him out of the way before battle while also gaining him recognition. Pepys described the young Penn as showing off French fashions, suggesting little surviving Calvinist influence on the lad.[38] Penn enrolled at Lincoln's Inn to study law but left after a few months because of the plague; he later denounced the dissipation of the Oxford and law students. King Charles restored to their previous royalist owner the lands that Cromwell had given the admiral but bestowed other lands with an income of £1,000, plus command of a fort and troops worth an additional £400. Because of disputes over titles and rents, the admiral sent his son to Ireland to gain experience in being a landlord by arranging rents and securing titles. (Penn later sympathized with and bought land from Native Americans, but he never reflected on how the English were seizing Irish land and showed no understanding of the causes of Irish poverty.)[39] While in Ireland, William socialized with English high officials and wealthy landlords and gained commendation for showing courage in helping put down a mutiny by unpaid English soldiers. He even considered becoming a soldier and asked his father to purchase him a commission in the army and give him command of the fort. The admiral refused.[40] In 1666/67 the twenty-two-year-old Penn went to his first Quaker meeting to hear Thomas Loe again, and this time he converted.[41] There is no information as to how much Penn knew about the distinctive beliefs and practices of Friends at this time.

THE QUAKERS

The Society of Friends originated out of the religious chaos and search for spiritual authority resulting from the end of print censorship in the Civil War, the abolition of bishops, and the failure of Parliament, the army, and later the clergy, meeting in what is now called the Westminster Assembly, to agree on church polity. The government failed to prevent a proliferation of sectarian groups, including Familialists, Anabaptists, Muggletonians, Grindeltonians, and Fifth Monarchists. The authorities saw the earliest Friends as just another one of these fanatical outgrowths and, unable to distinguish among them, hoped that all would just disappear. Bowing to necessity, Cromwell allowed freedom of worship but kept the parish system and a clergy supported by tithes.

In seventeenth-century England, virtually everyone assumed a Christian worldview, and most feared uncertainty and doubt about faith because this life was probation for the next, and the only options for Protestants were eternal punishment in hell or bliss in heaven. Heresy corrupted people and was to be suppressed because its consequences ruined one's future in both this life and the next. Getting Christianity right was of supreme importance, and the early Friends' claim that they were the only ones following the true path irritated virtually everyone else, who were also certain that only they had it right. Only a few acknowledged that maybe no one had perfect understanding. (Penn, as a young convert, was not among them, but as he aged he became more tolerant.)

Quakers attempted to institutionalize and make normative a distinctive religious experience that provided Gospel-mandated faith and practice in this world and salvation in the next. This was primitive Christianity rediscovered and authenticated by personally knowing an "Inward Christ." In the early 1650s, a few men and woman, George Fox most prominent among them, became convinced that they had a direct and unmediated experience of God that illuminated evil and gave them power to conquer sin, strength to practice Christian discipleship, and assurance of salvation.[42] They used many metaphors for this "experimental" knowledge: the Inward Light, Light of Christ, God Within, Holy Spirit.[43] (The term "inner light" is of late nineteenth-, not seventeenth-century coinage.) With intense missionary zeal, Quakers proclaimed that all people had within them an inward seed or receptacle, that at certain times God illuminated that seed, and that those who responded by silencing the will and letting Christ's Light rule (i.e., those who grew in grace) would be saved. Unlike Calvinists, who believed in the predestination of the elect, Friends preached that salvation was universally available but could be achieved only by complete surrender to the leadings of the Light (i.e., achieving over time justification and sanctification). The Inward Christ brought infallible knowledge gained through spiritual senses and understood through the conscience. Quakers condemned all those who denied direct revelation as distorting the Bible's teaching and succumbing to the devil or earthly temptations.

The essence of worship for Quakers was mental and spiritual. All true religion was inward, and so the physical aids and symbols used by false churches—baptism by water, Communion, hymns, ornate churches, a learned ministry, tithes—were no longer necessary because Christ had returned spiritually to teach his people. In Quaker worship services, termed "silent meetings," people entered and sat quietly, stilling their wills, until someone—man or woman—began to preach or pray words inspired by God. Silence did not mean that there was no speaking but that humans must silence their self-will in order to hear the "still small voice" of God (1 Kings 19:12). Those whom the congregation found speaking truth they called ministers. Within a few months of becoming a Quaker, Penn was recognized as an important minister.

From the inception of the faith, Friends developed "testimonies" that made them distinctive. By espousing Quakerism, Penn accepted all of these practices as divinely inspired and defended them as congruent with common sense and right reason. The first Friends offended their neighbors by refusing traditional forms of politeness and deference, including doffing one's hat, bowing to social superiors, and using such forms of address as "your Grace" or "my Lord," which they felt should be reserved for Jesus. They did not sign letters "Your humble servant" if the writer were neither humble nor a servant, nor did they use the second-person plural "you" (the correct way of addressing a social superior at the time) but addressed all people in the second-person singular, as "thee" or "thou." Jesus said, "swear not at all," and so Quakers refused to make any oaths requiring God's activity (e.g., "so help me God"). During the Commonwealth, many Quaker converts came from the army, and attitudes toward war varied, some continuing to serve until Cromwell purged all Friends, others denouncing all war as a product of sin. After a revolt against King Charles in 1661 by an apocalyptic sect called Fifth Monarchists, Quaker leaders issued a statement denouncing plotting or serving in the military, and the testimony against members' participating in war had become the standard by the time Penn converted.[44]

The earliest Quaker converts saw their mission as spreading the truth throughout the British Isles, the New World colonies, Europe, and even to Catholic Italy and the Ottoman Empire. Their successes, primarily in England and its possessions, their support for the most radical elements under Cromwell, and their defiance of law and custom made them appear threatening to other churches and state authorities, particularly after the Restoration. Although historians estimate that the total number of Quakers never exceeded forty-five thousand, contemporaries estimated their number as one hundred thousand, with a network of traveling ministers and meetings that could plot revolution.[45] The Cavalier Parliaments passed the Test Acts (the Clarendon Code of 1662 and the Conventicle and Quaker Acts of 1667), and individual judges applied old penal laws against Roman Catholics requiring loyalty oaths as a way of trapping Friends who would not take any oath. Unlike other dissenters who met in secret, Friends refused to be bowed and, as Pepys observed, were arrested like lambs.⁴⁶ As many as ten thousand Friends were imprisoned, and 366 died there, during the Restoration.

Penn's convincement required a refocusing of life that in his case meant reconciling his status, education, wealth, and manners to a spiritual equality with other Quakers and observance of their peculiar customs. Historian Mary Maples Dunn has argued that he was isolated from other members of his own class because of his distinctive Quaker dress and speech.⁴⁷ After his disinheritance and exile from his father's home, Penn embarked on a career as what we might call a professional Quaker and soon became a leading minister. He preached in meetings for worship, traveled in England, Ireland, and the Low Countries seeking converts, engaged in public debates with Baptist, Presbyterian, and Independent (i.e., Congregationalist) ministers, sent letters of encouragement to Friends, wrote long tracts attacking opponents, and defended Quaker doctrines and practices.

Penn joined the Friends at a time when they were evolving from a loosely structured movement led by charismatic men and women into a hierarchical organization with centralized authority.⁴⁸ This consolidation of spiritual power, necessary in all religious movements as they try to survive, came more quickly to Friends after 1660, as they dealt with the deaths of many early leaders whom the government had incarcerated. At the local level, there were meetings for worship on Sunday and at midweek; several of these meetings joined together to become a Monthly Meeting (MM) that supervised marriages, kept registers of births and deaths, enforced Quaker behavioral norms, and maintained property. Quarterly Meetings, composed of all the monthly meetings in a county, dealt with any matters not settled at a lower level and sent delegates to annual gatherings called London Yearly Meeting (LYM), which was the final authority on matters of faith and practice. Originally settled to coordinate responses to persecution and to deal with the government, the weekly sessions of the Meeting for Sufferings (MFS) in London became the primary administrative body of British Friends and, along with a Second Day Morning Meeting of Ministers (MMM) in London, supervised all publications. In addition, starting in the 1670s there were Women's Monthly and Quarterly Meetings.

The initiative for the pyramid, or Presbyterian-style, organization came from George Fox, who was supported by the early ministers, including Penn, who was involved in setting up the first formal London meetings: LYM, MFS, and MMM. Not all Friends approved of what seemed to them the confining of spiritual leadership to a bureaucracy and the creation of separate meetings for women. Penn sought by correspondence, attending arbitrations, and writing tracts to maintain the unity of Friends and to defend Fox's leadership.

Penn's responsibilities as an important and devout minister required a major commitment of time, because all of these meetings began with a period of worship, and decisions were made not by vote or consensus but by a "sense of the meeting," summarized by the clerk after listening to discussion in which all members waited expectantly for God's guidance. In Quaker business meetings, Penn had to learn to accept spiritual guidance from other Friends, none of whom had either his education or his social status. Penn defended George Fox and the early Quakers as similar to the apostles, who also were humble, uneducated men and received their authority directly from God through the Inward Christ.[49] Because Penn, as a Quaker, could not serve as a member of Parliament, justice of the peace, or soldier, his roles in the Society of Friends provided the experiences he used in early Pennsylvania. It was to be a colony dominated by Quakers, based on their principles and embodying Christian morality and harmony. It would also, Penn hoped, be a profitable investment.

Penn's first publication was an apocalyptic threat of judgment on all non-Quaker churches, which Samuel Pepys thought was nonsense. His second, a response to a public debate with a Presbyterian minister, titled *The Sandy Foundation Shaken*, criticized the satisfaction theory of atonement and the use of the nonbiblical word "trinity," and defended the universal availability of salvation against the Presbyterian doctrine of predestination. Pepys thought this essay was too well argued to have been written by Penn but saw the doctrines as dangerous.[50] The authorities agreed and arrested Penn for blasphemy and confined him in the Tower of London for nearly a year. The king sent Edward Stillingfleet, a moderate Anglican, to instruct him, and Penn clarified his thought in *Innocency with her Open Face* (1669) without recanting but now clarifying his belief in the divinity of Christ, God the Father, and the Holy Spirit. Either because he had quoted Stillingfleet or owing to his father's influence, Penn was released. He had written in the Tower and now published *No Cross, No Crown*, a defense of Quaker customs and a call for self-denial as the essence of Christian morality.

Penn met Gulielma Springett in 1667. A devout Quaker, also of gentry status (she was the daughter of Sir William Springett, who had died in the Civil War, and was raised as the stepdaughter of Isaac Penington, an important Quaker), Gulielma was in every way a suitable wife. She had a fortune estimated at £10,000 and, according to Thomas Ellwood, who had known her since childhood, was "in all respects a very desirable women," outwardly "comely" and inwardly of "extraordinary" intelligence and "abundant Affability, Courtesy and Sweetness of natural Temper." They were wed in 1672; both contemporaries and later historians have described the marriage as affectionate and happy. Penn wrote to her as he left for Pennsylvania, "Remember thou was the love of my youth, and much joy of my life; the most beloved as well as the worthy of all my earthly comforts." She supervised a house that Penn later described as having eight chimneys and three stories, capable of entertaining his family and from five to twenty guests. She managed his affairs when he was absent and bore seven or eight children (only three survived) over their twenty-two years of marriage. In a memorial written after her death in 1694, Penn described her as one in ten thousand women.[51]

ADVOCATE FOR RELIGIOUS TOLERATION

Penn first became famous among his contemporaries as an advocate for religious freedom, or toleration, terms that he used interchangeably but that always meant at a minimum freedom to worship. He gained legitimacy among Quakers and outsiders because he suffered for his beliefs, being imprisoned first in Ireland in 1667, then in the Tower for writing *The Sandy Foundation Shaken* in 1668, and again in 1670 for defying the Conventicle Act and preaching in the street after soldiers had locked the doors to the Quaker meeting house. (As late as 1686, it took a special declaration by the king to keep him out of jail.)[52]

In 1670 the authorities arrested Penn and William Mead, an ex-soldier turned merchant and recent Quaker convert, and charged them with causing a riot. In an account of the trial (which Penn denied writing but certainly influenced), the two men attacked the statute and made the judges appear foolish, arbitrary, ignorant of the common law, and intent on violating the traditional rights of Englishmen. When the jury acquitted both men, the justices imprisoned the jurymen in an attempt to force them to reverse their verdict. Ultimately, the Lord Chief Justice ruled that an English jury could not be coerced. The verdict did not help Penn, who was jailed for contempt of court. However, the Quaker version of the trial transcript dramatized persecution, picturing the young Penn as a kind of radical hippy of his day. It went through nine printings in one year and made him famous.[53]

In 1674, British Friends, including Penn, established the MFS to standardize Quaker responses to being arrested and to provide legal advice on how to fight indictments. Penn, on behalf of the MFS, approached the king, petitioning him to suspend the laws criminalizing religious dissent and release Friends and other dissenters from prison. Penn wrote and visited justices and nobles asking for relief, and he testified before Parliament seeking repeal or reform of the penal laws and exemption from being punished by laws requiring oaths that had been passed in Tudor times against Roman Catholics. The MFS backed candidates for Parliament who supported toleration, and Penn canvassed vigorously for Algernon Sidney in 1679. Like other Friends, Penn supported Charles II's and James II's suspension of laws on religious conformity, but he also wanted Parliament to pass a new Magna Carta of religious freedom and worked with James in 1687–88 to create an electoral majority to achieve this.

In addition to tasks for Friends' worship, Penn wrote many tracts defending religious liberty. Unlike his religious writings, these tracts were not submitted to the MMM for approval and were designed to appeal to the general public. Penn was not attempting to be original or write political theory but was addressing specific circumstances and seeking to persuade using a variety of arguments. All advocates of religious toleration after 1660 had to counter the widespread fear that religious differences had fueled the English Civil War, an experience few wished to repeat. Penn joined an ongoing debate on policies for churches in England. One solution, advocated by the Independent John Owen and the Presbyterian Richard Baxter, was to establish a comprehensive church with an educated ministry and supported by tithes that would include Anglicans, Presbyterians, and Independents. Left out would be Roman Catholics and various sectarians, including Quakers, whose enthusiasm and denial of the sacraments opposed reason and revelation.[54] Most members of the Cavalier Parliament opposed this idea, as did bishops who insisted that the Church of England already offered the essentials of Christianity necessary for salvation and that the issues in dispute were small matters. Even if a person could not accept everything, he or she could outwardly conform in order to ensure peace in the country and honor their fathers—traditionally seen as the king, magistrates, bishops, and actual fathers. No one could force conscience, but church and state working together could require correct moral and religious behavior in the interest of the public good.

The first Friends contributed no original ideas to the debate on religious liberty, but they did demand an end to their persecution. They did not advocate extending freedom to others, because everyone else was espousing worldly or corrupt religions. Quakers insisted upon their freedom to respond to the Inward Light and based their claims on prophetic certainty rather than political negotiation. George Fox proclaimed the "Word of the Lord" to Cromwell and ignored the practical implications of what religious liberty would mean to the whole country. Tithes were Jewish and should be abolished; the Bible forbade oaths, so none should be taken. Matters that Anglicans saw as indifferent Friends viewed as a product of the Antichrist, originating in the Roman Catholic Church and now enforced in England. Because all true religion was spiritual and nothing physical was legitimate in worship, the earliest Quakers wanted to destroy all other churches whose teachings and practices gave their members false assurance of salvation.

Penn's tracts started with the basic Friends' critique of persecution but expanded the scope of religious freedom to include all Protestants and those Roman Catholics who renounced the political powers of the pope. Quaker truth, for Penn, did not require the abolition of other churches. He began with theology but added arguments from the Bible, church history, human nature, English history, security of the kingdom, and utility to demonstrate that the survival of large numbers of dissenters and the growth of Quakerism proved that persecution did not work. Drawing upon the wide range of ideas first debated in England under Cromwell, Penn did not aim for or achieve originality but summarized and popularized. He added extensive quotations about the nature of religion from the church fathers (Tertullian and Origen), the Greeks and Romans, the Catholic Erasmus, and Protestant reformers, including Anglicans such as Herbert of Cherbury, the Cambridge Platonists, Thomas Cranmer, and Thomas Hooker.

He started with the Bible. Jesus preached love of enemies, resisted worldly power on the Mount of Transfiguration, allowed himself to be tortured and crucified, established his kingdom through the resurrection and early church, and now was re-creating his reign through the Quakers. Friends relied upon the parable of the weeds, or tares, in the field of wheat and interpreted these verses to mean that God alone would separate the good from the evil in the church at the time of final judgment. Jesus proclaimed the coming of a spiritual kingdom of God and was now resurrecting it in the hearts of faithful Christians. Israel's kings could force true worship, but now, in the reign of Christ, all that precedent had been abolished.

Penn continued with church history. The triumph of Christianity over Roman paganism came about when the apostles, Paul, and men and women of the early church preached, sent epistles, and traveled throughout the empire to proclaim the Gospel. They received no tithes and no state support (in fact, the opposite), and there was no coercion. Persecution came when Christians allied themselves with political authority under Constantine, the result being the corruption of the church, exemplified by the survival of the Roman Church's intolerant spirit in the Church of England, Presbyterians, and Independents.

Penn broadened his defense of religious liberty with arguments from human nature, English history, national security, self-interest, and utility, showing that persecution did not work. Rational nature or reasoning power mandated spiritual liberty because the origin of religion lay in conscience that could not be coerced. If any government tried to require religious conformity against a person's free consent, the result would be hypocrisy, dissatisfaction, and disobedience. Forced religion weakened civic virtue. Instead, the government's obligation was to enforce the morality required by the Bible, reason, natural law, and the common consent of humanity, summarized in the Ten Commandments. Freedom to worship did not mean freedom for immorality.

Forced tithes destroyed the rights of property. Penn argued that since the time of the Magna Carta, the English constitution had guaranteed that no man's property could be taken without his consent. Making a dissenter pay 10 percent of his earnings to a church he did not attend and a clergyman he did not hear violated property rights. The Roman Church instituted tithes after Constantine, when it became a servant of the state, and they were now a survival observed by the Church of England. Because Jesus, the apostles, and the first churches had survived by free gifts, so should the restored early church.

Finally, Penn used a utilitarian argument. All could see the effects of persecution: hardworking families went to jail for attending illegal services and for nonpayment of tithes and were thus reduced to poverty. The state that should be strengthened by its citizens' productive labor was weakened. And, of course, persecution had not worked. Presbyterians, Baptists, and Independents still existed, and Quakers continued to grow in number. The general sympathy of the populace to their neighbors' suffering made juries reluctant to convict on the basis of religion alone. Whatever their effectiveness among the literate population, Penn's toleration pamphlets had little effect on Parliament in the 1670s, and toleration remained elusive until after the death of Charles II in 1684.

PENN THE COLONIZER: NEW JERSEY AND PENNSYLVANIA

Penn's interest in the colonization of North America came after the Friends' meeting in 1676 appointed him arbitrator to settle the dispute between Quakers

Edward Billings and John Fenwick over who had what proprietary rights to half of New Jersey. After the English captured New Amsterdam in 1664, Charles II gave New Jersey to two courtiers, John Lord Berkeley and Phillip Carteret. Carteret sold his half to Billings, who, because he was in debt, borrowed money from John Fenwick to complete the purchase. When these two Quakers quarreled, Friends intervened to keep their dispute from going to court, and the arbitrators divided West New Jersey between them. Penn, with no financial interest at first, later bought a one-tenth share of West Jersey and joined with the Friends in Scotland, including Robert Barclay, in purchasing East New Jersey.

West Jersey was intended to be a Quaker colony, and in order to attract settlers, the proprietors published "The Concessions and Agreements of West New Jersey," probably written by Billings but signed by Penn and reflecting general Quaker attitudes toward government.[55] The Concessions was a radical document giving all power to an elected assembly, allowing all inhabitants to vote, requiring that all laws be written in English, and guaranteeing freedom to worship. There was no militia, no imprisonment for debt, and a drastic reduction in capital crimes to two: murder and treason.[56] Unfortunately for the stability of West Jersey, the legality of the Concessions was uncertain because only the king could grant the right of government, and so any claims by Fenwick and Billings were legally dubious. Settlement proceeded anyway; colonists created Salem and Burlington and continued the pattern of mutual but wary respect with the Lenape tribes that had been established with earlier Swedish, Dutch, and English inhabitants.[57] Penn's experiences in West Jersey gave him knowledge about colonization, but the uncertainty in government and the difficulties in dealing with men like Fenwick and Billings prompted him to turn his attention to the lightly settled area on the west bank of the Delaware River.

There is no good documentary evidence on how Penn persuaded Charles II to give him the largest grant of land ever given to a private individual, an area as large as Ireland. Penn claimed that the grant was made to pay off a debt of £11,000 (now grown to £16,000 with interest) to Admiral Penn for victualing the sailors in the Dutch wars.[58] Charles had many debts, essentially declared bankruptcy in 1672, and never paid most of them. During the period in which Penn petitioned the king (1680–81), Charles was preoccupied with maneuvering to escape Parliament's supervision, negotiating a secret treaty with a subsidy from Louis XIV, dealing with the anti-Catholic Titus Oates hysteria, and defeating Whig attempts to deny Roman Catholic James the right of succession. The king, by proroguing Parliament twice, stopped any prospect of a law for religious toleration. During the rest of his reign, Charles showed no sympathy for Quakers' desire for release from the Test Acts and penal laws and sought to reduce the autonomy of towns and colonies in order to increase his power.

Historians have suggested several alternative explanations as to why Charles acceded to Penn's petition.[59] One is that Charles sought to honor Admiral Penn, divide the Whig opposition and their Quaker supporters, and please London merchants. Other possible incentives included ridding England of Quakers, who, although not rebels, were troublesome subjects; paying off a debt at no cost; expanding the empire into what he saw as an empty land; escaping the cost of colonization or at least transferring it to others; and pleasing several courtiers. Penn later thanked Robert Spencer, Earl of Sunderlund, with whom he had traveled in France and with whom he discussed plans, for being the first to support his petition.[60] It may be that, like his brother, Charles admired or liked Penn as an honest man so different from himself and most of the personnel of the court. Finally, perhaps the most likely explanation is that Charles really did not care one way or another because he was ignorant of what or even where the Delaware River Valley was, and granting a colony to Penn was the easiest course.

Penn obtained his charter in spite of initial objections by representatives of the Duke of York (who owned Delaware), Lord Baltimore (who feared the grant would overlap Maryland's borders), the bishop of London (who disliked any favor that might privilege Quakers over Anglicans), and the Lords of Trade (who opposed proprietary colonies and wanted to centralize control of the emergent empire). Undoubtedly, we can conclude that Penn was aided by influential friends whom he had first known at Oxford, in Ireland, and in France and who as members of Parliament and government officials would support his proprietary government for the rest of his life.[61]

Unlike King Charles, Penn wrote hundreds of pages during the period between applying for a patent in 1679 and going to Pennsylvania in 1682: epistles to Friends, religious books, including *No Cross, No Crown*, draft constitutions that he sent out for comments, advertisements for settlers, descriptions of the land, and proposed laws. Sorting out Penn's motives and state of mind is not easy, for he adjusted his tone and content to his audience. One theme should be clear: Penn saw no conflict between his religious certainty that he was doing God's will and worldly aims such as making money from this new venture. In epistles from 1677 and 1679, Penn despaired because his hopes for toleration from Parliament had failed.[62] Blatant immorality in the court, in England, and on the Continent reaffirmed his fear of an impending apocalypse. As in ancient Sodom and Gomorrah, only a remnant of holy people stood in the way. After he received the charter in 1681, Penn hoped that Pennsylvania and its Quaker settlers could change the future. Whatever the outward causes, Penn knew, with the same assurance with which he experienced Christ in meeting, that God had given him this land, and his duty was to create a new Jerusalem, a city upon a hill, with a capital city named Philadelphia that recalled not only the Greek ideal of brotherly love but also the town pictured in the book of Revelation, where people did God's will.[63]

Penn's immediate responsibility was to establish a government that would attract the right kind of settlers. Led by Quakers and including devout people from many churches, the colony, with just laws, freedom of worship, and hardworking men and women, would prosper. "Let Men be good, and the Government cannot be bad, if it be ill, they will cure it. But if Men be bad; let the Government be never so good, they will endeavor to warp and spoil it to their turn."[64] After receiving the charter in March 1681, Penn, with what seems now like feverish industry, planned for the colony and prepared to sail to Pennsylvania in August 1682. He composed ten drafts and additional documents for a "Frame of Government" that he sent to lawyers and weighty Friends for comments. He wrote tracts describing the new lands to entice prospective settlers and letters to merchants and wealthy men who might not migrate but could buy large parcels of lands. Fearing that the colony could not prosper without an ocean port, he persuaded the Duke of York to grant him title to what is now the state of Delaware. He sought to reassure the Dutch, Swedish, and English settlers who already lived in the Delaware River Valley of his good intentions and sent a deputy to introduce himself to the Lenape and to begin the process of buying land from those who already owned the land the king had given to him.[65] And he somehow also found time to finish and publish a small pamphlet on Quaker church discipline and five hundred pages of moral instruction in a new edition of *No Cross, No Crown*, preach a farewell sermon before embarking on the ship *Welcome*, and send an eloquent epistle of love and affection to his pregnant wife and two children, who stayed in England.

Unlike John Locke, who postulated the human origin of government in a contract between ruler and people, Penn traced the beginnings of government to God's creation of Adam, who was to be his "Deputy to Rule" with "Skill," "Power," and "Integrity." Before the Fall, there was "no need of coercion or compulsion," and even now government remained "a Part of Religion itself a thing Sacred in its Institution and End," which was to crush the "Effects of Evil" and to "Cherish those that do well." It was not just a negative power but, like a private society, was "capable of Kindness, Goodness and Charity." "The great End of Government" was "to Support Power in Reverence with the People, and to secure the People from the abuse of Power." "Any Government is Free to the People under it . . . where the Laws Rule and the People are a Party to those Laws."[66]

Upon arrival in the colony in 1682, Penn summoned an assembly that functioned as a kind of constitutional convention, rejecting the proprietor's assembly of two hundred men and replacing it with thirty-six elected members and an appointed council scaled down from seventy-two to eighteen.[67] An Act of Union made Pennsylvania and Delaware one colony with one legislature. All those who believed in God were guaranteed liberty of conscience, freedom to worship, and no tithe or tax to any church. Male Christians who had not been convicted of a crime could serve in any office. The first official meeting of the Pennsylvania General Assembly the following year made liberty of conscience a fundamental law that could be repealed only by six-sevenths of the legislature.[68]

The laws of Pennsylvania reflected the experiences of Friends in England, principles derived from years of debate about the powers of Parliament and the executive, wishes of settlers for security of land titles and protection against tyranny, and Penn's desire to preserve his charter-given powers and the need to profit from this enterprise. The laws reflected agreements among Penn, colonists coming from England and those already in Delaware, and investors who bought large tracts of lands. In keeping with Penn's beliefs about morality, the law outlawed profane swearing, card games, gambling, cock and bull fights, plays, horseracing, and anything "which excite the people to Rudeness, Looseness & Irreligion."[69]

Citizenship or naturalization required making an affirmation of loyalty to the Crown and to Penn, but only those who believed in God could become citizens. Men needed a certain amount of property to vote, but, unlike in England, voting was by secret ballot. As with the West Jersey concessions, all subjects had the right to trial by jury and could defend themselves in court, two witnesses were required for conviction of a crime, laws would be easily understood and in English, no jailer could receive fees, and prisons would be workhouses. At the beginning of a trial, both parties had to declare that they were in the right (i.e., no paid lawyers were allowed). Treason and murder were capital crimes, but fines and punishments for other offenses would be mild and reasonable. Quakers in England had forbidden members to use lawsuits against one another before asking the meeting to appoint arbiters. In Pennsylvania, each county would have three peacemakers appointed to settle disputes. The historian William Offutt Jr. argues that Penn's reformed justice system functioned well and provided some stability in early Pennsylvania.[70]

By contrast, Penn's vision of the relationships among the governor, the Council, and the Assembly remained controversial and poisoned relationships between Penn and the settlers. In the drafts of the Frames of Government, the Council initiated all legislation, and the Assembly would occasionally meet, discuss, and then vote to approve, but could not on its own amend or initiate laws. Although not specified, Penn, as governor, was responsible to the Crown for all legislation and would exercise a right of veto. Penn's vision of lawmaking, probably drawn from the practices of London Yearly Meeting, was unlike the customs of the assemblies in other English colonies, which viewed themselves as modeled on English Parliaments, where the Commons had the right to initiate legislation, particularly on money bills. Penn wrote of his satisfaction with the initial Council and Assembly and the new laws. "I have held two General Assemblies with precious Harmony, Scarce one Law that did not pass with a Nemine Contradicente, and as our opening of them was deepe and with the word & prayer and men fearing god in power are both loved and feared, and god is adding dayly to us."[71]

The success of the new colony depended upon peaceful relations with the Native Americans, the Lenape, who initially probably viewed Penn as just another unwelcome intruder. Penn believed that the Indians, according to the laws of nature, had just title to the land, and so he was required to purchase it from them. The king and the bishop of London also insisted that he negotiate land sales from the Indians.[72] Penn's originality lay in his attempts to understand and appreciate the original inhabitants, and to guarantee that they were treated justly. In disputes between Indians and settlers, juries would be composed of equal numbers of both. Penn visited, ate, and ran races with the natives, sought to learn their language, and provided sympathetic descriptions of their customs. Unlike the Puritans and Virginians, he did not call them barbarous savages or devil worshippers and praised Indian morality, generosity, and eloquence.[73] If we, in retrospect, see the limitations in his approach and knowledge, particularly in concepts of land ownership, Penn, like Roger Williams, stands out as enlightened when compared with other colonizers.[74] The Lenape responded favorably to Penn, and for the next hundred years cited his policies as a way of maintaining good relations with Pennsylvania governments.

In 1681, neither Penn nor the first settlers knew very much about the land they were settling. Pleasing the first purchasers of lands proved troublesome. No one came to Pennsylvania intending to lower his or her station, and those who invested the most wanted the best land and the largest town lots. Even with the best of intentions and competent surveying, laying out the town lots and each man's farm took time, and the results did not please everyone.[75] Penn's policy was to require that owners of large tracts settle someone on them immediately in order to guarantee orderly settlements, but his grants to relatives and large investors violated this policy. He assumed that those who bought land from him would still pay quitrents, but those who cleared the land, built houses, and created farms saw no reason to pay once they had done the work. Controversy over Penn's demands for money would poison relations between the colonists and their proprietor landlord.

Penn established the "greene Country towne" of Philadelphia a few miles north of Chester/Upland between the Delaware and Schuylkill Rivers. In an attempt to avoid plagues and fires, he laid out large blocks in a grid system, with streets named for trees going east-west and numbered streets going north-south. The city was bisected by two large avenues, later named Broad and Market, and had five large parks. He assumed that the town would grow from the Delaware west to the Schuylkill, but instead population spread along the Delaware River, and his deep lots were divided up with additional streets. The area of Philadelphia was not as large as Penn advertised in England, and many of the original purchasers believed that they were entitled to town lots as well as outlying lands. Just before returning to London, Penn received a remonstrance from town lot owners complaining that they had not received what was promised.[76]

Penn's relationships with neighboring colonies were difficult. The governor of New York rebuffed his attempts to control the fur trade with northern Indians. Neither East nor West New Jersey welcomed his interference in its affairs, even though he was a proprietor. Most troubling was his attempt to create a satisfactory southern border with Maryland. A lack of knowledge of American geography resulted in years of controversy. When Charles II granted New York to his brother, the northern boundary of that state included half of Connecticut. Penn's border either began at the fortieth parallel, which was north of Philadelphia, or, to the south, included the mouth of the Susquehanna River. Penn and Lord Baltimore held several meetings without reaching a successful compromise and ended in mutual animosity. Both men appealed to London, and in the spring of 1683, Penn decided to return to England to prosecute his case.[77]

Although historians see emergent conflicts, Penn's letters show a positive attitude toward his and the settlers' accomplishments: a new Frame of Government, 164 laws, a town of one hundred houses, and a flourishing port in a colony of four thousand inhabitants (Native Americans not included), with more immigrants coming from England, Wales, Ireland, and the Low Countries. Penn appointed judges and sheriffs, laid out the borders of three counties, and established good relations with the Native Americans. In West Jersey, Delaware, and Pennsylvania there were fifteen Quaker meetings for worship, and Friends built meeting houses and duplicated the institutions of English Quakerism with monthly men's and women's meetings. A thousand Quakers attended a general meeting in Philadelphia, and in the epistle they sent to London, they "blessed God . . . that call us not hither in Vain & this was the testimony of Life," adding "that god was with us & is with us, yea he hath made our way for us, & proved & confirmed to us his word and faithfulness, for he hath adorned this Wilderness with his Presence."[78] Penn returned to England in August 1684, planning to return with his family to dwell in his manor in Pennsylvania. Unfortunately for Penn, his failure to return for seventeen years meant that he never regained the control or influence he had earlier exercised. He never understood why his failures contributed to the making of such an unruly colony.

POWER AND DISGRACE IN ENGLAND

King Charles welcomed Penn on his return, but he could do little to ease the widespread persecution of dissenters. Only after Charles's death in 1684, and the succession of the Duke of York as James II, did toleration seem possible, because James had told Penn years before that he favored freedom of worship. Even so, Penn was arrested three times and escaped prison and fines only after the king fully exonerated him and his family. For the next three years Penn exercised political influence as a confidant of the king.[79] The Lords of Trade confirmed his purchase of land and right of government for Delaware and set a border with Maryland, and Pennsylvania's charter was not threatened, nor was it included in the new dominion of New England, which stretched from Maine to New Jersey. Friends, including Penn, petitioned James for relief from persecution and thanked him for freeing twelve hundred dissenters from prison. Penn, who is now seen as the architect of James's strategy to grant toleration for Catholics and Protestants, persuaded him in 1687 to suspend the penal laws and Test Acts. Penn served as the emissary to William of Orange in an unsuccessful attempt to gain the ruler of Holland's (who was also James's son-in-law) approval of toleration of both Catholics and Protestants, which was already the practice in the Low Countries. There was widespread resistance to James's religious policy at the local level, and many suspected that Penn was a Roman Catholic plotting against English liberties.[80] Historian Scott Sowerby argues that in late 1687 Penn influenced the king in an attempt to create a parliamentary majority that would enact a new Magna Carta of religious liberty and supported his attempts to influence or pack the House of Commons with new members in favor of toleration.[81] Penn wrote several pamphlets trying to unify dissenters and to persuade members of the Church of England that toleration for both Catholics and Protestants was the best guarantee of peace and prosperity.[82] In the midst of what contemporaries believed was his influence with the king, Penn traveled in the ministry to Europe, Ireland, and the west of England and kept postponing his return to Pennsylvania.

The ruling class approved of James's initial declaration that he would protect and respect the rights of the Church of England and did not support the rebellion of the Protestant Duke of Monmouth, an illegitimate son of Charles II's. However, where Charles had been devious and careful on policy, James was headstrong and contemptuous of opposition. He appointed Roman Catholics as officers in a standing army in Ireland and as high government officials, suspended borough charters, and professionalized governmental administration. He replaced the Protestant president and fellows of Magdalen College at Oxford with Catholics and quarreled with, and then suspended, Parliament. In 1685 Louis XIV ended toleration for Calvinists in France and threatened war with Holland, causing Huguenot refugees to flee to England. James accepted a secret subsidy from Louis and favored France in this aggressive policy. Like his contemporaries, historians disagree on whether James wanted to emulate Louis's absolutist power and establish Roman Catholicism or just to guarantee Catholics and Protestants equal rights. Penn never questioned James's sincere wish for toleration or his close association with him, but he expressed reservations about the king's authoritarian leanings.

In his survey of this period of English history, Geoffrey Holmes argues that as late as December 1687 and even through midsummer of 1688, a revolution was not predictable.[83] So long as the succession after James would go to his Protestant daughter, Mary, the wife of William of Orange, a Protestant monarch was guaranteed. After a series of miscarriages, in July 1688 James's wife had a son who would be raised a Roman Catholic. A series of unwise actions by James prompted prominent nobles and Anglican bishops to ask William of Orange to intervene, and he landed with a small army in November 1688. When the king's English army deserted and joined William, James fled to France, and the relatively peaceful "Glorious Revolution" occurred. To contemporaries, the events seemed a miraculous deliverance from popery and absolutism, and a Convention Parliament made William and Mary joint monarchs. Penn, as a prominent supporter of James, was now persona non grata; he was accused several times of treason and briefly imprisoned in the tower. For the next four years, he spent time in hiding (emerging only to attend and preach at George Fox's funeral) and attempting to use prominent supporters to persuade the new king of his innocence. Penn did not deny his friendship with James but insisted that he had not plotted to restore him to the throne.[84]

"A MAN OF SORROWS": 1689–1694

The disorder prevalent in early Pennsylvania also characterized many other colonies. Virginia experienced Bacon's Rebellion in 1676; King Philip's War convulsed all New England in the 1670s; Maryland, New York, North Carolina, and Massachusetts overthrew either royal or charter governments in 1689. Even so, other colonies had forces promoting stability that Pennsylvania lacked. The governors of royal colonies were aristocrats and exercised authority in the name of the Crown; New England's religious uniformity meant that magistrates and ministers worked together to instill deference and obedience. By contrast, Penn was an educated commoner and a leading Quaker with considerable charisma, and, when present, was willing to listen and to compromise. Unfortunately for the colony, Penn was now absent, and there was no one else of "quality" or even with political experience gained in England to give legitimacy to the powers of the Council and Assembly. In addition, the Quaker settlers in England had ignored customs of social deference and only selectively obeyed laws that persecuted them. The yoking of Delaware and Pennsylvania into one colony created factions, as each population feared domination by the other. Delaware had few Quakers and more Presbyterians than Pennsylvania, and three-quarters of those who initially pledged loyalty to Penn signed their names with an X, indicating illiteracy. Most Quaker men and women were literate. The first laws of Pennsylvania enshrined so many Quaker practices that Anglicans and Presbyterians felt discriminated against. Religious liberty also contributed to political instability, as the few Anglicans and royal officials compared their subordination in Pennsylvania with the high status they had enjoyed under the established Church of England and sought to undermine Penn's position.[85]

Clear land titles were a prime requisite for stability, but Thomas Holmes, the surveyor, was slow, had failing eyesight, was frequently drunk, and was charged with taking bribes.[86] Penn appointed Thomas Lloyd, a Welsh minister and the only person in the colony with legal expertise, president of the Council, but Lloyd was present at only half the meetings because he married a New Yorker who preferred to live in New York. Penn hoped to create harmony by appointing political opponents to the Council who would work together, but the result was deadlock and animosity. As early as 1685 Penn complained that disorder in Pennsylvania was giving the colony a bad name and hindering immigration. He exhorted inhabitants, "for the good of the country, and me, be not so governmentish."[87] The editors of the *Papers of William Penn* observe that Penn soon replaced friendly solicitations and prayers for good will with demands, particularly as the settlers refused to pay quitrents or taxes to support the government.[88] He had been in debt before receiving the charter, and his sales of land had not enabled him to repay his debts. In desperation, in 1687 Penn appointed William Blackwell, a former Cromwellian soldier, as his lieutenant governor, but from the time of his arrival Thomas Lloyd and many leading Quakers defied Blackwell's authority, refused any cooperation, and ignored Penn's exhortations to live in harmony. Blackwell's main supporters came from among Delaware's inhabitants, who approved of his attempt to create a militia and wanted to be separate from Pennsylvania, and from a few Quakers who disliked the control exercised by a faction headed by Lloyd. Blackwell concluded that Quaker principles were incompatible with government and served mainly to justify extortion by the leading Philadelphia merchants.[89]

Penn had assumed that having a community of Friends would contribute to social harmony, but instead a religious and political dispute between George Keith and his supporters and most Quaker ministers convulsed Pennsylvania and New Jersey Friends in 1692. Keith, the best-educated and most prominent Quaker minister in the colony, sought to make sure that Quaker preachers emphasized the importance of the historic Jesus as well as the Inward Christ.

As a result, he was accused on two occasions of preaching two Christs and the meeting did not vindicate him. At this point, Keith, having discovered that many Philadelphia Friends denied essential parts of Christianity, published several tracts detailing their heresies and became the leader of a schismatic meeting. What began as an esoteric theological debate soon became political, as magistrates who were Quaker ministers arrested Keith and his printer, put them on trial, and confiscated the only press in the colony. Keith's tract essentially restated Bushel's case (see chapter 5), only this time the Quakers were cast as the heavy-handed judges who persecuted the innocent. At just the time that English government had guaranteed all orthodox Protestants the right to worship, Keith accused Friends of heresy and Pennsylvania government of persecuting a dissenter.[90] The English government, unhappy with Penn and the colony's disorder and irritated that Pennsylvania was providing no financial support for the war with France, revoked Penn's charter and appointed a royal governor.

One measure of a person is how he or she deals with setbacks, and from 1689 to 1694 Penn was, as he put it, "a man of sorrows":[91] in and out of prison and in danger of being arrested again, in debt that was made worse by receiving no rents after the devastation in Ireland caused by the war between William III and James II, distrusted by King William, blamed by many English Quakers for being too closely tied to James, suspected of being a Jesuit and a Jacobite, and forced to watch the slow decline, and then the death, of his beloved wife, Gulielma Maria Penn, in 1694.

While in hiding, he wrote eloquent defenses of Quaker beliefs: *A Key Opening the Way* in 1693, which went through four English editions within a year and two editions in French; prefaces to the collected works of Robert Barclay and John Burnyeat; "A Brief Account of the Rise and Progress of the People called Quakers" (included as a preface to George Fox's *Journal*, the "Brief Account" contains the best portrait of the religious impact of the Quakers' founder); a summary of Quaker beliefs; and the first attempt to place Friends in the context of the history of Christianity. With England at war, Penn also composed *An Essay on the Present and Future Peace in Europe* (1693), which proposed the creation of a European diet or parliament composed of representatives from all the major European nations, including Russia and the Ottomans, that would solve disputes among monarchs by examining and adjudicating claims and would have its own army to enforce its decisions. Finally, in *Some Fruits of Solitude in Reflections and Maxims* (also 1693), he composed a series of wise sayings as a guide to ethical living that has remained in print for three hundred years, demonstrating the continuing appeal of that kind of wisdom.

King William received Penn publicly in July 1693 and declared him exonerated. After promising to furnish men and money for William's war and to return to Pennsylvania, Penn regained proprietary rights of the colony. Even so, religious and domestic affairs occupied Penn for the next six years, including the loss, after a prolonged illness, of his eldest son and heir, Springett Penn, in 1696. Friends, like other Protestants, assumed that dying persons hovered between heaven and this life, and so recorded deathbed scenes as a way of promoting piety. Penn had done this for Thomas Loe and now he wrote a similar account of the dying words of his wife and son, presenting them as models of Christian submission, resignation to death, and assurance of life eternal.

Eight months after the death of his wife, Penn met and began courting Hannah Callowhill, the twenty-three-year-old daughter of a prosperous Bristol merchant. London Friends opposed the match because of the twenty-seven-year difference in age and wondered whether her £3,000 dowry was part of the attraction. When she hesitated, Penn insisted that her many God-given inner graces made her beautiful and that he had received spiritual testimonies as to the rightness of their union. We have Penn's eloquent letters professing his love for her, but not her responses. When they married, leading London Friends did not attend the ceremony, but many influential Bristol Quakers showed their approval by signing the wedding certificate.[92] Penn had agreed that they would live in Bristol, and when he returned to Pennsylvania Hannah accompanied him, even though she was pregnant. From all that we know now, the marriage was a happy one, although Hannah complained that Penn was often absent in London.[93] Before 1712, when Penn had his stroke, Hannah bore seven children, of whom three boys would survive. In his will, Penn left his second wife in charge of Pennsylvania until the sons came of age, and she proved a very competent proprietor.

If a few London Quakers blamed Penn for his political support of James, the response of others showed that he easily resumed his role as a religious leader. He traveled in the ministry in the west of England and Ireland, where he preached to large gatherings of Friends and outsiders. The Toleration Act made dissenters more respectable, and Penn preached in town halls to prominent citizens, mayors, and on occasion an Anglican bishop. The act had not relieved Friends from liabilities for refusing to swear allegiance or not paying tithes. The Meeting for Sufferings, including Penn, lobbied Parliament, and in

1696, with the king's backing, Parliament passed a law allowing distraint of property for tithes and an affirmation that could be used in business and in courts, except in cases of capital crimes. Quakers had wished for a plain declaration of "I Affirm" and had been willing to accept the words "in the presence of God," but Parliament added "the witness of what I say."[94] Many Friends thought this an oath, and though Penn was dissatisfied, he counseled using the legal form while working to get better wording. Penn served on delegations to the king and then to Queen Anne, and when Czar Peter the Great visited England and attended a Quaker meeting, Penn presented him with specially bound books.[95]

PENNSYLVANIA, 1694–1712

Penn's reluctance to return to Pennsylvania may have been due to his frustration with disorder there. In 1696 the Crown replaced the Lords of Trade, which had been composed of nobles who treated Penn sympathetically, with the Board of Trade, composed of bureaucrats less susceptible to his lobbying. The board disliked proprietary colonies, attempted to enforce the Navigation Acts, requiring that all trade go first to England and in English ships, and sought to make all colonies contribute to the war efforts against France. The board instructed Penn to stop smuggling, end disorder, and contribute a quota of money and men to New York for the war. In Pennsylvania, Benjamin Fletcher, the Crown-appointed governor, had allowed the General Assembly to initiate legislation but had been frustrated by the settlers' recalcitrance. Now, back under Penn, the Assembly, refusing to levy any tax, even for government, forced Penn's lieutenant governor, his cousin William Markham, to accept a revised Frame of Government granting the Assembly increased power, including the right to initiate legislation. The Quaker majority in the Assembly and Council also passed a tax to raise £300 for the war and eased their consciences by following Penn's advice to pretend that the money was for food for the Indians. Settlers from Delaware, supporters of Keith, a few Anglicans, and Crown-appointed customs officials opposed the Quaker-dominated Council and Assembly and sought repeal of the charter. Letters to England complained that Quaker justices denied equal rights to outsiders, aided, or at least did not hinder, pirates and smugglers, and ignored immorality and vice. Penn's exhortations that Pennsylvanians work together had no effect, and he complained that he had received no financial support or quitrents for years and had spent £6,000 on the colony.[96]

In 1699 Penn and Hannah came to Pennsylvania, and during the next two years he grappled with but could not solve the controversies over who owned what land and the boundary between Maryland and Pennsylvania. Philadelphia merchants complained about being harassed by royal customs officials and corruption from the new admiralty court judges, who decided cases without a jury. The Board of Trade had instructed Penn to remove from office David Lloyd, who as attorney general had defied the authority of the Crown. But Lloyd was a Quaker and the only skilled lawyer in the colony, and as Speaker of the Assembly he would lead an assault on proprietary privileges for many years.[97] Penn also could not end the animosity between Delaware settlers who wanted a militia and a fort and Pennsylvania Quakers who saw no need for either.

Letters between Penn and Hannah show them making extensive renovations to Pennsbury, their estate twenty miles north of Philadelphia, and ordering food, wine, rum, and chocolate to be sent up the river. In one letter, Hannah called the area "desolate," but she gave birth to a son and experienced better health than she had in Bristol.[98] It is clear that Penn intended to make a permanent home there, and he seems to have been busy and happy working with the Assembly to pass a new code of laws, settling land disputes, appointing officials, meeting with the Native Americans over land sales, planning a new settlement on land near the mouth of the Susquehanna River, and meeting with governors of other colonies to address the issues of pirates, smugglers, and currency.[99] He even proposed, once again, creating an assembly of representatives from all of the colonies to settle disputes among them and to create a common policy for dealing with war.[100] Most reluctantly, he granted a new Frame of Government in 1701 that allowed the Assembly essentially full power to create and enact legislation, weakened the Council, and permitted the inhabitants to decide the separation of Delaware from Pennsylvania.[101] Fearing that a proposed law in Parliament would make void all charter colonies, Penn sailed for England in the fall of 1701. He promised to return but never did; attacks on his control of Pennsylvania, mounting debts, ill health, and perhaps the reluctance of his wife kept him away.

In his final decade, before his stroke in 1712, Penn's letters show that what little happiness he had stemmed from the birth of two more sons and grandchildren. Billy, now his oldest surviving son, had married at age nineteen a woman who his father said brought neither wealth nor wisdom to the partnership. Billy was to be proprietor of Pennsylvania, and in 1702 his father sent him there, complaining to his agent James Logan that the young man was unsteady and too easily led astray but hoping that with the example of Friends a reformation would occur. Instead, Billy became a companion of the newly appointed lieutenant governor of Pennsylvania, John Evans, a former soldier who was about the same age. Evidently, their behavior so irritated everyone that one evening at a tavern, someone blew out the candles and proceeded to give them a beating. Billy renounced Quakerism, started wearing a sword, and returned to England, where he planned a career in Parliament or as a soldier but did neither and soon was living in France. Hannah seems to have taken care of Billy's wife and children as well as her own children and parents. She complained about her husband's frequent absences, and Penn regretted that he was home less than half the time.

In his haste before leaving for Pennsylvania in 1681, Penn had signed several papers increasing his debt with compound interest to his steward Philip Ford.[102] He tried to borrow money from the colonists, but James Logan informed him that they had none because the war had hindered trade, stopped migration, and caused the price of land to fall. A shortage of specie and the colonists' unwillingness to pay rents or taxes meant that no help could come from America. Penn sold his large home and moved into a more modest dwelling. In 1702 Ford died and his widow and heirs tried to collect the debt. Penn claimed that the amount they demanded was fraudulent and went to debtors' prison rather than pay. Eventually, a court set the amount, and a group of wealthy Quakers, including his father-in-law, paid a revised settlement in return for a mortgage on Pennsylvania. In the 1690s Penn had advised the proprietors of New Jersey not to sell the rights of government to the Crown, but now he offered to sell back the power of government to Pennsylvania. His price of £30,000 was what he estimated the colony had cost him, but his initial offer was too high and left him with too many powers. He insisted on preserving liberty of conscience and demanded that Quakers could continue to serve in government. Otherwise, they would sacrifice their birthright in creating and building up the colony. The negotiations continued as Penn lowered the price, but his stroke stopped the process; the Penn family would control Pennsylvania until the American Revolution.[103]

Penn was an unsuccessful businessman, but beginning with the Virginia Company none of the absentee proprietors made money because colonization was expensive, with few immediate returns. That he was essentially bankrupt helps explain the self-pitying, whining tone of his later letters. The War of the Spanish Succession (1701–14) increased conflict in Pennsylvania. Settlers in Delaware wanted a fort and a militia, and the English government wanted money and soldiers. Anglican settlers and royalist officials saw the noncompliance of the Assembly as a sign of the incompatibility of Quaker principles and government. They also refused to participate in courts where defendants and plaintiffs could take affirmations rather than oaths. When Governor Evans attempted to create a voluntary militia, few responded. After Evans spread a false rumor that French ships were coming up the river and attempted to raise a force, Penn recalled him in disgrace. Because Penn's governors obeyed his instructions against the Assembly's wishes, it passed few laws. The only election favorable to Penn occurred in 1710, after London Yearly Meeting rebuked the colonists for their behavior. The motivation for the Assembly's strong opposition to Penn is unclear. It could have been simply a quest for power against an absentee landlord, or a belief in the need to obtain rights before Penn sold the government. Penn saw it as ingratitude and a betrayal of all that he had done. The safest conclusion is that Penn did not understand the colonists' needs and wishes, and that they did not appreciate his efforts in creating and protecting their rights and privileges.

Jasper Batt, an important Quaker, warned Penn in 1683 that concentrating on the outward business involved in creating and maintaining a colony was a danger to his religious purity.[104] This was not true at the time but seems the best explanation for Penn's lack of effort on behalf of Quakers after 1702. He wrote a few introductions to books, composed broadsides for Parliament, revised *Some Fruits of Solitude*, and led the Friends' delegation to Queen Anne in 1702. He engaged in no religious controversies, and when George Keith accused him of being a deist, he wrote no refutation. Penn went to local meetings but did not travel in the ministry, rarely attended the MMM or the MFS, but always went to the LYM. We can only hope that his new family and his abiding confidence in experiencing the Inward Christ sustained him through his disillusion over the failure of his "Holy Experiment" in Pennsylvania.

In 1712, after what may have been a series of minor strokes, Penn suffered a major seizure while writing to his very demanding, greedy son-in-law. With his memory impaired and his mental powers compromised by this stroke, he could do no public business.[105] He lingered for six years, attending local meeting, where he occasionally delivered a few "short, but very Sound and Savoury Expressions," and died in 1718. The memorial minute from Reading Quarterly Friends Meeting described him as "Learn'd without Vanity, Apt without Forwardness, Facetious in Conversation, yet weighty and Serious, of an Extraordinary Greatness of Mind, yet Void of the Stain of Ambition."[106]

Chapter 2

CONVINCED

Penn's conversion to the Quaker form of Christianity in Ireland around 1667 enraged his father, disappointed his mother, and surprised his acquaintances. He could no longer aim for a title or a seat in Parliament or be a diplomat or courtier to a king. In any social setting, except among other Quakers, his clothing, speech, and moral rectitude made him stand out and isolated him from others of similar wealth and standing. But he was still a "Gentleman of quality," as a noble observed.[1] The interplay between his religious beliefs and practices and his social status is the key to understanding him.

A major issue for historians is to understand why the son of an upper-class naval hero joined the despised Quaker sect. The first section of this chapter discusses the sources, while the second deals with early accounts of Penn's joining the Friends, and the third focuses on Penn's writings about conversion. Unfortunately for biographers (many of whom made up stories to fill the void), we have only scattered records of Penn's early life. Unlike many Quakers, Penn left no journal that has survived, not even a commonplace book, which he recommended others keep. During his journeys to Ireland and the Low Countries, he kept an itinerary of the kind that other Friends used as a basis for journals. He published his German journals almost twenty years later, in 1694, perhaps after the death of some of the people mentioned in them, or as a recruiting device for inhabitants of the Low Countries, whom he encouraged to migrate to Pennsylvania. To create an autobiography, he could have relied upon a sufficient number of letters and writings preserved in his letter books, as George Fox did in writing a journal.

Joseph Besse, in his introduction to the *Collection of the Works of William Penn* (1726), referred to Penn's "Private Memoirs," and there are two brief fragments titled "Accounts of my life" that were published in 1836, one concerning meetings with King Charles and the Duke of York in the 1680s and the other his earlier imprisonment.[2] If the two fragments are typical, the memoirs were secular in tone. It is puzzling why he wrote a secular history unlike that of other Friends. Still, it is unlikely that the memoirs contained information about the conversion, or Besse's account of it would not be so cursory. Thomas Clarkson's 1813 biography, based upon Penn's writings, did not go beyond Besse's remarks. It may be that Penn never found the time to write as he aged and had less energy, but he had enough stamina to sire seven children between ages fifty-five and sixty-one (three boys and one girl survived to adulthood). He clearly was not expecting a debilitating stroke at age sixty-eight that diminished his mental capacities for the remaining six years of his life. He had leisure while in hiding after 1689 to have written a journal. One of the enigmas of William Penn is why a man who wrote so much told us so little about himself and his family. This must have been a conscious decision—perhaps, like his refusal to have a portrait painted, because it would appear a sign of vanity. At any rate, there is a gap in the record, because the conversion was neither discussed nor described in Penn's published writings.

At some periods in his life, Penn was not reluctant to talk about himself. When Fox, Penn, Robert Barclay, George Keith, and others traveled in the ministry to Holland and Germany in 1677, they visited Princess Elizabeth, James I's granddaughter. She had asked Penn to provide an account of his life, religious exercises, and sufferings. He says that he began recounting after a period of silence at 3:00 PM. He talked until supper, to which the princess invited the other Friends, and then began again, continuing until 10:00. If we allow two hours for supper, a less formal meal than midday dinner, that is still around five hours. Penn says he could have said more but left out events because of shortage of time and lapses of memory.[3] It is difficult to reconcile the journal, published years later, with a letter Penn wrote at the time. In this letter, addressed to the Countess of Herford (Besse's spelling), after religious exhortations that take up four pages in Besse's folio edition, he wrote, "Something rose in my Heart, to write of my own Convincement to you, with what Entertainment I received from Kindred, Acquantance [sic], Rulers etc. The many Circumstances belonging to my Conversion and Travail, which though inferior to your *Quality*, might not be ungrateful or unserviceable to you."[4] Penn refrained from going further because this letter was already very long.

If, after many hours of Penn's talking about himself, he still needed to say more to the princess, then it is hard to fault Bishop Gilbert Burnet's negative opinion of Penn as a "talking vain man." Burnet added, "He had such an opinion of his own faculty of persuading, that he thought none could stand before it: tho' he was singular in that opinion. For he had a tedious luscious way, that was not apt to overcome a man's reason, though it might tire his patience."[5] Burnet was a Church of England clergyman (later a bishop) who did not like Quakers, thought Penn might have been a Catholic, and met him as James II's emissary to persuade William of Orange to support religious toleration and end the Test Acts for Catholics. Burnet opposed this too.[6] Given the eminence of the other Friends on this European trip, including Fox, it is remarkable, but not unusual in Quaker travel documents, for the author—in this case Penn—to concentrate largely upon himself. To the frustration of historians, ministers recorded in their diaries where they went, the content of meetings, and their spiritual leadings, but they rarely discussed daily life.

Penn's energy level as a mature man is evidenced in one day's itinerary on his German trip. After a full day meeting people, the party of Quakers left at 8:00 at night, walking six English miles to reach "Duysbergh" (Duisburg), but when they arrived sometime between 9:00 and 10:00, the gates were shut. They lay down in a field, "receiving both natural and spiritual refreshment." They arose at 3:00 AM and walked for two hours to the city, entering when the gates were opened at 5:00 AM. They went to an inn, where Penn wrote a letter, four pages long in the *Papers of William Penn*, of "comfort and exhortation" to a "persecuted Countess," and then met with some interested individuals; the group left at 4:00 and walked another eight miles to the next town, where they stayed the night.[7]

Clearly, an explanation is needed for why so vigorous a man came to espouse a religion that required stilling the will and silent meetings.[8] In a letter to Princess Elizabeth, Penn wrote that his religious yearnings were solitary and that no one else in his family was spiritually inclined—not his father, mother, sister, or younger brother. The portraits of the Penn family in Samuel Pepys's diary seem to confirm this, suggesting no great religiosity on the part of the admiral, his wife, or the children—the young William Penn included.[9] In fact, the admiral and his wife seem rather typical Restoration figures; for example, Pepys described romping on the bed with Lady Penn and other ladies and what seems to have been his unsuccessful attempt to seduce her and her daughter.¹⁰ The admiral, whom Pepys called a "rogue" and an "atheist" (this is certainly incorrect), was a trimmer in politics, and the British navy was no place for the squeamish.¹¹

The one influence that the father had on his son William was unintentional. The admiral, in exile with his family on an estate in Ireland earlier given by Cromwell, invited Thomas Loe, a traveling Quaker minister, to speak to his family and guests. Penn said that his father wanted to be able to judge the Friends' faith for himself, but it is equally probable that the admiral viewed inviting a Quaker as entertainment. Such a practice was unusual, because normally Friends approached seekers or those likely to be sympathetic, and Admiral Penn was not that kind of man. In no other records does Loe appear as a particularly distinguished preacher. At the admiral's, Loe's "doctrine" so affected the Penn family's Negro slave that he cried, and "looking on his Father saw ye Tears running down his Cheeks also; he thought in himself wt if we all became Quakers [blank space, illegible]."¹² There is no record of any other contact between the young William Penn and the Quakers until ten years later, after the admiral sent William to Ireland to bring order to his newly granted estates.¹³

When William learned in Cork that Thomas Loe was preaching nearby, he attended the meeting, was emotionally affected, and began frequenting services immediately thereafter. The Harvey manuscript (see below) does not say what in Loe's preaching appealed to Penn. In fact, when Penn discussed his early spiritual awakening, he sometimes said that it predated, and at other times that it coincided with, his childhood sojourn in Ireland. In 1673 he wrote, "the knowledge of God from the Living Witness from 13 years of Age hath been dear to me, from 16 I have a great Sufferer for it at the University."¹⁴ At age thirteen, Penn was in Ireland with his father. On other occasions, however, he dated his first glimpse of God to the ages of nine, twelve, thirteen, and fourteen.¹⁵ So either he had multiple spiritual awakenings or his memory was uncertain. In retrospect, Penn believed that his later knowledge of God confirmed and allowed him to understand his childhood experiences.

CONVERSION

The first account of Penn's spiritual awakening appears in John Aubrey's *Brief Lives*. Aubrey began writing his biographies in 1680 and died in 1697. Aubrey, a non-Quaker, described Penn at Chigwell School at age nine and alone: "he was so suddenly surprised with an inward comfort and (as he thought) an external glory in the roome that he has many times sayd that from thence he had the Seale of divinity and Immortality, that there was a God and that the Soule of man was capable of enjoiying his divine communications."[16] The schoolmaster was not impressed. According to Aubrey, Penn had similar "meditations ravished with joy, and dissolved into tears" at ages thirteen and fourteen. This story "that he has many times sayd" could be what happened again in Ireland and what Penn told Princess Elizabeth and others, and it explains his search for a church that would legitimate his repeated experiences as a youth, as a direct encounter with what he later called the Word/God.

The earliest histories of how Penn became a Quaker are two accounts written long after his death. Joseph Besse published an "Account of Penn's Life" in his 1726 *Collection of the Works of William Penn*. A manuscript titled "An Account of the Convincement of William Penn" is a thirdhand account; that is, Penn told it to Thomas Harvey, tentatively identified as a Bristol Quaker, who told it to someone else in 1729, some fifty years later. In seeking to understand Penn's convincement, we will start with an analysis of what can be learned from these two sources and then examine Penn's early writings in which he described the contours of being born again. My assumption is that Penn made his own "experimental" knowledge normative for all Friends.[17] Besse's description of Penn's conversion at age twenty-two tells us little:

> Being at Cork, he was informed that one of the People called Quakers, that Thomas Loe . . . was to be shortly at a Meeting in that City; he went to hear him, who began his Declaration with these Words, There is a Faith that overcometh the World, and there is a Faith that is overcome by the World; upon which Subject he enlarged with much Clearness and Energy. By the Living and powerful Testimony of this Man, which had made some impression upon his Spirit Ten Years before, he was now thoroughly and Effectively Convinced.[18]

Thomas Loe was an Oxford tradesman who made several visits to Ireland. His initial message seems unexceptional, but Penn—caught between his unsatisfied spiritual quest, guilt at what he would later term a frivolous gentleman's life, and desire for religious certainly—found in that Quaker meeting the truth that would govern his life.

The most detailed account of Penn's conversion is the thirdhand manuscript—told by Penn in 1697 to Thomas Harvey, who later told it to an unnamed and unidentified person who wrote it down in 1729. The unnamed writer is careful to say that the narrative was recounted "in a brief manner as well as his memory would serve after such a distance of time." In spite of a couple of mistakes, the document does have the ring of truth.[19] It contains anecdotes that would be easy for a Friend to remember, and it provides no introspection, no biblical passages, and no theological or psychological analysis, and thus is unlike most Quaker conversion narratives.[20] A logical explanation for writing it down was the superficial account of Penn's convincement in Besse's introduction to the collected works.

Penn was in Cork, Ireland, managing the admiral's estates, when he went into the shop of a Quaker woman, told her he had heard Loe ten years before, and said he would go a hundred miles to hear him again. The woman told the young gentleman that Loe would be at a meeting the next day. The Harvey manuscript relates that when Penn attended this meeting, "another appearing first [in the ministry,] he was not Effected with his Testimony but when T. L. stood up [Penn] was exceedingly reach'd so that he wept much and it seemed to him as if a Voice sayd stand on thy feet, How dost [thou] know but somebody may be reach'd by thy tears so he stood up that he might be seen."[21] Young William, like his father and the Penns' slave, wept. His tears showed a deeply felt emotional and cultural link with a childhood memory; perhaps he had also cried as a child in Ireland upon hearing Loe. Unlike Besse's account, the Harvey manuscript provides no information on the contents of Loe's preaching.

What conclusions can be derived from these two secondhand stories? First, they convey the importance of a vivid memory. As a young adult, Penn sought out Loe. He had heard Loe as a boy and seen his impact on his father and his slave, who both shed tears. Aubrey states that Penn cried as a child. (It is more plausible that the admiral, who had seen combat, would cry, because Charles I, James I, the Duke of York, Oliver Cromwell, and General Fairfax were public weepers.)[22] The thirdhand Harvey manuscript twice refers to weeping, either as a sign of authenticity or because by that time it was unusual among Friends. Going to buy some cloth, Penn engaged the Quaker shopkeeper in conversation and expressed a desire to see Loe again. The coincidence that Loe was in Ireland and in the same town as Penn struck him as providential. He attended a worship service the next day hoping to rekindle his boyhood experience. The first preacher had no impact, but (in Besse's edition of Penn's collected works but not in the Harvey manuscript) Penn later recalled Loe's theme: "There is a faith that overcometh the world, and there is a faith that is overcome by the world." Young William, like his father and the slave, wept. The tears authenticated the verse's impact and established a link with an adolescent memory. Loe's topic was derived from 1 John: 5:4, and, if his sermon was typical of Quaker messages, he would have quoted the text from memory: "For this is the love of God, that we keep his commandments; and his commandments are not grievous. For whatsoever is born of God overcometh the world, and this is the victory that overcometh the world, even our faith."

The meaning was clear: a person who had truly experienced God would receive the power to keep the commandments (probably the Ten Commandments, notably love of God and love of neighbor). Much later, Penn would refer to the light as a "principle" and the essence of Quakerism as "duty."[23] (Notice how prosaic these terms are.) The ability came from God, not the human being. A person's "victory" would be to overcome the temptations of this world and gain eternal life. In this verse we see the themes that would characterize Penn's religious writings: the necessity of a religious experience that gave power; the strength to conquer worldly temptations; a strong emphasis upon morality and Christian ethics; pleasure in obedience to God; and victory over sin that would result in eternal life. In short, self-denial or mortification in this life would result in eternal life; that is, no cross, no crown.

What the two surviving documents about Penn's conversion miss is any record of his later constant emphasis upon God's purging of sins as an initial stage in conversion, which is compared to a sword or a "refiner's fire."[24] He never described his own "dark night of the soul" or wrote of fearing God's wrath and feeling unworthy of God's blessings, either because he never had these feelings or he did not feel it was necessary to talk about them. Penn was familiar with the "lusts" of the world, but unlike Puritan spiritual autobiographers, he did not bewail his constant shortcomings or confess his continuing sins.

In retrospect, it seems clear that Penn's lifelong study of religion and law, management of his father's estates, and tourism had not satisfied him, and that he felt guilty for enjoying the theater, playing cards, and being attracted to young ladies.[25] Penn maintained a relationship with Loe and attended him on his deathbed in 1668, and his account of Loe's deathbed sayings were later included in a collection titled *Piety Promoted*.[26] However, in none of Penn's early published writings did he mention Loe or his impact in his converting to Quakerism. Not until the publication in 1694 of his 1672 travels in Germany did Penn discuss Loe, and the reason seems clear. Loe was only the human instrument; all credit belonged to God.

Penn committed himself to Quaker worship and attending meeting but not to observing other testimonies on plain dress and speech; soon thereafter, when he was arrested in Ireland, he attempted to throw the arresting soldiers down the stairs and had to be rebuked by a Friend who stressed their religion's peaceful nature. The magistrate later observed that he knew the young man and that his clothing was not like that of other Friends, but Penn insisted that he was a Quaker. Because of his rank, the Earl of Orrery, an old acquaintance, released the young man but also wrote to the admiral, who summoned him home. Irritated because Penn did not return promptly, his father sent a second letter dated ten days later reiterating the command. At this time, Penn was still dressing like an English gentleman, but "his manner of Deportment and Solid Concern of Mind" proved his new religion.[27] Although the Harvey manuscript and Besse's edition of Penn's works give accounts of the external events, they do not say what Penn thought or why Loe was so persuasive.[28] So both need to be supplemented by statements Penn made after his conversion. The difficulty with relying on Penn's postconvincement statements is that they reflect his commitment to Quakerism.

One of these documents was written to Mary Pennyman, who seems to have charged Penn with being boastful of his book learning and theological acuity. (Of course, standing up after hearing Loe certainly gives the impression of a young man very aware of his social standing and self-importance.) Penn countered, "I never addicted my selfe to School-Learning to understand Religion by; but allwaies even to their Faces rejected & disputed agst it. I never had any other Religion than what I felt, excepting a little Profession, that came wth education."[29] This assertion that Penn did not study religious books in school to define his religion, and was little influenced by them, is clearly false and ignores what seems to have been his deep attachment to Reformed or Calvinist religion, an attachment that shows in several themes of his writings after his conversion. In fact, a year later, Penn claimed to have "had a Conversation with books" and cited DuPlessy, Grotius, and Amyraldus,[30] along with early Christian writers he probably read at the Protestant Academy in Saumur.[31] He later praised David Blondel, who taught at Saumur, for proving spurious some of the accounts in which the Sibyls prophesied about Christ.[32]

It would be easy to make the case that Penn almost became a Puritan. At Oxford, he had attended private meetings of students, probably for study as well as devotional exercises, at the house of Dr. John Owen, a Puritan who had previously been vice chancellor of the university and was now residing close by. Owen had also written a great deal and was almost a physician of the soul interested in cultivating a life of prayer, Bible reading, and morality.[33] Penn's later comments on Owen, and also on the French Calvinist Moses Amyraut, were respectful, but he never mentioned his time in Saumur or his study with either man. Nor did he criticize the students or teachers at the Protestant Academy, unlike his reaction to Oxford and the Inns of Court. We are taught now to look for the silences as well as the emphases in people's writings. Penn quoted neither Amyraut nor Owen in his *Treatise of Oaths* or the second edition of *No Cross, No Crown*, where he compiled citation after citation on various topics, and he rarely mentioned them elsewhere. To do so would have been to admit to other influences than the direct experience of God on his religious life.

Like the young George Fox and many Puritans, Penn wanted to make a sharp contrast between his life before and after conversion. At the same time, however, he presented himself as outwardly very moral—no one could say that he had "ever . . . seen me drunk, heard me swear, utter a Curse, or speak one obscene word. . . . I speak this to God's glory that has ever preserv'd me from the power of those pollutions, & that from a Child begot an hatred in me toward them."[34] For Penn, such behavior, while moral, clearly had little to do with the salvation that came from the experience of grace.

In order to infer what Penn believed happened to him during Loe's preaching, a logical strategy is to look at his very early writings. One such document was a letter in which he attempted to justify to his father his new course of life. For this, he needed an authority that the admiral would accept, and so he ignored his subjective religious experiences and distinctive Quaker beliefs and practices, including the Inward Light, silent meetings, and plain speech and dress. Instead, he cited Bible verses to distinguish between the spirit of the world and the spirit of Jesus Christ.[35] His strategy required that the admiral either accept his son's life choices or oppose the Bible's precepts and teachings, particularly since the young man presumed to lecture his father about a Christian lifestyle.

The letter contained two lists, one enumerating qualities belonging to the spirit of the world and the other naming qualities in keeping with the spirit of Christ. The first list included persecution, mockery, profane swearing, drunkenness, wantonness, and pleasure (in other words, an implicit condemnation of things to which the admiral had subjected him and a rebuke of his father's lifestyle).[36] Christ's spirit brought love, silence, holiness, chastity, temperance, forbearance, modesty, and moderation. The scriptural references ranged widely and drew on both testaments, but they were also selective. On the immorality of the world, Penn cited the prophets Amos, Isaiah, Jeremiah, and Ezekiel, the Psalms, and the Gospel stories of the torture and crucifixion of Jesus. To illustrate the spirit of Christ, he used the synoptic Gospel verses to contrast persecution with the command to love one's enemies and cited the parable of the tares. Penn ignored parables and miracles in the synoptic Gospels and never cited John, although it was many Quakers' favorite book. Instead, he relied upon the strict ethical teachings in the Pauline and pastoral Epistles[37] and attested that by the "holy Spirit have I been made daily desirous of dying to all the Sin, Pomp, & vain Fashions of this World."

The letter is an apologia for young William and a sermon to his father about worldliness. Penn often insisted that God provided the power to transform one's life, and he condemned the lifestyle of both his parents. The Harvey manuscript says that after he returned home, Penn told the admiral that if not for the forfeit of worldly advantages, he would have become a Quaker after first hearing Thomas Loe. No wonder his father disowned him, but they reconciled—although exactly when is uncertain—and the boy was made principal heir even before the death of his younger brother.

A second source for understanding Penn's recollection of his convincement is his later invocation of it as a source of authority. He gave essentially the same account at least three times. Here is his account ten years later:

> The Lord first appeared unto me, which was about the 12th year of my age, Anno 1656, how at times betwixt that & 15, the lord visited me; the divine impressions he gave me of himself, of my persecution at Oxford; how the Lord sustained me in the midst of that hellish darkness & debauchery; or my being banisht [from] the Colledge. The bitter usage I underwent when I returned to my Father, whipping, beating, & turning out of Dores, in 1662. Of the Lords Dealings with me in France; & in the great plague in London; in the fine the deep sense he gave me of the vanity of the world; of the irreligiousness of the religions of it. . . . How after all this the glory of the world overtook me, & I was ever ready to give up myself unto it; seeing no such thing as the primitive spirit & church in the earth; And being ready to faint concerning my hope of the restitution of all things, [and] that it was at this time, that the lord visited me with the Quakers.[38]

None of his convincement narratives mentions Ireland, any Quaker meeting for worship, or Thomas Loe. All stress the early experiences of God, the suffering, and the final "knowledge of that Inward tender Principles, that overinclined me to Righteousness, Mercy & Peace." Note that there is no ecstasy or weeping mentioned here. Compared with the conversion narratives of George Fox and other early Quakers, Penn's account has no drama, no excitement. Penn subordinated history to theology here, and he provided no actual details of the context because he wanted to describe a process that would provide a universal pattern of overcoming outward authority by inward assurance.

The final sources helpful in understanding Penn's view of his conversion are some of his early writings in defense of Quakerism, particularly since some of these were directed at Presbyterians and Independents. These letters and tracts help to explain why Penn became a Quaker in spite of his education. Some but not all of them date from before the time Quakers began supervising all publications, and we know that Penn wrote quickly, sometimes dictating as the type was set. "I write & speak as I feel it, & not in demure Images."[39]

He makes clear that convincement is not sudden but occurs in stages: "He first wounds, and then heals: afterwards he Atones, Mediates, and Restates the Man in the holy Image." Elsewhere he says that what is needed is "godly sorrow, true mourning, and that repentence." "Holy awe in your Hearts," "a Divine Sense of his Presence in your Souls," "Godly Sorrow, that worketh unfeigned repentence, the only way to Eternal Life."[40] These phrases show that convincement came gradually; equally striking, these stages would be the same for a Puritan like John Owen. Note that there are no surviving documents that show Penn undergoing a process of spiritual turmoil or agony before or after he heard Loe.

The immediacy of the experience was so strong that a language of the senses provided analogies: "Do you see with this Divine Light? Have you searcht your Hearts with it? . . . Is [Jesus] your Eye, your Head, your Wisdom? Do you live, move, and have your life and being in him, in Praying, Preaching, and Singing, yea in your whole conversation? . . . And have you heard his Voice, and seen his Shape?"[41] Penn insisted that the experience required suffering and yet was pleasant: "hide his Living Word in your hearts; though it be as an Hammer, a Fire, a Sword, yet it reconcileth, and bringeth you to God, and will be sweeter to you, that love it, than is the Honey, and the Honey-Comb. Fear not, but bear the CROSS."[42]

Grace was not an intellectual experience; Penn cautioned against images of the mind that came from the self, but the end result was knowledge, peace, and assurance: "My Friends, disquiet not yourselves to comprehend Divine Things; for they that do so, are of the Flesh: But wait in Stillness, . . . and then shall you have a true feeling of him, and of that which feeds the Soul, and giving the Saving Knowledge, viz. That knowledge which is Everlasting . . . likewise Peace, and everlasting Assurance goes along with it."[43]

His earliest, longest, and most subjective description came in 1668:

> I am necessitated to declare, (and be it known to all that ever knew me) that when the unspeakable Riches of Gods eternal Love visited me, by the Call of his Glorious Light, from the dark Practices, wandring Notions, and vain Conversation of this polluted World, and that my Heart was influenced thereby, and consequently dispos'd for the more intimate and sincere Reception of it; those very Habits, which once I judg'd impossible, whilst here, to have relinquished, (as well as I was unwilling) and did allow my self Liberty therein, because not openly gross or scandalous, I thought my self excusable became not only burdensome, and by that Light manifested to be of another Nature than that which I was called to the Participation of; but in my faithful Adherence to its Holy Counsel and Instructions, I was immediately endued with that Power and Authority as gave Dominion over them, and being in Measure redeemed from that to which the Curse is pronounc'd, I sensibly enjoy'd the Blessings that attend a Reconciliation. . . . And as I have the Seal of God's eternal Spirit of Love upon my Soul, as an infallible Assurance.[44]

What were the dark practices, wandering notions, and vain conversation to which Penn refers here? Is the reference to the Calvinist theology he had encountered at Saumur, or the open immorality practiced by King Charles and his courtiers at the Restoration court, or something in Penn's past? He clearly had rejected the card games, theater performances, and dinner parties described in Pepys's diaries. Of course, the clear distinction between godly and sinful practices may be only theological rhetoric needed to convey a stark contrast between good and evil.

At Saumur, Moses Amyraut had modified the strict form of predestination endorsed by the Synod of Dort and had been tried for heresy and acquitted. At Oxford, Owen disliked Amyraut's easing of the harshness of predestination. Both men opposed the sectarian groups, including Quakers, that had arisen during the English Civil War. For Quakers, Penn among them, the concept of predestination was absurd in any form, a libel against God's mercy expressed through Jesus Christ. The simplicity of Quaker worship was the antithesis of the emphasis on liturgy enforced at Restoration Oxford by Dr. John Fell. Penn in retrospect felt guilt about the life of leisure he had been living but was unable to renounce it until he gained "power" and "authority" from God. A consistent theme in Penn's later writing was the Inward Light's power to overcome temptation, and he would rely upon its authority in countering dissident Quakers.

What is a modern scholar to make of Penn's analysis of conversion? We can say that it was characterized by at least seven points:

1. A clear debt to Puritan stages of conversion that was not acknowledged.
2. A close relationship between the Light and the purging of sin.
3. An experience that was, like sensual knowledge, self-authenticating—a call, a feeling, harsh but sweet, in the heart or soul—yet was duplicated by all Quakers who had been implanted by God with a receptacle for spiritual senses.
4. The conviction that the Light gives "power and authority" to give up not only sinful practices but what previously were thought of as innocent pastimes.
5. An embrace of suffering as essential.
6. The belief that the Light is absolutely pure and provides direct contact between God and the person.
7. Knowledge that authentic religious experience gives "knowledge," "Peace," and "everlasting Assurance."

No good Puritan or Anglican would agree with numbers 3, 6, or 7, with their affirmation of a direct, unmediated (what Penn often calls an "experimental") knowledge of God. Unlike most Calvinists, Penn insisted that the individual knew for certain whether he or she encountered the Word/God. His conversion required rejecting Puritanism and testing the validity of all other religions, a requirement that he expressed in his first published work, *Truth Exalted in a Testimony against all those Faiths, Worships, and Religions that have been formed in the Darkness of Apostacy* (1668). The seven points do not tell us how Penn became a Quaker, but they are similar to the conversions of other late seventeenth-century Friends. Given his education, Penn should have become a Puritan, and perhaps he would have had he come of age ten years earlier. During the Restoration, the Puritans were demoralized, and had little sense of the triumphant discovery of truth or the bold willingness to suffer that appears in Quakers' first writings, including Penn's.[45]

In conclusion, we are left with Penn's assertion that he found in the Quaker claim of the availability of direct encounter with God a description that answered the immediacy of divine presence and gave power and purpose to his life.[46] He felt God's presence as a child and did not find the same assurance among the Anglicans, Puritans, or Calvinists of England and France, but as a young man in Ireland he found a certainty among Friends that he appears never to have questioned for the rest of his life. Penn had wavered between the gentleman's role his father desired and his need for moral purity. There is no evidence that he ever questioned the validity of the Inward Light of Christ that he found within the Society of Friends.

Exactly why Penn, in the thousands of pages he wrote, never described his conversion remains a mystery, particularly since he offered to provide one to Princess Elizabeth. That he was too busy and intended to write a journal but failed because of his stroke at age sixty-eight is unlikely. After all, he kept and published journals of his traveling ministry in Holland and Ireland. An explanation is needed for why he decided not to describe what happened in Ireland, and there are several possibilities. Two are theological: first, he may have feared that telling his story would make people rely upon his example rather than on the Inward Light. His few remaining sermons show that, unlike other Quaker preachers, he rarely provided many details about himself.[47] This reticence could have been reinforced by the second possibility—his sense of himself as an aristocrat influenced by Stoicism and rationalism, a man who believed that a person's interior life should be kept private. A gentleman disciplined his passions and kept his thoughts to himself because the ideal life required self-discipline, not self-disclosure.[48] A third possibility is that Penn's initial experience in Ireland seemed no more important to him than what he often experienced in meetings for worship. A Christian was to emphasize his or her growth in grace toward sanctification rather than the initial conversion. Quakers believed that justification and sanctification occurred concurrently during a Christian's pilgrimage through life. Conversion was only the first step and, by itself, not all that significant. In his writings, Penn presented himself as a spiritual, moral, rational, thoughtful Quaker Christian, and he may have believed that those who sought more information indulged in idle curiosity.

The most plausible explanation as to why Penn became a Quaker is that beginning in childhood, both before and after hearing Thomas Loe in Ireland, he experienced what William James termed mysticism and what theologians call a "sense of the numinous."[49] Neither at Oxford, nor at Saumur, nor in Anglican services had he found again that personal awareness of God's presence, and he was unwilling to rely upon external authority—father, king, or established church. As a young man, he was uncomfortable with the leisured life of a gentleman and the moral tone of the court and English society, and he sought meaningful activity. Hearing Loe again in Ireland, he was transformed, finding the spiritual power to change his life as he conformed to the teaching and practice of the Society of Friends. In Quakerism, Penn found a religion that affirmed the validity of his youthful experiences of God. He now embraced a biblically based moral rigor within an organization that allowed a layperson to be a minister with the authority to preach, debate, and write. The last words on his spiritual autobiography should be Penn's: "I can no more get rid of it [the spirit of God], if I would, than of myself, or my own Nature; so present is it with me, and so close it sticks unto me."[50]

Chapter 3

THE DISSIDENT QUAKERS

> And never since I have been conversant with their Principles . . . have I found one Article that did not receive a full and satisfactory assent from that very Grace, Spirit, or Light of God, which first called me from the gross Impieties vain entertainments, tempting glories and will-worships of this Generation.
> —"The Guide Mistaken," 1668

Penn combined his individual and subjective journey to spiritual assurance with opposition to those Quakers who demanded religious liberty in the meeting for practices he opposed. How, having been a religious radical, could he now become a conservative authoritarian and remain so the rest of his life? The evidence comes from Penn's writings in response to those who, having once been Friends, now became critics and began worshipping in separate meetings and publishing against the main body of Quakers. The disputes were named after the ministers who initiated them: John Perrot, John Wilkinson, and Thomas Story.[1]

Before he could become a spokesman for his new faith, Penn needed to become a "weighty" member, a person whose deportment in life and spoken messages in meeting gained the approbation of leaders. Our knowledge of Penn's life in the years immediately after his conversion is fragmentary at best.[2] He remained in Ireland and attended meetings before being arrested and released because of his status, but the Earl of Orrery, the lord president of Munster, with whom Penn had previously socialized, ignored young William's first defense of religious liberty and wrote Admiral Penn about his son.[3]

Summoned home by his father in two letters dated ten days apart, he paused in Bristol for two months (a sign of reluctance to face a wrathful parent). There Penn gained the support of two "weighty" ministers of high social status who already knew the admiral. George Bishop, a former Cromwellian magistrate and a prolific author of tracts, including *New England Judged*, about the persecution and execution of Quakers in Massachusetts, wrote Admiral Penn.[4] Josiah Coale, who had traveled in the ministry to America and also defended Friends in print, accompanied Penn to meet his parents. Joseph Besse recounts stories of several hostile confrontations with the admiral, who disowned the young Penn,[5] but we do not know how long the estrangement lasted, how Penn supported himself, or even where he lived during the next few years.

According to Besse, Penn, recognized as a minister in 1668, participated in a debate along with George Whitehead, already an important Friend, with the Independent-turned-Anglican Thomas Clapham, and in a second debate with Presbyterians Thomas Vincent and Thomas Danson.[6] Penn wrote to Isaac Penington about the death of Thomas Loe, whom he had visited on his deathbed. There is no record of when Penn first met George Fox, who was released from prison in 1668, but he had a conversation with Fox and Margaret Fell before their wedding in October 1669 and journeyed to meet Fox in 1671 as he prepared to leave for America.[7] Penn wrote to Fox in November 1669, and Fox replied to Penn in May 1671, instructing him to complete a tract.[8] Within three years of becoming a Quaker, Penn had published a prophetic judgment against all other churches, proved his theological sophistication in two tracts, and defended Quaker morality and customs. He was now recognized as a leading Friend, engaging in debates against Baptists and Independents, traveling as a minister, being imprisoned for heresy, being released from prison, and reconciling with his father. A year later he had become famous as an advocate of religious toleration. Now he became a consistent defender of the policies of George Fox and other leaders who sought to create an organization capable of surviving a persecution that led to the incarceration and/or early death of many prominent ministers. Although our focus is on Penn's religious defenses of spiritual authority within the meeting, his gentry status and education inclined him to expect deference and order in the general society. Whether in England or, later, in Pennsylvania, Penn believed in respect for existing authority.

To survive, new religious movements need to agree on their beliefs and to provide internal mechanisms for solving theological and behavioral problems.[9] Working out internal controversies among Friends became difficult because the Restoration Parliaments denied their right to worship publicly and used laws and the mob to enforce conformity to the Church of England. Penn lobbied the king, Parliament, and influential nobles for repeal of punitive laws, relief from imprisonment for refusal to pay tithes, and exemption from oaths. Within the Society of Friends, he helped create and support organizational structures to deal with those in prison, define a strategy for dealing with courts, and establish Quaker order and policies. He served on committees that met with dissenters, sent letters rebuking "false" policies and seeking harmony, and attended the first gathering, in 1672, of what became London Yearly Meeting.

The evidence on Penn's attitudes toward dissident Quakers comes from a letter and two treatises on the Perrot division and two pamphlets on the Wilkinson-Story division.[10] All of these writings are relatively short, at least as compared with Penn's voluminous tracts on theological controversies. Because the dissenters in both disputes claimed to be authentic Quakers, Penn assumed, unlike in his tracts against Presbyterians and Independents, that all agreed on fundamental beliefs and practices, including the Inward Light and silent meetings, that ministers spoke under the immediate prompting of God, and that the Bible and the example of the early Christians remained normative. By worshipping together, all knew the truth of Quakerism.[11]

PENN, PERROT, AND MUCKLOW

Penn first wrote letters, and then two tracts, on a dispute that arose in 1661 when Quaker John Perrot returned to England after being released from prison in Rome, where he had gone in the hope of converting the pope, had fallen into the hands of the Inquisition, and been imprisoned and tortured. In his years of isolation, Perrot had arrived at a self-assured spirituality that resisted outward forms. In Britain, Quakers had followed the Calvinist practice of leaving their hats on in preaching during worship, but in prayer, both the speaker and the congregation removed them. As Penn phrased it, preaching was for the people but prayer was for God, and removing one's hat was an expression of honor to the Deity.[12] Perrot, who had the prestige of a suffering martyr, refused during meetings for worship to remove his hat in prayer, insisting that this custom was an outward form. He rested his dissent on his experience of the Inward Light, and, while he did not object to others' keeping their hats on, refused to conform as a matter of religious liberty.[13] Perrot attracted followers in England, but he left for Barbados in 1662 (a condition of his being freed from an English jail), and there he abandoned Quaker plain dress and served as a military watchman.

In response to the Perrot schism, Penn replied in 1672 to a letter from William Mucklow, hoping to solve the issues involved. Instead, Mucklow attacked Penn in *The Spirit of the Hat* (1673); Penn counterattacked in *Judas and the Jews* (1673); Mucklow answered in *Tyranny and Hypocrisy Detected* (1673); Penn responded in *The Spirit of Alexander the Copper-Smith* (1673).[14] These writings illustrate a contrast between Penn's advocacy of freedom of conscience for all and his restriction of liberty within the meeting to the counsel of those with spiritually sensitive correct consciences—that is, the leading ministers, including George Fox. Penn's problem, as for all Friends, was to preserve the infallibility of the unmediated experience of the Inward Light for the individual and group, deny the claims of Quaker opponents who sought freedom within the meeting, and refute the claim of Presbyterians, Baptists, and Independents that Quaker principles led to spiritual anarchy.[15]

Before Penn joined the Friends, influential ministers condemned Perrot's practices and there seemed little lasting effect, but in 1672 William Mucklow sent Penn a letter (now lost) listing thirty-eight reasons for defending Perrot. Penn did not know Mucklow and had not been involved in a controversy that seemingly had ended, but he was already identified with what could be called an emergent Quaker establishment, primarily George Fox and those who attended the Second Day Morning Meeting of Ministers (MMM) in London.[16] Both Mucklow and Penn claimed to be seeking truth, writing in Christian love, and seeking reconciliation. As a "member" of Friends, Penn saw his role as reclaiming a lost soul who could return to the true faith and thereby escape damnation. In disputes among Friends, all sought to preserve the testimony of the first Friends, which they saw as the latter-day embodiment of primitive Christianity, and claimed assurance of having received guidance from the Holy Spirit. Penn's writings in disputes with dissident Friends convey a mixed message of compassion and irritation, care and arrogance. His self-righteousness, like that of Mucklow, made it easy to judge harshly the other's motives, and while the issue appeared to be doffing one's hat during prayer, ultimately, for Penn, the larger issue was the authority and unity of inward revelation for all Friends. At the beginning of his long letter, Penn judged Mucklow, Perrot, and their followers as schismatic and, in a paraphrase of Jeremiah, complained, "thou delightfully play'st the Harlot every day."[17]

Penn reduced Mucklow's thirty-eight articles, which he saw as redundant, to three: (1) Were any forms or ceremonies allowed in the true church? (2) Was removing the hat during prayer an outward form? (3) Was the Quakers' disowning of John Perrot and his followers an infringement on religious liberty and a sign that Friends had betrayed spiritual worship by following the examples of persecution set by Roman Catholics, Anglicans, Presbyterians, and Independents?[18] Complicating Penn's task was the fact that Quakers proclaimed that all true worship was inward and spiritual and denounced traditional Christian physical practices and forms, including baptism by water, Communion, and liturgy. The only outward forms Friends retained were set times to begin meeting for worship, standing to preach, and, for men (but not women), removing their hats during prayer. Perrot had taken the basic Quaker belief in worship as spiritual to its logical end by refusing to take off his hat during prayer. He also raised the issue of the binding authority of an individual's subjective inward revelation against the collective judgment of any organization, even that of the earliest and most important Friends.

Penn agreed with Mucklow that Friends had repudiated any "Ceremonies Typical which show forth a future Glory" or any "mystical Dispensation: forms or observances dependent upon further revelation."[19] All customs originating in the Jewish faith, for example, tithes, Christ had abolished. When he precluded new revelations from any individual acting alone, Penn undercut Perrot's assertation that his practice was legitimated by inward spiritual certainty. (In the Wilkinson-Story controversy, Penn and the main body of Friends discovered and defended new revelations.)

Unlike his debates with non-Quakers, Penn in his letter used scripture but cited no proof texts. Mucklow did not deny that humans had bodies that were physically present during worship. Both also agreed that even though the body was involved, any earthly or bodily origin of practice in worship was unacceptable. Penn added, by contrast, that it was "rational," "true," and "lawful" to involve something of the body in response to a spiritual leading. "Till bodies are excluded any share in Divine Worship, bodies ought to have, and will have exterior as well as Soul's interior acts of Divine Reverence." It was acceptable to have set times for worship and some forms or ceremonies, but all such actions must originate in a spiritual leading. They could not be "Typical, Legall or Superfluous" and, by analogy, were not the "fruit" but the "leaves" of religion. "In short, as the Soul worships, so does the Body," and an exterior or bodily motion that arises from the interior is "Lawful, & that the Spirit of the

Lord has unity with, & has led to, & had countenance in." Any custom that arose from the body or earth or an unworthy motive, however, "under the pretense of religious liberty" or further revelation, "the Lord judgeth and not we" as "delusive, Imaginary, unsubject, self separating & rending Spirit."[20]

Then the issue, as Penn defined it, was whether removing the hat during prayer was a spiritual response. When an outsider doffed his hat before an acquaintance, it was an act of deference to the pride to a social superior, a custom that had originated with the Fall. Quakers refused to acquiesce in such an earthly custom. By contrast, taking one's hat off to God was an act of worship, of reverence, and grew out of spiritual discernment. Perrot had allowed those who felt free to remove the hat to continue the custom as a form of religious liberty. Penn countered that if Perrot allowed other Friends to remove their hats, he had admitted that the custom could have a spiritual sanction. Because Friends and Perrot agreed that the issue was of minor importance, why could Perrot not accept the spiritual guidance of most Quaker ministers? For Friends, the answer was clear: Perrot's custom sprang from pride in his own revelation and a will to power. He had succumbed to a bodily or earthly form, even while claiming it to be spiritual. Penn claimed that the same action could at times be either "necessary [or] indifferent." When he preached, Penn kept his hat on, although he had the freedom to remove it, but when addressing God, as a sign of respect, he removed his hat, explaining, "The Objection about the hat in prophesie [preaching] is not to purpose, for in that state men speak from the Allmighty God to mortall men, & in prayer they speak as mortall men to the immortal Glorious God."[21]

The third issue involved religious liberty. Why had leading ministers testified against Perrot on a matter that both sides agreed was a "slight thing"? Penn answered: first, because John Perrot had shown disunity, judging George Fox and other Friends by keeping his hat on before even discussing the issue. This showed that Perrot had placed his judgment above that of all other Friends. If, as Perrot conceded, this was a small matter that had no effect on "Life & Salvation, nor to the Edification of the Body," then why did he persist in disrupting the harmony of the members by keeping his hat on during prayer? The danger was that Perrot might innovate again under his imagined claim of inward inspiration. If Perrot had prevailed "in this one conceit, he would have drew in his own Body, & Mass of imaginations, till the blessed Truth had been overrun with his Ary Dreams," Penn asserted. Such practices would make Friends "a just derision to all sober Men."[22] In short, Perrot had fallen from the "pure spirit," and Penn, like other ministers, had seen the source of his infatuations and, under the guidance of the Light, had followed the judgment of God.

If Penn believed that he was persuasive, he learned otherwise when Mucklow, in *The Spirit of the Hat* the following year (1673), accused Friends and Penn of betraying the Inward Light by creating a "papish hierarchy." Mucklow argued that the main body of Friends had stayed loyal to the first witness, but they remained silent cyphers while George Fox and the ministers, particularly those in the MMM, sought power. "In the true Church, Unity stands in diversities; But in the false, Unity will not stand without Uniformity." In essence baiting his opponent to reply, Mucklow charged that the Independent John Faldo had bested the supposedly better educated Penn in their debates, and he labeled George Fox a leader with Penn his Hector—a follower doomed to failure.[23]

Mucklow sought religious liberty within meeting and asked for a "medium" policy between expulsion for those who could not remove their hats and approbation of the custom. Citing the examples of Peter and Paul in early church debates over whether to retain Jewish customs on meat eating and circumcision, the tract asked for "diversity" in the spirit rather than "uniformity" by decree. Quakers had refused to remove their hats as a sign of deference to social superiors but now disowned those whose inner spirit found no freedom in removing them during prayer. They had argued that they showed no disrespect to their social superiors in keeping on their hats; why, asked Mucklow, wasn't the same true with respect to God? After all, there was no scriptural warrant for such an outward form as removing the hat in prayer but not in preaching, and it was possible to show reverence with the hat on or off. If true religion were spiritual, then it should make no difference what a Quaker did with his hat. Why had the ministers made such an issue of the practice, disowning those who found no spiritual leading to continue a practice long observed by Presbyterians and Independents? Mucklow charged that George Fox and the ministers, in claiming the authority of Jesus Christ for their decisions, had destroyed the witness of the first Friends. "G. F. and the rest of this Councel have endeavored to subvert the Royal Law of Liberty, and to introduce an Arbitrary and Tyrannical Government over the Conscience, over the Flock of God."[24]

Given the standards of theological debate in the seventeenth century, Penn's initial letter to Mucklow had been restrained and reasonable, but his response to *The Spirit of the Hat* expressed outrage that an "apostate" had made Friends' disagreements public. Mucklow was a follower of Satan, a Ranter, a Judas who had sold Christ for silver, an Alexander the Coppersmith—who had opposed the Apostle Paul—and his tract was filled with "Rancour of Malice, Fury, and Revenge and with Folly too." The title of Mucklow's pamphlet was fitting, for he had "so little Head, or at least no more Brains than in an Empty Hat."[25] At a time when Friends were being persecuted and imprisoned for not attending Anglican services and being attacked by Anglicans, Baptists, Presbyterians and Independents, Mucklow had enlisted in the devil's campaign to overthrow true religion.

The later pamphlets, filled with charges of scandalous behavior by Friends' enemies, shed little light on the underlying issue of the hat. Penn insisted that if some Friends wore hats during prayer while others did not, this would create disorder and would disgrace Friends in the eyes of their opponents. God, particularly a God of order, would not inspire some Friends in meeting to wear their hats while others bared their heads. This would be Ranterism, not Quakerism. Inward revelation was not disorder; it was unity under the guidance of the Holy Spirit. Perhaps because he was embarrassed by the trivial nature of the dispute over the hat, he shifted his focus to the nature of the church. Penn used two kinds of argument here. First, he made a political defense. The church as a civil society needed authority to define its beliefs and practices and to enforce them on all within it. The church had power over its members but not on outsiders. Second, he gave a theological defense. Friends believed that "every Man is enlightened with a sufficient Light to Salvation," and that all faith and worship should depend "upon the Convictions and Leadings" of the Light. The "leadings of the Light" controlled the body, not the other way around. All agreed also that Christ gave the church, "consisting of faithful Believers," the ability to judge all innovations and to beware of "false prophets," no matter how innocent in appearance. The church also had the right to admonish "any dissenting or innovating persons" and to deny them for acting in a "wrong Spirit." Such persons might agree with these precepts about the Light but still be motivated by a "wrong Spirit to divisions," and the church should judge them. Penn concluded that the Quakers, not "those few stragling Fellows of John Perrot," were the true church.[26] God had given the true ministry to the Quakers, and after reasoning with and then admonishing John Perrot, they disowned him.

THE WILKINSON-STORY CONTROVERSY

The Wilkinson-Story division is named after two ministers from the north of England who opposed the establishment of separate business meetings for women beginning in the 1670s. They sought to worship in secret so as to avoid persecution and to hide goods so that informers would not seize them, and they wanted the names of those who had been disciplined by the meeting kept secret. Above all, they disliked what they feared was an emerging authoritarian, hierarchical organization of LYM and the creation of the MFS as a kind of executive body.[27] An epistle signed in 1675 by most attenders of LYM, including Penn, condemned these separatists. Later, Penn was one of those delegated to meet with them in an attempt to end the dispute without, however, agreeing to their demands.[28] During the early phases of the controversy, Penn wrote no pamphlets, perhaps because he was busy advocating religious liberty, electioneering for the Whigs and Algernon Sidney, mediating disputes over West (New) Jersey, and seeking a charter, writing laws, and recruiting colonists for Pennsylvania.

Why Penn wrote *A Brief Examination, and the State of Liberty Spiritual* in 1681 is not clear. There was no immediate publication for him to answer; at least, he does not mention any.[29] Robert Barclay's *Anarchy of the Ranters* (1676) provided a clear theological defense of the main body's rationale, and although an initial agreement with the two ministers failed, Story was reconciled to Friends before his death. Separatist meetings continued to exist in Bristol and Westmoreland. If the audience for the second edition of *No Cross, No Crown* (1682) was entirely Christian (including those who might migrate to Pennsylvania), the readers of the *Brief Examination* were Friends alone. It seems likely that, although the primary audience was the schismatics, Penn also attempted to guard the new colony from the divisions that plagued Quakers in England by guaranteeing unity, restricting the meetings' power over nonreligious matters, and promising no religious persecution. (Both books could have been read in Pennsylvania; in 1688 William Bradford, the only printer there, listed them both for sale.) Penn sought "obedience to God, our Superiours, to the Houshold of Faith, and to all Men and Creatures," and made a clear distinction between outward religious toleration and "Christ's Liberty, [which] is obtain'd through Christ's Cross; they that would be his Freeman must be his Bonds-men, and wear his blessed Yoke. His Liberty is from sin."[30] Note the hierarchy of authority: God, "our Superiours" (political authorities), and the "Houshold of Faith," which must be obeyed as "Bonds-men" (indentured servants) to Christ. Penn reinforced a hierarchal view of society here: king, proprietor, father as outward authority, and Christ and his ministers as spiritual masters.

Although the intellectual content of *Brief Examination* is the same as that of the two anti-Mucklow tracts, the arguments there are presented calmly and, for Penn, succinctly, perhaps because he hoped for reconciliation. Building upon the premise that Friends reincarnated the early church, Penn argued that Jesus exercised authority over his followers and that, as described in Acts and the Pauline Epistles, his disciples exercised similar spiritual power in defining beliefs and practices. Using a metaphor derived from Paul, Penn insisted that the present body of Jesus was the visible church, and a physical body could not function if the head, arms, eyes, mouth, and feet were not unified. And, of course, all parts of the body had to obey the head.[31] The members of the church were like parts of the body, each one having a function and place; for example, a well-functioning body required that the arm not attempt to replace the head. Within the church, members had diverse gifts and places; disorder would come from those, like Perrot, Wilkinson, and Story, whose pride made them discontented. Some had a "gift" for preaching, others for visiting the sick, comforting the dying, helping the poor, providing counsel, or sitting quietly in worship. Just as a minister who had the gift of eloquence could outrun his inspiration, so anyone, no matter how outwardly saintly, could be mistaken in her or his understanding of the Light. It did not matter that Perrot and Wilkinson and Story had once been ministers in unity with Friends; now they had fallen, and their pride and self-will had vitiated the Light of Christ.[32]

Penn's fear of disorder made him insist that Jesus would not have left either the first- or seventeenth-century Christians without a means of controlling the outward church. Just as the church was both visible and invisible, so humans were both body and spirit, and the outward body of the church could be controlled by the inward, spiritual, direct, infallible revelation. All Christians must submit to guidance from the Light and thereby obtain true freedom. Because God was eternally constant, giving the same counsel in all periods, the Bible, early church, modern Quakers, and any individual's revelation had to agree. Those who had founded Friends, who had stayed true to their gift, suffered, and endured, could now provide spiritual insight. They joined collectively after worshipful silence and received from God the authority to judge, with no appeal from their decisions. So long as ministers and elders waited for guidance from the Light, they could not err. (The dissenters pointed to the resemblance of this doctrine to practices by the Roman Catholic, Anglican, Presbyterian, and Independent churches that Friends had often denounced.) Penn insisted that the main body of Friends had "absolute right" to judge the validity of any member's individual revelation. True Christian liberty meant obedience to the "One God, one Spirit, one Faith, one Baptism."[33]

What if a person believed that the ministers were wrong? Penn suggested that honest self-examination would reveal whether ignorance, complacency, carelessness, or self-will had led to this conclusion. After praying for guidance and sitting in worship, a sincere seeker who had conquered self-will would receive the truth and conform. Because of the variety among people, there was always diversity within the meeting, but never spiritual disunity. If a person strayed from the fellowship, he or she went "out of the light," and the meeting needed to disown those who undermined unity. "God is not the God of Confusion, but Order."[34]

Complicating Penn's authoritarian stance was his commitment to spiritual freedom, and so he insisted that the meeting could impose no outward penalty except disownment. Freedom from persecution based on religious belief was a natural right, because a person's conscience could not be coerced. Penn quoted George Fox, who disliked the term "religious liberty" because that was external; what he wanted was true freedom, and that was submission to Christ.[35] Beyond the bounds of the meeting there was freedom for Quakers and all others. Here, the rules for behavior were universal and based upon reason and morality, because the Inward Light applied only to religion. Normal life—how one earned a living, where one lived, what one ate—should be decided by moderation, and the test here was keeping with the moral law.[36] A government could foster ethical living by enacting laws that promoted a healthy society, but it had no responsibility for regulating matters of conscience. Penn had proved, at least to his and most other Quakers' satisfaction, that he had reconciled religious liberty for all, the authority of inward revelation, and the unity of Friends.

In 1692 Penn again addressed the supporters of Wilkinson and Story, who continued to worship separately from the main body of Friends, but now the context differed. Penn was in hiding, suspected of treason, and the theological dispute with George Keith and his supporters preoccupied LYM. Wilkinson, Story, Barclay, and Fox—the main personalities in the dispute—were now dead. Whether Friends should respond to persecution by meeting openly or secretly, a major issue in the 1670s, had become irrelevant because the law guaranteed freedom of Protestant worship. Now, as Penn saw it, the only issue troubling the "dissatisfied Quakers" was separate women's meetings, and, as he had earlier argued, this was not a matter of faith and worship, upon which there could be no compromise, but an outward issue involving civil society and due order but not spiritual freedom. Penn's language was gentle, as he wrote in "Sense and Sorrow" and with "Charity" and "Tenderness" at the "Distance and Dissatisfaction" between the groups; he sought not "Victory" but through "Peace and Love" hoped to end the division and restore "precious Fellowship and seamless Garment."[37]

As in the earlier tracts, Penn's task was made easier because all agreed that the original vision of the first Friends restored true Christianity, and the issues did not involve faith, worship, or morality but only outward practice. Yet he sought reconciliation without admitting that the original complaints had merit or that Fox and the ministers in LYM had undermined freedom of conscience and betrayed the authority of the Inward Light by creating a centralized system requiring conformity. Penn did admit that there was misapprehension about motives and small matters that had been magnified in the "heats," "zeal," and "fear" of the dispute.[38] He effectively ignored the earlier claims of Fox and the ministers that they acted under the direct guidance of the Inward Light and New Testament precedents. By confining the dispute to civil society and ignoring all issues except women's meeting, Penn could insist that liberty of conscience had been preserved.

Drawing upon the language he used in the second edition of *No Cross, No Crown* (1682) and *General Rules* (1681), Penn restricted the power of the monthly meeting over commerce, dress, houses, and other private matters—so long as there was moderation. However, Friends, like other religious groups, needed an organization to deal with feeding the poor, visiting the sick, supervising marriage ceremonies and funerals, maintaining order within the meeting, and ensuring the purity of members. All agreed that men and women constituted the church, shared responsibility, and should cooperate as helpmeets. (Penn mentioned that there were more women than men in the church.) The only matter in dispute, he argued, was whether outward tasks could be better performed with men and women meeting together or separately. There were many matters "relating to their own sex" that women were better qualified than men to discuss, and they would welcome the opportunity to speak freely among themselves.[39] Penn did not specify these issues, but, based on women's meetings' minutes, we can assume that he meant dealing with poor widows and orphans and investigating whether a maiden had been sexually active, become pregnant, or made promises of marriage to more than one man. It was logical for the woman and man intending to marry to come before the women's meeting first and then the men's. Penn did not say so, but the men's meeting controlled disownment and most expenditures. (Women's meetings had funds for charity and even made small loans.) Whatever one concluded about separate men's and women's meetings was of minor importance compared with the necessity of love and unity among Friends.

In his earlier tracts about the separation, Penn quoted the Bible extensively and relied upon precedents from the early church. Not so here. Only in the final paragraph did Penn cite any scripture, and then he mentioned (but did not quote) fifteen verses, all in the New Testament, none from the four Gospels, and all from Paul and the pastoral Epistles that advocated charity and harmony within the church.[40] Submission to due authority was missing.

CONCLUSIONS

The rebel Penn was also an authoritarian Quaker because he could not believe that God had created a world in which humans could not know religious truth with certainty. A loving God would not make Christian behavior in this world and eternal bliss in heaven depend upon earthly knowledge gained from the Bible, reason, moral law, and conscience. The devil could read and quote scripture; avarice, self-will, emotion, and above all pride could overcome natural reason and the moral law.[41] His personal and shared experience of the "Word-God" in conscience was Penn's solution to religious and moral relativism. God had convinced Penn individually, but it was the communal feeling and spiritual knowledge gained in meetings for worship and later in monthly, quarterly, and yearly gatherings that gave Friends certainty. Those who opposed publicly the "weighty Friends"—George Fox and other early Friends and more recent converts like Penn, Whitehead, and Barclay—denied the infallible knowledge available to spiritually sensitive leaders. Penn would not tolerate their errors.

Whether Penn's tracts had any influence on dissident Friends is uncertain, but in time most separate meetings ended, either because the members left Friends for other churches, or died, or rejoined the main body of Quakers. From the 1670s to 1692, there is consistency in Penn's main argument: that the policies of Fox and the ministers did not infringe the power of the Light or freedom of conscience. Because they were the living embodiment of the early church, Friends, whose leaders exercised authority only under the guidance of the Light, retained the right to define faith and practice as described in the New Testament. In later tracts, Penn emphasized that the dispute was over outward matters and did not question the motives of the dissidents. In addition, the tone of his writings in the 1670s is strikingly different from that of later tracts. In the 1670s he wrote with scorn and vituperation, defending Fox's authority and resisting persecution, whereas in 1681 he stressed concern for obedience and fear of disorder, and in 1692 he expressed a desire for peace and harmony and an end to disputes over small matters.

His convincement confirmed in Penn a certain style of rebellion—a readiness to defy his father and to flout the religious authority of Presbyterians, Anglicans, and the Crown. As he proclaimed in the Tower, "my prison will be my grave before I will budge a jot."[42] Paradoxically, the man willing to die in jail for his spiritual freedom and to defend religious toleration even for Roman Catholics showed no understanding or sympathy for those Friends who defied the leadership of George Fox and what might be called the emergent Quaker establishment. If Loe was Penn's first "father-confessor," Fox later occupied a similar role as the prophet who rediscovered true Christianity. Fox had the prestige of starting the religious awakening and, to Penn's mind, embodied the virtues of Quakers, and so he supported Fox's condemnation of Perrot for refusing to remove his hat during prayer and approved Fox's initiation of women's meetings and a hierarchical structure of monthly, quarterly, and yearly meetings. Whether confronting the followers of John Perrot or the Wilkinson-Story critics, Penn demanded submission. (The style of dealing with discontent that Penn learned in Quaker meetings did not work well in England and would be even less successful in early Pennsylvania.) By 1692, the confidence Penn had expressed in the earlier tracts had been tempered by his failures with King James II and in Pennsylvania. The authoritarian now sought peaceful reconciliation.

Penn's conversion did not dampen his respect for authority or his desire for order. We know little about the household in which he was raised, but his authoritarian father undoubtedly expected subordination, and so did the young Penn in London and Ireland. He criticized pride in family but was not a social leveler. The young man's rebellion was not against the privileges of birth but was confined to the demands of his new religion. Women and men were spiritual equals, but within the meeting members had different gifts and should defer to those with deeper spiritual insights. In his later political tracts, Penn defended an Englishman's traditional rights, but he was never a republican who opposed monarchy. He had better relations with Charles II and James II and nobles in the court than with the gentry of Charles II's first Parliament, who insisted upon the persecution of dissenters. The only hierarchy Penn consistently opposed was that of the Church of England, where, he claimed, bishops and other clergy debased the free Gospel of Christ by taking tithes, imprisoning Quakers, and seeking political power. Because Quaker ministers did none of these things and because he was one of them, he supported their defense of social order. George Fox and the first Friends had discovered the authentic Christianity that Penn experienced in worship. He found a community of faith among the leading Quaker ministers, and neither he nor they would compromise or betray truth. Penn, like many others before and since, reinforced Friends' religious confidence by silencing dissenters.

An explanation for the young rebel's later submission to the totality of Quaker principles and practices comes from his description of them. They were "sound in Principles, zealous for God, devout in Worship, earnest in Prayer, constant in Profession, harmless and exemplary in their Lives, patient in Sufferings, orderly in their Affairs, few in Words, punctual in Dealings, merciful to Enemies, Self-denying as to the World's Delights and Enjoyments, and to sum up, Standards for the God of heaven."[43]

No wonder Penn became and remained a Friend. As a historian of Quakerism, I wonder whether the behavior of Pennsylvania Friends many years later changed his mind, not about his or their religious experiences but about the colonists' Christian virtues. By offering to sell to the Crown the right to govern Pennsylvania and Delaware in 1702, Penn surrendered his efforts to create a holy commonwealth. His reforming efforts would be restricted to maintaining the witness of the first Friends in the meeting.

Chapter 4

THE BUSINESS OF QUAKER MEETING

There is no record of any seventeenth-century person's becoming a Quaker because of the thrill of participating in the meeting for business. Even so, religious movements need an organizational structure to create and implement policies involving church buildings and other property, raise money, establish norms of behavior, address the discipline of members, navigate relations with outsiders, and, in Restoration England, deal with persecution and politics.

A major omission in the scholarship on Penn concerns his role in the business of Quaker meetings. Such business included setting policy for dealing with challenges posed by both Friends and outsiders, working to end persecution, and adjusting to the changing political and religious landscape from the 1660s until 1712. Was Penn active in setting policy? Was he primarily a follower or a leader? Did his roles within the business meetings change over time? Were certain tasks reserved to him? Were there others in which he was ignored? Although the meeting minutes present Penn as a weighty Friend who undertook many business tasks, on four occasions his contributions stand out: first, during the reign of James II (1685–88); second, in the debates on George Keith in London Yearly Meeting in 1694; third, in the controversy among Friends on the response to Parliament's 1696 affirmation law; and, finally, in the circumstances surrounding a memorandum that Penn wrote and presented to the Second Day Morning Meeting of Ministers in 1701. These events are the major foci of this chapter.

Penn's roles during the meeting for worship will not be discussed, because they are unrecoverable. With a few exceptions—mostly sermons that were taken down by outsiders—Quakers claimed to be speaking under the direct influence of the Inward Light of Christ and did not write down the spoken messages.[1] It is ironic that we have no firsthand descriptions of what it was like to hear Penn speak, because in "A Brief Account of the Rise and Progress of the People called Quakers," he provided the best descriptions of George Fox in prayer or preaching.[2] All that is certain is that he was an eloquent preacher whose appearances while traveling attracted large crowds. My emphasis in this chapter is on the slightly more mature man who became recognized as a minister, a leading apologist for Friends, and a member of the three organizations centered in London: London Yearly Meeting (1672), the London Meeting for Sufferings (1677), and the Second Day Morning Meeting of Ministers (1673). My primary sources here are the minutes of some forty years' worth of meetings during which Penn was an active and important Friend.

A major difficulty for any historian is that Friends did not officially accept human authority, and certainly not any individual's domination in business meetings. They believed in the guidance of the Holy Spirit, and in ascertaining and following the knowledge furnished by the Inward Light of Christ, available to all. However, within this theological perspective, Friends, following Paul in 1 Corinthians (12:4–31), distinguished between the gifts of ministers and other weighty Friends, who would later be officially recognized as elders and overseers and whose leadings had special significance, and the main body of Friends. In other words, God gave to a few the gift to speak in meeting, to others the ability to arbitrate business disputes and lobby Parliament, to some a calling to help widows and orphans, and to many the role of worshipping in silence while striving to be Christians. In 1702, LYM discouraged "backbencher" members from attending and stated that the only persons authorized to attend were ministers, members of the MFS, and delegates from the various Quarterly Meetings.[3] Long before Penn became a convert, believers had created an unofficial hierarchy of power relations among Friends.

In controversies of the 1670s, opponents, most of them former Quakers, complained about the dictatorship of Fox and his supporters, including William Penn and George Whitehead, in creating an organizational structure of yearly, quarterly, and monthly meetings, the MFS, the MMM, and women's meetings.[4] At the national level, the basic issues facing the leadership were alleviating persecution and dealing with those who for theological and other reasons resisted Fox's leadership and new structures he created. As a supporter of Fox's authority, Penn was involved in both of these issues. After Fox's death, a 1690s satirical etching of LYM focused on the power of Whitehead, Penn, and a small group of Friends seated at what Friends called the facing bench, behind a head table with Fox's *Journal* in the center, receiving the prominence that would normally have been reserved for the Bible (see fig. 2, p. 100).[5] For the purposes of this chapter, I agree with those who saw a human power structure within the meeting and seek to understand Penn's role in it.

A second difficulty in determining leadership was the way in which minutes were kept and tasks assigned. Elias Hookes, who became the first paid employee of LYM in 1674, kept minutes for LYM, MFS, and MMM, and he recorded decisions but not the content of discussions or disagreements.[6] Tasks were allocated to groups rather than individuals, often with a notation that any three of the five or six persons named should do the work. Although we know little about how clerks were chosen in the seventeenth century, then as now the clerk probably named the committee and asked for volunteers, but the meeting as a whole approved the composition of each group. Penn was sometimes appointed when he was not present; he sent written reports of a completed mission and its success or failure and occasionally had to be reminded to finish the task. A word of caution is in order regarding interpreting my findings: if it were easy to discern Penn's various roles from the minutes or his correspondence, this would have been done long ago. Minutes show only final agreement on issues; they camouflage individual input and discussions. Those who disagreed kept quiet, whether because they accepted the authority of the leaders, ignored those leaders' decisions, or stopped attending meetings for business.

Penn's roles in his local monthly meeting are not of importance here, because the major decisions came from the three London-centered meetings. In addition, the published minutes of two local meetings where Penn resided (Lower Bucks and Bristol) show few activities by him and nothing unusual. The more significant was in Bristol, where he was a visitor to the Latin School and met the master, James Logan.[7] (The pupils must have been terrified to recite before their distinguished scholarly visitor.) Historian Mary Maples Dunn describes Penn as a restless man, and he had permanent residences in Bucks, Sussex, Bristol, and Bedford, as well as lodgings in London on several occasions. His first wife, on her deathbed, exhorted him not to give up his traveling ministry in order to stay with her, while his second wife regretted how frequently he was absent.[8] He seems to have been a constant traveler in the ministry, visiting various local meetings on first days, taking prolonged journeys to Ireland and the Continent, going to America twice, and spending several months in debtors' prison and time in the Tower after the publication of *The Sandy Foundation Shaken*. He also went into hiding for several years after the 1688 Glorious Revolution. Even had Penn wanted to take an active role in local meeting affairs, he was often absent.

Penn was present at the first gathering that became LYM and also at the first MMM; he may also have attended the first MFS, though there is no hard evidence of this. Attendance records were kept for the early years of the MFS, but not for the other two organizations. At the beginnings of LYM, Penn was present when he signed (with others) the epistle.[9] In 1681, London began recording the names of delegates from the Quarterly Meetings; Penn was almost always present, often from Sussex but also Bristol and Bedford. He was absent only when he was in hiding or in America. Members of the MFS and MMM gathered every week on different days. Penn often lived not far from London, but it would still have taken a major effort to journey to the city twice a week. He had lodgings in London during the reign of James II, the period when he was most active in the MFS. His attendance at both the MFS and MMM can best be described as erratic. He would not appear for months, but there were brief periods when he was always present.

The activities of the three organizations were in theory separate but often overlapped. The MMM, composed only of male ministers, had as its primary tasks supervising the ministers in London and reading over and editing manuscripts; it could recommend publication, changes, private circulation, or suppression. Depending on the need, originality, contents, and perhaps the prominence of the author, the MMM might adjust the length or change the focus of a manuscript. A couple of members might privately edit it, but generally all members would read the manuscript aloud in order to make sure that it represented the position of Friends. In Penn's case, the MMM read his primarily religious writings but not his tracts on toleration, politics, or Pennsylvania, *Some Fruits of Solitude*, or the *Essay on the Present and Future Peace of Europe*. Friends may have approved these writings but did not say so publicly. They were officially endorsed by Friends as canonical when they were included in the 1726 collected works.

The MFS, composed of both male ministers and prominent laymen generally living in or near London, dealt with all matters between sessions of the LYM. After the debacle caused by inconsistent and overlapping attempts to get George Fox out of prison, LYM created the MFS to coordinate responses to persecution by compiling lists of those who suffered, offering legal advice on how to proceed in various courts, and approaching the authorities to gain relief.[10] LYM was the final authority and, in theory at least, approved the decisions of all subordinate meetings. There was significant overlap in the membership of all three groups, particularly among ministers who could attend all three, and prominent Friends like Penn, George Whitehead, and Ambrose Rigge participated in all three. But laymen and women did not attend the MMM. It was responsible for worship in and around London, and for making sure that too many ministers did not show up at the same place of worship and that too many Friends did not attend and overcrowd Grace Church Street Meeting when a prominent minister was there. In 1678, however, the MMM told Friends to vote as a unit for members of Parliament who would end persecution. Later members showed that they were aware of their restricted mandate over politics when a submitted manuscript advised King Charles on how Friends should be treated. It was referred to the MFS.[11] In theory at least, all published works about religion had to be approved by the MMM, which then referred the manuscript to the MFS, which paid for its publication and determined how many copies would be printed and where they would be distributed.

The position of a person's name in the list of attendees was one means of assessing the standing of individuals in the MFS during its early years. This Quaker practice can also be seen in other conventions; in colonial-period marriage certificates, for example, the bride and groom's names have pride of place over their parents' signatures and all other names. In the MFS minutes, George Fox, when present, was almost always listed first, and when he wasn't, this was probably either because Fox came late or because the clerk remembered that Friends did not believe in hierarchy. George Whitehead's was the name most frequently written after Fox's. Penn was never listed before Fox and only rarely before Whitehead. There was at least one meeting where Fox and Penn head the list.[12] Penn, like Fox, had special status. When Penn made his second visit to America, the minutes referred to him as "beloved brother," and the MMM granted him a special certificate for travel.[13] No one else received such treatment. In all three meetings, from their formation in the 1670s, Whitehead emerged as the most significant leader of Quaker business. Whitehead, a grocer who resided in London, had the leisure to attend all of the three meetings because he married a wealthy widow. He was as active as Penn in representing Friends to the king and Parliament, even during the reign of James II. Fox had more importance as the writer of tracts and letters, sometimes included with LYM's official epistle, but he was rarely quoted as actually speaking about business.

Penn brought unique skills to Quaker business meeting. He was a gentleman, the son of an ennobled naval war hero. King Charles and the Duke of

York had known him since his youth, and he remained the valued acquaintance of influential noblemen. The Earl of Sunderlund, whom Penn had known at Oxford and in France, became an important adviser to Charles II, James II, and, later, William III. Penn was also well educated, fluent in Latin and with some Greek, and had read extensively in Christian theology as well as political and social treatises. Although Keith and Barclay were more rigorous theologians, no other Quaker shows a similar depth of learning in so many areas. Penn had also early acquired the social graces of an English gentleman accustomed to upper-class society. His letters to non-Friends show that he could adapt Quakerism's rough edges to the demands of polite friendship. Prominent men, including George Villiers, Duke of Buckingham, welcomed Penn as a houseguest, and Henry Sydney, Earl of Romney, enjoyed his conversation.[14] Finally, he was rich and willing to spend freely in the service of Quakerism, even when he was living beyond his income. For example, after the MFS approved Penn's treatises on Quakerism, he often paid for their printing.

THE QUEST FOR RELIGIOUS TOLERATION

Penn's most important role in the MFS was to defend Friends' right to practice their faith publicly. Since his convincement in 1667 and his famous trial for public preaching in 1670, Penn had become the most prominent Friend to use tracts, the courts, and appeals to the king and Parliament to ease Quakers' suffering.[15] Normally, Penn did not stand out from other Quaker leaders in policies advocated in the MFS. During the Wilkinson-Story controversy, Penn was one of those delegated to meet with the dissident Friends in Bristol. Although Penn and Thomas Rudyard had legal training, MFS sent them to apply to "learned council" for instruction in tactics to use in trials, including what courts to avoid and how to appeal to which court.[16] Penn also sent instructions to all meetings on how to record their persecutions so that their accounts could be combined with others in tracts designed to appeal to Parliament.

Because he was already known to many powerful men, the MFS used Penn to approach authorities. He met with Lord Baltimore over restrictions on Quakers' voting and refusing to take oaths in Maryland; with the commissioners of New England over persecution of Friends in Massachusetts and Connecticut; and with Lord Carlisle, the new governor of Barbados, about penalties being applied to Friends. Local meetings asked to have Penn write to or meet with a sheriff, justice, or nobleman.[17] Friends sought redress from being imprisoned by appealing to King Charles and Parliament. After 1660, Charles was on occasion willing to suspend laws on persecution. But when Penn sought to persuade the king to end the financial burden of fines on Quakers (originally directed at Roman Catholics), Charles cynically replied that only Parliament could grant such relief. Penn was one of the Friends who presented to Parliament the Quaker petition for relief from penalties for refusing to take the oath of abrogation of Roman Catholicism and nonattendance at Anglican services. Even after he had gained Pennsylvania, Penn was arrested as a non-swearing Roman Catholic, and he obtained from the attorney general a certificate, recorded in the MFS minutes, attesting that he was not a papist. During James II's reign, Penn was again arrested on the charges of a woman informer, but this time neither the mayor nor the courts would prosecute.[18]

Penn's leadership stands out during the reign of James (1684–88), when Quakers made full use of his close relationship with that monarch.[19] After James suspended the penal laws against all dissenters, including Friends and Catholics, Penn presented the official thanks of LYM to the king, which Friends then printed. Thorough studies of James's efforts on behalf of toleration credit Penn with persuading the king to try to establish toleration by parliamentary act. For Penn, enshrining toleration in law would be to establish a new right comparable to those enumerated in the Magna Carta. Penn wrote tracts advocating a new law, the only Quaker known to have done so, and accompanied James on his tour to gain electoral favor, where he spoke in favor of the policy. With Penn's support, the king also attempted to purge from corporations those voters who might elect members of Parliament who were likely to oppose toleration of Catholics and Protestant dissenters. James appointed commissioners, often Baptist ministers, to conduct examinations of the views of voters and MPs. In one of the only surviving letters of this process, Penn wrote to fellow Quakers on how to select those who should be elected to Parliament.[20]

During James's reign, Friends had easy access to the king, primarily through Penn but also through Whitehead. The MFS petitioned the king opposing the use of recusancy statutes, the falsehoods of informers, and on not taking the Crown's one-third share of fines for violations of the Conventicle Act. Through the use of his suspending power, James accommodated Friends' desires. Penn informed the king of the inconveniences and suffering caused by the tendering of oaths in assizes, exchequer, and bishops' courts or as a qualification for office. At the instruction of the MFS, Penn told the king about the nuances of Friends' testimony on oaths, and he presented copies of a treatise on oaths to seven men of influence. In response, James instructed Sunderlund that Friends could qualify for any office without an oath. Friends sent copies of the king's declaration to Quarterly Meetings and made sure that the mayor of London received a copy.[21] The LYM's 1687 epistle thanked the king for toleration and complained about "ungrateful prejudicial persons" who valued "their own interest more than the public good"—that is, who opposed the king's toleration policies.[22] In March 1688 Yorkshire Friends asked MFS if Friends could serve on, or recommend Friends or Roman Catholics to serve on, commissions of enquiry. MFS referred the issue to Penn for his advice and later instructed Friends that they might nominate and serve on the commissions unless the members had already been chosen.[23] This is the clearest example of Penn's playing a leadership role in meeting for business.

Since the 1670s and at the time of the Exclusion Parliament, Friends had received advice instructing them to vote for those who favored toleration, but the policy of having Friends in political office was a clear change. It is uncertain whether most Quakers supported engaging in politics in 1688, because of increasing fears of James's pro-Catholic policies. LYM faced this issue in August of that year. As this was one of the few times that a debate was recorded, it is worth quoting the minutes in full:

> Bray Daily, proposes about chusing Parliament men and about Accepting of Offices, As justices of Peace &c.
>
> 1. S Crisp As to making Use of their right, 'tis left to freedom not expected that all must be alike in that use of Priviledge.
> 2. Men Capable, and way made open, with a Clear Conscience in their Testimony may be Imployed. But yt is not yet.
>
> G. F. not safe to conclude such things in a Yearly Meeting But Keep to the power of God, and discourse of such things among themselves that are concerned therein.
> W. P. some to be appointed with whom to Advise thereof. Nothing to be a bond of Unity, but the Truth, But circumstances differ, wch need Advice to keep.
> G. F. It was not in the wisdom of God to propose such things here. Serve all Men in Truth and Righteousness.

> S. C. We all have Liberty to give Advice one to another in straits.
>
> W. P. They to come to the Testimony the Testimony not to them.[24]

Why this matter needed to be discussed in LYM is unclear, since the MFS had already decided that Friends could serve in office. Was the question asked out of ignorance or out of opposition to the policy? Why the clerk preserved only this discussion is also unknown: was he trying to vindicate Fox or to discredit the political Friends? Note that the LYM debate was inconclusive. How difficult it must have been to debate when Fox invoked the "power of God" for his position. Was Fox giving the same advice that he gave in 1659, when he instructed Friends to steer clear of supporting the defenders of the Commonwealth? Having lived through two revolutions already, perhaps Fox sensed the dangers of a third? Was he only objecting to the public nature of the debate, or was he reacting to the dangers of mixing politics and religion? Stephen Crisp advocated allowing Friends who were clear in their minds to work for political change, as Penn was already doing. Penn desired a special advisory committee to discuss the issues with members who were uncertain what to do. In spite of what Fox advocated, Crisp and Penn continued to insist that testimony should not be imposed either for or against politics, because "Liberty" meant consent rather than coercion. Later in the same yearly meeting, Penn, knowing that Friends were still suffering and that many were still imprisoned by local authorities who opposed James's policies, wanted again to approach the king who would be sympathetic.

Irish Friends asked whether using the king's dispensation on oaths when appearing in chancery courts would violate the testimony on swearing. After a discussion in which Fox participated, the meeting announced no decision, instead referring the matter to a committee of fourteen, including Penn, to draw up a paper on oaths and tithes.[25] This discussion clearly prefigured the 1690s controversy over what kind of an affirmation to accept.

William of Orange's invasion and James's flight to France in December made the debate in the summer of 1688 irrelevant, and the next LYM advised Friends to behave quietly and wisely, "giving no offences nor occasions to those in Outward Government nor way to any Controversies, Heats, or Distractions."[26] The revolution brought popular opprobrium on Friends, made Fox's view appear prudent, and discredited Penn, who was charged with treason. The new king persuaded Parliament to grant limited freedom of conscience to Protestants. However, the opportunity for Friends to play a political role disappeared and would reappear only in Victorian Britain.

LYM DEALS WITH GEORGE KEITH

From 1689 until 1693 Penn kept a low profile, not attending any of the major meetings. He did read one manuscript for the MMM, preached at George Fox's funeral, and wrote seventeen publications, including testimonials to Fox, *A Key to the Scriptures,* and *Some Fruits of Solitude (FOS).* In the summer of 1693 Penn emerged into prominence again, having been received by the king and queen. He attended LYM as a delegate and was appointed to the epistle-writing committee. In the list of names for the epistle-writing committee in 1695 and 1696, Whitehead's name came first and Penn's second.

The main issue for LYM in 1694 was what to do about George Keith, who had appealed his denunciation and disownment by Philadelphia Yearly Meeting, which had accused him of leading a schism between Pennsylvania and New Jersey Quakers and publishing several tracts libeling Friends. Keith had earlier been a close associate of Penn's, Whitehead's, and Barclay's and a leading defender of Quakers in London and America. He now insisted that his only fault was defending essential Christian beliefs always affirmed by Friends. Moreover, he accused Pennsylvania ministers of heresy, of downplaying the Christ's outward atonement, and of denying the resurrection of the body. After the formal close of LYM, a special session of leading ministers, including Penn, heard from Keith and his opponents over the course of six days, read over manuscripts and tracts, and listened to the conclusions of important ministers.[27]

William Mead, a minister, a frequent attendee of MFS and MMM, and Fox's son-in-law, was Keith's most prominent English defender. Mead had long been a public opponent of Penn's. While some have wondered whether this was because he feared that Penn would overshadow Fox in public opinion, the more probable cause was controversy over business involving Algernon Sidney, in which Penn was a mediator. An additional possible cause was Penn's rejection of a proposal whereby Mead would purchase a large tract in northern Pennsylvania for £6,000 and thus gain control of the Indian fur trade. In 1693 Mead refused to read Penn's "Brief Account of the Rise and Progress of the People called Quakers," or to allow it to be attached to the second edition of Fox's *Journal.* Mead spoke before and after Penn, blaming the schism on Thomas Lloyd and Pennsylvania Quakers and arguing that Keith's trial by a civil court in Philadelphia was an unparalleled example of oppression "on a double Account in Church and State." Even so, Mead did not defend Keith's publications about the dispute. After Penn spoke, Mead told the assembly not to be swayed by Penn's "multitude of fine words."[28]

Penn's statement, the longest recorded by the clerk, carefully ignored the theological issues Keith had raised and praised the comments of William Edmundson, an early convert and respected Irish Friend, who had argued that by publishing against Philadelphia Friends, Keith had violated Quaker procedures and provided arguments to the enemies of truth in America and England. Keith's unusual way of preaching Christ had departed from the simplicity demanded by Jesus and practiced by other Quakers. Penn did not say that what Keith preached was heretical or against the faith of Friends. Instead, he invoked the unity of Friends, noting that meetings in Pennsylvania, Maryland, Rhode Island, and Barbados had condemned Keith; if LYM exonerated him, it would disrupt the Quaker unity. Still, Penn said, he cherished Keith and hoped that unity could be restored because Keith had affirmed his loyalty to Quakerism and his belief in the efficacy of the Inward Light to save, and—even if his manner was extreme—he could humble himself and remain a Friend.[29]

In essence, Penn expressed what became the general sense of LYM on Keith: he should not have published or separated and must collect and destroy his recent tracts, and he must clear Friends of the charge of preaching heresy. Philadelphia Friends should condemn any unorthodox sentiments expressed in Keith's writings and should not have used the civil courts. Both sides were guilty of extreme behavior, acting under duress. To make sure that the outside world knew that Friends believed in orthodox Christianity, the LYM reaffirmed belief in the virgin birth and in Christ's suffering, miracles, atonement, resurrection, and intercession.

Keith remained dissatisfied and was soon preaching and publishing against the LYM's decision (he specifically blamed Whitehead and Penn) and creating a separate meeting. The next year, when Keith appeared and read a statement, Penn interrupted him to demand that he repudiate the offending tracts. However, Whitehead, who spoke often, led the opposition to Keith. LYM now unanimously disowned Keith, who would become the ablest opponent of the Society of Friends.[30]

THE AFFIRMATION DEBATE

In 1696, Friends disagreed about their response to Parliament's passing a law allowing Friends to affirm "in the Presence of Almighty God the Witness of the Truth of what [we] say." The Act of Toleration allowing freedom to worship had not stopped Quakers from being imprisoned for nonpayment of tithes or refusing to take an oath in court, although they were allowed to affirm loyalty to King William and Queen Mary. The MFS delegated men to lobby Parliament, but no relief could be obtained until the king intervened and a law was passed allowing distraint rather than jail for nonpayment of tithes and permitting an affirmation to be used in civil but not in criminal cases. Friends had wanted a simple "I affirm," as was the law in Pennsylvania, and they had earlier offered to accept "in the presence of God." After all, God was constantly present. Opponents, who did not like or trust Quakers, insisted on adding "the Witness of the Truth of what I say."[31] The question before Friends was simple: was this form really a surreptitious oath that they could not accept? The issue became complicated because there was no agreement on what constituted an oath.[32]

Penn was not involved in the negotiations with Parliament, perhaps because he was living in Bristol, but he had co-written *A Treatise of Oaths* (1675), appeared before Parliament in 1678 asking for relief from oaths designed against Roman Catholics, and expanded his arguments in "The New Athenians" (1692). In 1675 he drew on his usual sources for proof: the Bible, reason or pragmatism, and sayings from great men past and present. Jesus said, "Do not swear at all. . . . Let what you say be simply 'yes' or 'no'; any more is evil" (Matt. 5:33, 37). Swearing dishonored the Deity and sought his involvement for trivial reasons (such as saying "So help me God" or placing one's hand on the Bible). Requiring oaths also flew in the face of reason. In short, Penn argued that oaths were of heathenish origin and did not work because everyone knew that liars often swore. Friends, as a peaceful, moral people, sought to affirm their allegiance and truthfulness in a way that did not violate their conscience. Their complaint was against the "form not the matter," and they were willing to declare their loyalty and accept the same penalties as disingenuous swearers. After ten pages (in Besse's folio edition of Penn's works) of intellectual defense of the Quaker position against oaths, Penn followed with fifty pages of citations of ancient and modern thinkers complaining about swearing oaths.[33]

The Bible did not say what constituted an oath, and nowhere in Penn's early writings was there a clear definition. When he testified before the House of Lords in 1678, Penn "solemnly Declare[d] in the Presence of Almighty God."[34] In 1692 Penn dealt with this issue because Anglicans claimed that in the Old and New Testaments, God, the prophets, and Paul had sworn. Penn answered that what God promised was not an oath, because an oath required invocation of a superior being and there was no such entity. Any swearing in the Old Testament was voided by Jesus's command. Paul's "God is my Witness" (Rom. 1:9) and "God knowth I lye not" (Gal. 1:20) were not oaths because they were used in a church matter and not a court. Penn clearly hedged here: an oath was a matter of "Degree, if not a Form," and "the same Words, being an Oath, and not an Oath, as they may be used and applied in different manner."[35] Four years later, the ambiguity in Penn's definitions would allow Quaker representatives to defend Parliament's wording. Although "in the presence of God" and "the witness of God" are found in earlier Quaker writings, no one previously had linked the two phrases together or used them in court. Making God a "Witness of Truth" required the same kind of activity as swearing "so help me God."[36]

In order to persuade Friends to accept the new form of affirmation, the MFS decided to issue an epistle using quotations from Fox, Penn, Ellwood, Barclay, and Penington. The letter held that the present affirmation allowed by Parliament was "without question, the Principle of Practice of Friends" and was not swearing.[37] So not only could a Quaker use the affirmation in "good Conscience," but, the epistle added, "Let none . . . call this a subjecting our Testimony to the Will of Man, seeing God hath so far subjected Man's Will to our Christian desire."

It is uncertain whether Penn knew of the decision to issue this epistle before he wrote two letters of his own. His first letter probably went to the MMM, which initiated and must approve the contents of the new publication; the second was addressed to the MFS, and Penn recommended that they not publish any statement about the new affirmation. These are the only records of Penn's privately opposing a decision of the LYM. As usual, he gave several overlapping reasons. Enemies (Keithians, Anglican bishops) would profit from any public show of disunity. The government would in the future distrust any negotiations with members of the MFS, and this would weaken any future attempt to get better wording. Penn insisted that he was not criticizing the Quaker lobbyists because they had tried to get a simple yea or nay, even though they failed. However, the tract was "overbearing" and showed impatience by blaming "little ones" of tender conscience who refused to take the new affirmation. "For peace and Unities Sake, & let things rest as they Lye quietly, and Friends use their Freedom" until a new law was passed or opponents become "more generally easie with what Authority has been . . . kindly pleased to Exact for us."[38]

At the 1696 sessions of LYM, where Penn was a delegate, reports from the Quarterly Meetings, after declaring thanks to the government and those who worked with Parliament, showed that a significant minority of Friends opposed and/or refused to take the new affirmation. Recognizing the disunity of Friends, LYM decided that Friends who could take the affirmation should do so and that those who opposed it would not be coerced. Neither side should criticize the other. Because the affirmation law needed to be repassed, Friends would, in the future, seek a simple yea or nay.[39] Penn's position, in which the form either was or was not an oath, prevailed. In 1660 such a division would have created a schism, but by 1696, a year after disowning Keith, as British Friends adjusted to toleration, theological consistency was less important than harmony among Friends.

THE MORNING MEETING OF MINISTERS

The ministers at the first MMM in 1673 instructed Penn and Whitehead to obtain copies of all books written against Friends and to supervise the press. Although Penn's attendance at this meeting was inconsistent, he regularly submitted epistles and manuscripts for approval and served on committees that read the writings of both prominent and obscure Friends. Penn helped edit tracts by Fox, Barclay, and Whitehead. He collected the printed works and letters for the collected works of John Gratten and Isaac Penington. He edited the tributes of Mary Penington for her husband and added one of his own. Penn wrote to Bristol Friends about issues in the Wilkinson-Story separation and helped arrange, and then attended, the meeting with those two men and their followers in Westmoreland. When such efforts proved futile, Penn signed the LYM epistle against them and wrote a pamphlet about true and false spiritual liberty.

Before his death in 1691, Fox left instructions that Penn should help supervise the printing of his works. Penn probably read Ellwood's edition of Fox's *Journal* before publication, although there is no certain evidence, but he wrote the "Brief Account of the Rise and Progress of the People called Quakers" as a preface to it. Fox had chosen Penn as one of the readers who selected and edited Fox's epistles and doctrinal works before publication, a task that took several years. In an effort to standardize Quaker beliefs on major Christian doctrines and to prove Friends' agreement with orthodox Protestant beliefs, the MMM appointed individuals to read the collected works of all major Quaker writers, including Fox, Penn, Whitehead, and Barclay, and to compile an index and bibliography of their works. Penn helped read over the works of Ambrose Rigge. The writings of Penn and Whitehead together required a committee of six.[40] As part of a similar effort to defend Friends, Thomas Ellwood was instructed to prepare an answer to George Keith's book accusing Penn of being a deist. After some time and several complaints by the MMM, Ellwood confessed that he could not see his way clear to completing the task.[41] Evidently, Ellwood had discovered what later scholars confirmed: that Penn was often ambiguous in his writings advocating religious toleration, downplayed the necessity of the historical Jesus, and on occasion seemed to reduce Christianity to a rational religion very similar to deism. Alternatively, Ellwood may have objected to Penn's separation of the divine and human in Christ, in which he held that only the humanity of Jesus died on the cross.[42] The MMM, instead of defending Penn against Keith, used his writings as an exemplar of what Quakers believed by reprinting *No Cross, No Crown* and sending copies of *Christian Quaker* and *Key to the Scriptures* to the colonies, influential men in Parliament, and Czar Peter, and had them translated into French and Danish.[43] Until his stroke in 1712, Penn periodically read manuscripts and provided testimonials or introductions to books by other Friends.

An indication of Penn's growing conservatism came upon his return from a second trip to Pennsylvania in 1701. After attending the first meeting of the newly formed Yearly Meeting of Ministers, he submitted a manuscript and served on the MMM committee to edit it, but he was not listed as a signer. The epistle, designed for the use of ministers, was then sent to all counties and towns but was not circulated to laymen and -women. The epistle contained twenty articles, ten concerning general guidelines for behavior (be careful in business, have plain furniture, do not be overly familiar) and ten that sought to make Quaker preaching conform to acceptable standards of behavior:

1. Against undue and Restless behavior under another Ministry whilest in the unity of the Body.
2. Against Long frequent and Unnecessary Preambles.
3. Against pretending to a few Words, or a Brief Declaration, and Apologizing for a short Conclusion, and contrary wise prolonging the same People etc.

4. Against Misquoting and Misapplying Scriptures . . .
5. To be carefull how they fall upon Disputable Points or Dialoguing in their Testimonies and making unfair objections and such as they don't clearly Answer.
6. Against all affectation in Speech, Tones, Sounds, and Gestures not agreeable for Gravity & affecting and seeking Popularity in Speakings to themselves. . . .
15. That the Women friends be carefull not to hinder their Brethren in their Service in publick Meetings, and that ye Brethren have Charity towards the Women and not to discourage them in their Respective Service. . . .
18. That all be Cautious of laying too great a stress on their Testimony by pretending divine Motions and too often Repeating the Same to be credit when it is not really soe.
19. That None follow their owne Spirits and presume to Prophesse therein, against any Notion, Towne, City, People or Person.[44]

It is easy to sympathize with Penn and elite ministers, in this new yearly gathering, who for years had to sit through what they saw as bad sermons: lengthy, cliché ridden, pious sounding, theologically simplistic, poorly delivered. Such preaching had led to the Keithian controversy in Pennsylvania and provided fodder for critics in England. A late eighteenth-century Friend observed that one of the worst ways to be tortured would be to be preached to death.[45] However, for an early eighteenth-century young female or male minister, reading over the list should have had challenging implications, making more stressful the already awesome Quaker belief in declaring the mind of God. A speaker in meeting for worship who could not prepare in advance now had to consider the content, the delivery, the time in meeting, the length of the message, and whether he or she understood the theological implications of any distinctive or controversial Quaker belief, such as spiritual baptism or Communion. Although thinking rationally had long been unacceptable in ministering, now messengers of God could neither prophesy nor too often claim divine inspiration. The clear superiority of male preaching was, if not directly stated, clearly implied.[46] Early Friends, including George Fox, Edward Burrough, James Naylor, and even the young Penn, would have rebelled at such a disciplining of the spirit of God. That Penn initiated and the ministers now approved such a document shows that early eighteenth-century Friends had become fearful and conservative.

CONCLUSIONS

All authority within the Society of Friends derived from the experience of the Inward Light in the meeting for worship. The business of Quakerism at the national level depended upon the support of members of local meetings. The three meetings discussed here provided directions for, but were not directly involved in, the daily activities of monthly meetings—recording births and deaths, supervising marriages and burials, maintaining buildings, and enforcing Quaker testimonies. Instead, they dealt with political authorities, set policies, printed books, and presented the public face of Quakerism.

Penn learned to subordinate his strong personality, privileged rank, education, and wealth to the combined spirituality of those within these corporate bodies. He had to become not a powerful, eloquent individual but a humble seeker after truth. Agreement came when all leaders shared a sense of what was right policy after seeking the guidance of the Holy Spirit, because they saw business meeting as a form of worship. Penn would have been pleased that it is impossible for us, some three centuries later, to discern from the minutes when he disagreed with decisions of these three meetings or the extent to which he initiated policy. His commitment to working for religious toleration through appeals to king and Parliament and to engage in electioneering had the support of Quaker leaders from the 1670s through 1688. Like Penn, the other leaders rejoiced in the religious liberty brought by King James. Although Penn was the Quaker most closely identified with James, his lobbying had the support of the MFS, at least through the spring of 1688. The one occasion on which we can be confident that Penn's advice determined Quaker policy was in his public support of King James in 1688 and his advocacy of Friends' seeking office. Of course, the 1688 revolution meant that he lost and was blamed for damaging the reputation of Friends. From that point on, Friends, including Penn, abandoned electoral politics and relied upon ties with men of influence—or what we would call lobbying—as a way to protect Pennsylvania and to gain relief from oaths and imprisonment for failure to pay tithes. Penn argued that supporting James was worth the risk because religious liberty needed to be based upon parliamentary statute. King William's toleration law allowed worship but restricted Friends from holding office and attending universities. It granted nothing to Roman Catholics.

Penn was initially perplexed over the Keithian controversy, unable to understand why so influential a leader had caused such animosity. However, after both sides presented their arguments in the 1694 LYM, Penn's perspective aligned with those of other ministers. He condemned both sides while seeking reconciliation, and a year later advocated Keith's disownment. By 1695, as Penn's roles in the affirmation controversy proved, his primary goal had become achieving harmony within the Society of Friends, even at the cost of consistency. Finally, Penn supported and helped lead the reaffirmation of Quaker alignment with mainstream Protestant beliefs after the Keithian controversy and the virulent attacks on Friends in the 1690s by Keith, Francis Bugg, and Charles Leslie.[47]

In 1667, Penn's experience of the Inward Light brought religious certainty, transformed his self-understanding, and made his identification with Friends so unbreakable that to voice public dissent, let alone to separate, would be unthinkable; it would destroy his personhood. Through all the turmoil in Restoration England, and the evolution of the Society of Friends from radical persecuted sect to an almost respectable and singular denomination, Penn enjoyed being in harmony with Quakers. His ability to share leadership in the meeting for business came from subordinating himself to a religious community.

Chapter 5

THE QUAKER QUEST FOR RELIGIOUS LIBERTY

Americans often give thanks for religious liberty and the separation of church and state and attribute these practices to Thomas Jefferson, Roger Williams, and William Penn.[1] These men and many others deserve credit, but their accomplishments rest upon the writings, struggles, suffering, and even martyrdom of obscure women and men, including not a few early Quakers. Penn's contributions built upon the efforts of the first English Friends during the Commonwealth under Oliver Cromwell. Persecution in the 1650s was sporadic and local compared with the suffering after the restoration of Charles II in 1660, when Parliament attempted to force all dissenters to worship in the Church of England.[2] After his conversion in 1667, Penn emerged as an influential advocate of religious toleration in England, and starting in 1681 he had the opportunity to translate his ideas into practice in Pennsylvania. This chapter discusses Quaker ideas about liberty during the Commonwealth and the Restoration in the period before Penn's conversion, considers the originality and main emphases of Penn's writing under Charles II and James II, and examines how his ideas were put into practice in Pennsylvania.

Before Penn converted in 1667, Quakers had a fifteen-year tradition of seeking religious freedom under different governments, and he drew upon these efforts as he responded to evolving conditions in England, West New Jersey, and Pennsylvania. He desired success, not innovations in tactics or arguments. By insisting upon their legal rights, the Christian obligation to preach anywhere, and the necessity of practicing their religious beliefs openly, early

Friends joined an ongoing debate on religious freedom. The immediate context was the recently ended Civil War, in which bishops, monarchy, and the House of Lords had been abolished and the king executed. To understand the origins of Quaker beliefs about religious liberty, one must begin with English history in the 1650s and 1660s.

In the 1650s, Cromwell, the New Model Army, and Parliament attempted to solve perplexing constitutional problems concerning executive and parliamentary powers, at the same time seeking a religious settlement that would preserve freedom of conscience and keep the peace. Although the Puritans considered the liturgy of the Church of England papist and in need of reform, the Articles of Religion, first drawn up under King Edward VI and modified under Queen Elizabeth, defined belief in a Reformed idiom. Presbyterians, Independents, and Particular Baptists agreed on most of the theological principles that would be enunciated in the Westminster Confession, but their profound differences over church organization doomed attempts to legislate religious unity to failure. Recognizing the diversity of religious opinion in England, the inability of these Protestants to compromise, and the failure of members of Parliament to agree, Cromwell and the army sought a settlement that would penalize no religious body's freedom of belief. Cromwell's policies preserved the traditional parish pattern, in which tithes paid the salaries of educated clergymen and maintained church property. Tolerance did not extend to Anglicans who wanted to restore the monarchy, Roman Catholics, who owed political allegiance to the pope, or Fifth Monarchy Men, who sought to overthrow Cromwell so that King Jesus could reign. However, these groups could worship in private in their homes so long as they did not use religion as an excuse for political actions.

Because the growing number of Quakers seemed to threaten stability, local justices who shared the popular dislike of the beliefs and tactics of Friends imposed fines, imprisonment, and beatings, but this did not stop Friends from seeking redress from Cromwell and exhorting the army to follow the guarantees of the "Good Old Cause"—that is, promises of religious liberty made during the Civil War.[3] After the restoration of Charles II in 1660, Friends repeatedly cited his Declaration of Breda, in which he promised no religious persecution, but Parliament, against the wishes of the king, attempted to force all to worship in and pay tithes to the Church of England. Parliament feared that allowing religious diversity might cause another revolution and therefore used fines and imprisonment to quell dissent.

Quaker efforts for religious liberty consisted of enduring suffering, loudly denouncing and documenting persecution, and reiterating arguments made during the English Civil War. Later, Penn's writings on toleration drew upon a wide variety of sources, including many written by Quakers. This section examines Friends' writings on freedom of conscience before 1667 as a prelude to understanding the arguments Penn continued and those he ignored.

Influential early Quakers, among them Richard Hubberthorne, James Nayler, Edward Pyott, and John Whitehead, had earlier served in the New Model Army. George Bishop participated in the Putney debates in 1647, in which lower-ranking soldiers and officers demanded freedom of conscience, debating what that meant besides the end of persecution and freedom to worship. Initially, Quakers cited Parliament's 1651 Instrument of Government, which guaranteed freedom to worship, and Cromwell's declaration that one of the four fundamentals of his government was the "natural right" to liberty of conscience.[4] Persecution originated not from the central government but from local justices of the peace and conforming parish priests, who now constituted the Church of England and received tithes. Early Friends defined those who opposed their beliefs and practices as apostates under the power of Satan. They claimed the right to oppose false worship in the market and at the end of church services. Because all Quaker beliefs were authenticated by the Inward Light, any compromise would jeopardize the purity of the true church of Christ. Only gradually did Friends extend their demand for religious freedom to others. The clearest example of the change was Edward Burrough's appeal in 1659 to delegates from all churches to meet and formulate policies for each to have religious freedom.[5]

Some of the methods that early Friends used do not reappear in Penn's writing. Penn did not advocate symbolic gestures such as wearing sackcloth and ashes or going naked for a sign, denouncing a minister in church, or declaiming against hireling ministers in the marketplace. (However, for Penn, just appearing in court in plain dress, refusing to bow, and using "thee" and "thou" instead of "you" were visible signs of his faith.) John Camm, Francis Howgill, George Fox, Margaret Fell, and George Bishop had interviews with Cromwell in which they tried to convert him, informed him of Friends' beliefs, sought his intervention in freeing prisoners, or denounced his increasing conservatism and desire for a crown.[6]

Quaker Samuel Fisher's approach to Parliament illustrated the differences between early Friends' political tactics and those of William Penn twenty-two years later. In 1656, Fisher, a well-educated former minister, felt commanded by God to speak to Parliament and relied upon the Deity to give him the right words. After Cromwell's speech insisting that he knew of no religious persecution, Fisher began preaching, but the crowd and soldiers silenced him. He soon came again, with the same result. So he published what he would have said had he not been shut down. In what reads like a stream of consciousness, with no discernible organization, Fisher condemned the false religion and sins of members of Parliament, called on them to convert, described religious persecution, contrasted the immorality that went unpunished with the suffering of Friends, proclaimed Quaker principles, and issued a warning of God's impending judgment.[7] By contrast, when Penn appeared before Parliament in 1678, he came for a scheduled hearing as part of an official delegation of Friends. His testimony was a deferential and well-organized summary of why Friends should not suffer from legislation directed at Roman Catholics. He advocated religious toleration and complained about the ill effects of persecution, which contrasted with dissenters' work and wealth, which, he argued, strengthened the realm. Penn did not condemn the religion of members of Parliament, insisted that Friends agreed with the essential beliefs set forth in the Anglican Articles of Religion, used no apocalyptic imagery, and presented Friends as peaceful and obedient subjects. He made no assertion that Friends had rediscovered the original truth of Christianity.[8] Fisher acted like a prophet and cleared his conscience, Penn like a politically astute supplicant.

During the war and the Protectorate, censorship of the press became ineffective, and Friends took full advantage of freedom to publish broadsides, short pamphlets, and substantial books in which they condemned apostate religion, exalted the power of the Inward Light of Christ, described their suffering at the hands of malicious prosecutors, and warned that pervasive immorality would doom England. Tracts by George Fox and James Nayler relied upon biblical exegesis and church history to advocate a freedom of conscience that included outlawing tithes, allowing affirmations instead of oaths, and granting freedom to preach in the marketplace.[9] Fox and other prophetic ministers continued beyond 1684 to write essays that read almost like stream of consciousness, or what is called an incantatory style, with frequent repetition and no overt organization.[10] We find a contrasting approach in Edward Burrough's 1661 *Case of Free Liberty of Conscience*, which uses theological and biblical themes to prove that the Antichrist was responsible for all persecution, even of heretics. Two tracts by four of the so-called First Publishers of Truth gave, respectively, sixteen and twenty-nine defenses of toleration based on the Bible and the definition of authentic Christianity, adding only a few pragmatic defenses in conclusion.[11] The style and content of Penn's biblical and theological arguments for freedom of conscience resemble these 1661 publications more than they do Fox's writing.

Like early Friends, Penn also drew upon Quakers' appearances in law court and their discussions of English legal history, in which they defended themselves by claiming the rights of freeborn Englishmen ("1. Life, 2. Liberty, and 3. Dowre"), trial by jury, and the inviolability of private property.[12] Two former justices of the peace and Quaker converts, Gervase Benson and Anthony Pearson, attacked paying tithes to support ministers and church buildings that Friends did not use. Pearson spent two years reading all previous writings on the tithe before he wrote his treatise, citing the Magna Carta, medieval and recent English statutes, and modern commentators, including Edward Coke's *Institutes*.[13] Richard Farnsworth combined legal and theological arguments in a 1661 pamphlet designed to aid juries and local authorities dealing with Friends.[14] When he addressed lawyers in 1660, George Bishop, a former soldier and an influential politician in Bristol, cited examples from English history along with natural law and reason.[15] The earliest pamphlet to invoke "reason" and "unreason" as a primary defense against religious persecution was allegedly written by George Fox in 1658.[16] In tone and argument, Penn's later advocacy of religious liberty most resembles Pearson's and Bishop's arguments, being based on "reason" rather than on the purely spiritual concepts of Fox, Nayler, and Penington. Most Friends who sought liberty of conscience during the Commonwealth and Restoration saw no contradiction in mixing apocalyptic, political, scriptural, historical, legal, and prudential arguments for religious freedom. Because he was writing within Quaker tradition, Penn could include all these grounds; his primary novelty was the amount of documentation he provided for supporting freedom of conscience, namely, the works of ancient, medieval, Christian, and contemporary authorities, including Roman Catholics and Anglicans.

SEEKING TOLERATION: TACTICS, ARREST, TRIAL, FAME

The best sources in which to assess Penn's views on toleration, religious liberty, and freedom of conscience, terms he used interchangeably, are the many documents he produced in political campaigns. In this context, he joined an ongoing debate in which the repetition of a few attractive ideas might lead to success, and so originality was not as important as being persuasive. Penn tailored his writings to various audiences, using different personas, avoiding discussion of certain implications, and ignoring inconvenient truths when it suited his purpose. Historian Mary Maples Dunn has argued that religious toleration was a consistent theme throughout his life, an observation echoed more recently by the historian and political scientist Andrew Murphy.[17] But there are differences between what he advocated in England, where there was an established church, and what he later created in Pennsylvania. Although the focus here is on ideas, Penn also published accounts of the suffering of individual Friends, lobbied judges and influential noblemen, and testified before Parliament and Charles II seeking relief. In all of these activities, the community of Friends represented by LYM or the MFS authorized Penn's activities. Unlike his purely religious writings, which had been read and approved by the MMM, Penn's political writings on toleration did not receive an official imprimatur. However, because Quaker printers often reprinted them and Joseph Besse included them in his 1726 edition of Penn's works, we know that influential Friends approved.

A major difference between the tracts of all other Friends and Penn's is the tone. Penn wrote as an educated gentleman for men of his class, asking for debate, appealing to reason and nature, and sprinkling his text with examples from classical and modern history. His university education, wide reading, and social position flavored his Quakerism. Penn believed in God's intervention in history with apocalyptic wrath, and in his earliest pamphlet he threatened prophetic judgment on all non-Quaker churches, but he seems to have realized that such a stance would not get him very far with the king, courts, or Parliament. He was perhaps the first Friend to recognize, at least in print, that their movement would remain a small minority in a larger world of dissenters, and that therefore Friends would need to enlist allies from other churches, even those with no faith and little morality. Penn socialized with, and defended in print, the Duke of Buckingham, who advocated religious toleration, even though the duke's brazen sexual immorality scandalized even the king. He also supported Algernon Sidney, who believed in ending persecution but also at times wanted armed rebellion and favored a republic over monarchy.[18]

Penn gained fame as a Quaker advocate of religious toleration in 1670 in a tract that provided what appeared to be a verbatim account of his and fellow minister William Mead's trial for causing a riot.[19] The pamphlet was reprinted twelve times in its first year and many times since. Even today it amuses undergraduates and has been presented in theatrical form by lawyers from Philadelphia as a way of educating high school students in the workings of the jury system. Its popularity was and is deserved because it was good political theater, sharp satire, and as close to humor as one finds in seventeenth-century Quaker writing, with an innocent hero besting corrupt power. The judges become incompetent villains—arbitrary, overbearing, ignorant, and foolish—refusing to provide a copy of the indictment, not knowing the common law, bullying witnesses and jury, and failing to silence Penn.[20] He and, to a lesser extent, Mead were witty, intelligent, and knowledgeable as they upended court proceedings, defied the judges, proclaimed their innocence, and defended English liberty. By disputing both the legitimacy of the statute and the factual basis of their alleged crime, the two men stood against injustice and became minor martyrs; even after the jury found them not guilty, the judges sent them to jail for contempt of court for refusing to remove their hats.[21]

The trial occurred as a result of Parliament's passing the Act of Uniformity (requiring worship using the Book of Common Prayer), the Quaker Act (mandating a loyalty oath to the king), and the Conventicle Act (which forbade public worship of more than five nonfamily members outside a private home, disobedience bringing a sizeable financial penalty). After soldiers locked the doors to the Quaker Grace Church Street Meeting House in London, Friends, among them Penn and Mead, held a worship service in the street in which both men spoke. When soldiers arrived to break up the gathering, disorder ensued—perhaps caused by the normal street rabble—and the authorities arrested Penn and Mead, charging them with causing a riot. Had they been accused of preaching, the justices could have fined them and sent them to jail, but causing a riot required a jury trial with witnesses and a conviction for plotting by at least two people. The witnesses recounted that Penn and Mead were present and that both men spoke, but the noise was so great that no one knew what they said. The jury found Penn guilty of speaking but did not convict Mead—a verdict meaning that neither man could be convicted. In the seventeenth century, jury trials almost always resulted in a conviction. Furious with the jury, the judges tried to force a guilty verdict and locked up the jurors. In time, Bushel's case (named for the foreman of the jury) marked a significant milestone in English legal history because the Lord Chief Justice ruled that an English jury could not be coerced. Publishing a popular pamphlet using tactics based on making an English court look foolish, and praising a sympathetic jury that found Penn not guilty, was not the best way to influence a Parliament whose members often served as justices of the peace and presided over similar trials. They would not wish to grant liberty to radicals whose fervor and disrespect of authority reminded them of the origins of the Civil War.

RELIGION, REASON, LAW, INTEREST: PENN DEFENDS FREEDOM OF WORSHIP

In order to capture the nuances of Penn's ideas about religious liberty, this section focuses on treatises written in 1670 and 1675, when Penn addressed the strongly Anglican and intolerant Cavalier Parliaments. His tone changed in a tract written in 1679, when the newly elected Parliament seemed more sympathetic to toleration, and again in 1686 and 1687, when he wrote supporting James II's efforts to change the law. Penn emphasized the same themes, but he now linked religious freedom to a more moral and harmonious society.

Early in 1670, while in Ireland on a preaching tour and observing persecution of Quakers firsthand, Penn wrote a treatise addressed to the king titled *The Great Case of Liberty of Conscience*. After being tried and jailed in England, he rewrote this tract in a succinct form and addressed it to both king and Parliament. He defined religious liberty as "the free and Uninterrupted Exercise of our Conscience in the Way of Worship" that God has required of us.[22] Penn made a religious argument based on theology, scripture, and church history; a legal case using English history, natural rights, and necessity; an economic argument on creating wealth; and a pragmatic argument based on the fact that persecution had not worked and that the people remained religiously divided. Penn did not desire religious liberty because he was s secularist or skeptical of religious claims to truth but because he wanted to make English society more Christian, moral, prosperous, and peaceful.

In the English edition of *The Great Case of Liberty of Conscience*, Penn summarized the content of not only this but virtually all of his writings on liberty of conscience: persecution on religious grounds impeached "the Reverence due to God, Respect for the Nature of the Christian Religion, the Sense of Divine Writ, the Great Priviledge of Nature, the Noble Principle of Religion, the Justice, Providence and Felicity of Government," and the "Judgment and Authority of a whole Cloud of Famous Witnesses."[23]

First, he addressed the nature of God. Penn started with the Protestant principle that God was the author of true faith and reached out to humans in their consciences. Persecution besmirched God's "divine Prerogative" by imposing human authority and thereby interfering with what God required of his faithful disciples, who suffered fines or prison merely for following God's instruction. Alternatively, if they belied their faith and conformed, they risked forfeiture of eternal life. Indeed, for a government to play God required a belief in its infallibility that was characteristic of Roman Catholicism, not Protestants.[24]

Second, he tackled the "nature" and "practice" of the Christian religion. The kingdom of God was a spiritual reality, spread by Christ's teaching and example, not by force.[25] Jesus, who in the temptation stories and on the cross could have called down powers from heaven, refused all carnal aids. The early church grew from the preaching and example of the apostles in spite of Rome's antipathy. The Bible also testified against persecution, and Penn cited many verses from the Old and New Testaments, including Jesus's "Render unto Caesar," the parable of the tares, and the golden rule.[26]

Third, he took on the nature of man. The "Priviledge of Nature" meant that forced belief destroyed what it meant to be human. God made humans rational and intelligent and gave them a universally shared instinct for the Deity.[27] The seat of religion was in the mind, in conscience, and could not be coerced. "In Order to believe, we must first Will, to will first we must Judge; to Judge any Thing, we must first Understand; if then we cannot be said to Understand any Thing against our Understanding, no more can we Judge, Will, or Believe against our Understanding." If the state attempted to force religion against a person's will or understanding, the resulting faith would have no value. No person could be saved by another person's religion. "Force may make a Hypocrite; 'tis faith grounded upon knowledge and consent that makes a Christian."[28]

Fourth, Penn considered the nature of law.[29] All statute law, he argued, originated in "fundamental laws"—a philosophical and theological doctrine originating with the Stoics, reiterated in medieval Scholasticism, continued in natural law, and reiterated by Edward Coke.[30] The technical name that Penn used was "synteresis," a term he may have learned in law school but more probably from a 1660 pamphlet by George Bishop, who had written Penn's irate father on behalf of the new convert.[31] Synteresis was the belief that there was a universal innate form of knowledge that was the "Corner-Stone of Humane Structure, the Basis of Reasonable Societies." Its principles were discoverable by right reason and were summarized in the Ten Commandments and natural law. The teachings of Jesus were to live honestly, not to hurt one another, and to give all people their rights. Like George Bishop and the Neoplatonists, Penn identified it with the innate "Principle of God," the Logos of Christ, and the Inward Light.[32] Like natural law, synteresis survived for centuries not because of its philosophical rigor but because it was vague enough to be reinterpreted to serve various needs. In case a persecutor claimed that king and Parliament were not bound by the traditional understanding of English rights, Penn insisted that any law passed by Parliament that violated synteresis, fundamental law, was not legally binding.[33]

For Penn, English law originated in these fundamental rights and had embodied them in three distinctive principles: "Ownership, and Undisturbed Possession" of property; "voting of every law," whereby the rights of property are "maintained" by representatives in Parliament; and a "real share" in "Judicatory Power" through juries.[34] The rise, survival, and flourishing of these liberties began with the Romans and continued through the Anglo-Saxons, Normans, Tudors, and Stuarts. He quoted churchmen, legal commentators, and kings. The conclusion was clear: in all eras, property rights did not depend on religious adherence. For example, in all the changes of religion, beginning with Henry VIII (from Catholicism to Anglicanism), through Edward (Reformed Protestantism), Mary (Roman Catholicism), Elizabeth (Anglicanism), the Stuarts (the rise of Puritanism), and the Commonwealth (Presbyterians and Independents), no one had claimed that Englishmen lost their right to property because of false beliefs. Being a bad churchman did not make one a bad landlord. After all, what if England should undergo another change of established religion, as had happened in the past? A right to property, not attendance at church or right theological belief, was the foundation of the English state. The state existed before the church or any religion, and a Christian living in a Muslim state, or vice versa, did not forfeit his property. "No property out of the Church is a Maxim; the plain English of publick Severity, that belongs not to the holy Law of God, or the Common Law of the Land."[35]

Fifth, Penn took on the question of interest. Penn attempted to persuade the king, Parliament, other dissenters, and Anglicans that religious freedom was in their "interest," which meant ignoring morality and reason and relying on gain. Since 1661, laws had outlawed all religious practice other than attendance at the Church of England, but a variety of religious "interests" continued, and persecution had failed.[36] So even if religious uniformity might be a desired outcome in theory, it was impossible to achieve in practice. Since the

Reformation and Henry VIII, religious diversity had become a constant fact of life. Now, with England so factionalized, the government needed a policy that would compel all Christian churches—each of which feared being dominated by others—to look to the government for security. The government had little to fear from a variety of churches, but an overmighty denomination's "interest" would seek its own benefit and might threaten the throne. The Church of England had numerical superiority in England but not in Scotland, and on its own might not withstand the threat posed by Roman Catholicism. Because the king and his government wished to strengthen the realm against the papacy, they should favor freedom of worship for all Protestants.

A wise policy for king and Parliament was to "balance" religious groups against one another so that no individual church could threaten the government. If Roman Catholics were to be feared, then all Protestants should unite, for they would have overwhelming numbers. And if Anglicans should threaten the government, dissenters would provide a counterweight. Prudence required uniting all Protestants in toleration but dividing them in case one church's clergy should seek too much power. Just as in nature, neither hot nor cold was best, and so in a family neither force nor weakness was good, so balance and moderation should prevail within the kingdom.[37] Prudence, not purity, brought safety.

Persecution undermined the purpose of government and weakened a kingdom by fining or imprisoning for alleged heresy those who paid taxes and contributed to the realm by hard work. Religious dissent did not affect a person's loyalty, but harsh punishment might turn people against the state, particularly since the penalties enacted were disproportionate to the fault. A state that relied on physical force in religion would create poverty, disunity, and plotting, but tolerance would bring loyalty, peace, plenty, and unity.[38]

Sixth, Penn marshaled the wisdom of ancient authorities. Penn believed that ancient and modern history and the testimony of wise men (he cited no women) proved that permitting freedom of worship was not new. Ancient kingdoms and peoples that allowed many forms of religion included Jews, Romans, and Egyptians; more modern examples included France after Henry IV and Germany following the Thirty Years' War. Holland's rise to prosperity was helped by its welcoming of religious variety. (Even now, Penn observed, England was inconsistent, in that Huguenot and Lutheran immigrants in London worshipped in their own churches.) Among the ancient authorities Penn cited were the Romans Livy and Tacitus and the Christian church fathers Justin Martyr, Tertullian, and Jerome. Turning to modern authorities, he noted Martin Luther's declaration before Charles V, John Calvin's address to Francis I, and Hugo Grotius. From English history, Penn quoted medieval anticlerical writings, among them a poem allegedly by Chaucer (he liked Chaucer's sentiments but not his poetry), John Wycliffe, and William Langland's *Piers Plowman*. Recent luminaries included two important Anglican divines, Henry Hammond and Jeremy Taylor.[39] Finally, Penn quoted long passages in which the king's grandfather James I and his father, Charles I, seemed to endorse toleration. One wonders why Penn assumed that Charles II, who knew the real attitudes of his ancestors, would be influenced by these passages, but Penn quoted them repeatedly.

Why did Penn, in his theological, devotional, and political writings, frequently, almost incessantly, invoke ancient authorities? His belief in synteresis is one key. The God of the New Testament was the eternal Yahweh pictured in Hebrew scripture; his counsel remained the same in both testaments. Penn also believed that a few witnesses in all generations knew the golden rule, natural law, and inward revelation. So the testimonies of Socrates, Plato, and Marcus Aurelius remained relevant. Penn also praised the Albigensians and Waldensians and Roman Catholic mystical writers such as Thomas à Kempis and Johannes Tauler as evidence that God had never abandoned a few saints, no matter how pervasive apostasy seemed to be. Because truth was unchanging, the task was to rediscover it, not to create something new. The result was that even when Penn amassed historical evidence of religious tolerance, he was being ahistorical, seeking a universal truth that at least some men had always known.

Seventh, Penn made an argument about the power and importance of emotion. Since the 1650s, Friends had published accounts of their suffering at the hands of the established church and state. Penn frequently cited the indiscriminate and excessive nature of the fines imposed on Friends, including the seizure of property, for their refusal to attend Anglican church services: "Flocks of Cattel driven, whole Barns full of Corn seized . . . Parents Left without Children; Children without their Parents. . . . The Widdow's Mite hath not escaped their hands; they have made her Cow the Forfeiture of her Conscience, not leaving her a Bed to lye on, nor a Blanket to cover her. . . . The Poor Helpless Orphan's Milk, Boiling over the Fire, has been flung away, and the Skillet made Part of their Prize."[40]

Eighth, he made an anticlerical argument. Penn claimed that religious persecution began when Roman Catholic bishops sought to gain political power, and it had continued through what he termed the "insatiable Appetites of a Deciminating Clergy."⁴¹ The intolerant spirit of Rome had infected the Church of England and also corrupted the Presbyterians and Independents who sought wealth and power in alliance with the government. Penn did not consider that by attacking all educated clergymen he was alienating a still powerful force in English society.

In 1679, animosity between Charles II and two newly elected Parliaments seemed to presage a new civil war. The primary issues, apart from the Crown's demands for more money for foreign policy, were whether James, the king's Roman Catholic brother, could be excluded from the succession, and whether persecution for non-Anglican worship should end. In 1679 Penn published *An Address to Protestants*, laying out his vision of a Christian society in which the government enforced and the people willingly obeyed a strict moral code,[42] the churches became voluntary societies supported by gifts from worshippers, the clergy repudiated pride and became humble servants of Christ, and all enjoyed freedom to worship. The solution to religious animosity was to return to a biblical faith. All Protestants, asserted Penn, agreed that the men who wrote the Bible were passive instruments under the guidance of the Holy Spirit and that the text was thus infallible. Not all parts of the scriptures were equally weighty, but all were true, even those verses difficult to understand. "Who can speak better, to express the Mind of the Holy Ghost, plainer than the Holy Ghost?" he asked rhetorically. If Protestants would make their confessions of faith and state their creeds by quoting directly from the Bible, then man-made wisdom would be conquered by God-made truth.[43]

Penn's hopes for religious toleration in England failed, because King Charles, after receiving a secret subsidy from Louis XIV, prorogued Parliament, preserved the succession of his brother, and ended the threat from the Whig faction. For the last four years of his reign, the king ruled without Parliament and allowed increased persecution, including of Quakers. The *Address to Protestants* had little influence in England because its proposals seemed unrealistic and too much like Quakerism, but it is significant as a guide to Penn's ideas for a new colony.

PENN AND JAMES II, 1685–1688

Penn returned to England from Pennsylvania in 1684, intending to stay a short time in order to settle a boundary dispute with Lord Baltimore over his colonies' southern border and rights to the area later called Delaware. Even after receiving a favorable ruling (although the border between Pennsylvania and Maryland would not been settled until the Mason-Dixon line was drawn in the mid-1760s), he remained in England because the accession of James II in February 1685 increased the prospects for religious liberty. (Admiral Penn had served under James in the second Dutch War and had entrusted the care of his son to the king's brother.) James, who had earlier informed Penn of his commitment to religious toleration, was king, even though he was still legally barred from serving in Parliament, in the army or navy, and in any government office. Naturally, he wanted to end the disabilities of his fellow Catholics and sought the aid of Protestant dissenters, including Penn.

Now, many perceived Penn as a favored courtier and sought to use his access to James for religious liberty. On behalf of the MFS, Penn petitioned the king to release Friends from prison, but getting them freed was time-consuming and was sometimes frustrated by local magistrates. James had supported Charles's short-lived suspension of the penal laws and Test Acts in 1672, and in 1687 he again suspended them. Some contemporaries and many historians today credit Penn with writing the official supporting declaration, and though there is no proof, the language and sentiments in that document echo the arguments he had used for years. Penn accompanied a delegation of Friends thanking the king and helped organize letters of gratitude from other denominations, chiefly Baptists and Independents. Hoping to make toleration secure and perpetual, James, with Penn's support, sought to purge Anglican MPs opposed to toleration in order to create a parliamentary majority that would pass a law guaranteeing religious freedom forever, or what Penn called a new Magna Carta. (Opponents suggested that any new law could be repealed by a later Parliament or suspended by a new monarch.) James sent Penn on what turned out to be an unsuccessful secret mission to William of Orange, seeking his backing for religious toleration similar to what existed in Holland. Penn accompanied James on a royal procession to the west of England in an attempt to influence public opinion and made speeches supporting religious toleration. One document shows Penn listing men, primarily Baptists and Quakers, who could be appointed commissioners to canvass MPs as to whether they would vote for religious liberty as the king desired.

In 1686 and 1687, Penn issued two tracts under his own name advocating religious liberty and defending James.[44] Because the king had appointed Roman Catholics as his advisers and as commander of his army in Ireland, Penn expanded his definition of religious freedom to apply not only to public worship but—as with the law in Pennsylvania—to the right of Christians to hold any office. As an example of a king's right to choose the best men regardless of their faith, he pointed to Charles II's employing former Cromwellians like Admiral Penn and other naval commanders who had served the monarch faithfully. To Penn's mind, ability and moral rectitude, not religious faith, should be the requisites for office. The two tracts reiterated his arguments of the previous twenty years, including the anticlerical case, as Penn asserted that "Interest," defined as political power and wealth, motivated clergymen, whether Roman Catholic, Anglican, Presbyterian, or Independent, to practice persecution. All Christians, he asserted, believed in the Apostles' Creed, the divinity of Christ, and morality. All denounced hypocrites who exploited religion for power or wealth, and all believed in obedience to government. The existing laws against plotting and rebellion provided sufficient security for government.

Penn sought to reassure Anglicans that toleration would not threaten their property, status, or role in society. To dissenters who feared unity between the Church of England and Roman Catholics because of similarities in liturgy and a mutual commitment to persecution, he insisted that history, since Henry VIII and the firmly Protestant Articles of Religion repudiating the papacy and transubstantiation, made such collusion impossible. Similarly, he said, Presbyterians, Independents, and Anglicans could not create a comprehensive church because of their profound theological differences. The Church of England, for its part, need not fear the minority of dissenters given its legal protections, traditional role in society, and the devotion of its numerous adherents. Penn sought to prove that many Anglicans, as early as the reign of Queen Mary, had written in favor of toleration. Statements from Elizabethan bishops he had used before, but now he added long passages from three of the most eminent living clergy, all of whom would become bishops: Edward Stillingfleet, who had counseled Penn in the Tower and was reputed to be the best preacher in England, Gilbert Burnet, a historian and an adviser to William of Orange, and John Tillotson, named archbishop of Canterbury after the Glorious Revolution. All were known to be moderate, Broad Church, or Latitudinarian,[45] and Penn quoted again the pious Jeremy Taylor and Henry Hammond. He also recycled his quotations from James I and Charles I and pointed out that Charles's sentiments were from the Civil War period.

Although James's support gave impetus to the quest for religious liberty, the king's Catholicism remained a major obstacle. Penn needed to persuade a populace reared on tales of "bloody" Mary Tudor, the Inquisition, and Guy Fawkes and reenforced by Louis XIV's 1685 revocation of the Edict of Nantes and persecution of Huguenots, who were now fleeing to the Low Countries and England. He had to prove the compatibility of Roman Catholicism, Protestantism, toleration, and domestic peace, and to do so without repudiating his earlier fear of the pope's political power and Catholics' universal loyalty to Rome. In Poland, Holland, and the Germanic parts of the Holy Roman Empire—even in places where there were prince-bishops—Catholics and Protestants lived together in peace. Because Protestants outnumbered Roman Catholics in England by a ratio of 200:1, there need be no fear of the Catholic Church's future establishment.

Most important, claimed Penn, was the security provided by the character of King James, a man of integrity who had suffered for his faith. Penn argued that James was devoted to toleration and the protection of the rights of Englishmen. He had promised at his enthronement to preserve all the rights of the Church of England and to provide clemency to dissenters. The dispensing power the king exercised was within his prerogative, but obtaining a law of Parliament would guarantee no prosecution in the future. It would have been imprudent for Penn to say that James, who became king at age fifty-two, was an old man who would not live long, but he did mention that his only children were two Protestant daughters. Promoting toleration was in the king's "Interest," because religious liberty brought balance among the different denominations so that that no one could threaten the monarch. Each denomination's "Interest" in preserving its liberty would mean supporting the Crown; also, there would be no secret plotting against the throne, because all religious services would be open to outsiders.

Few in 1687 saw that a revolution against James would occur by the end of the following year. The birth of a male heir who would be raised as a Roman Catholic guaranteed the prospect of a Roman Catholic dynasty. James's actions in rescinding borough charters, promoting Catholic officers, forcing Catholic fellows upon Magdalen College, and centralizing administration made many fear that the king was imitating Louis XIV. James unwisely attempted to force all clergy to read his Declaration of Indulgence from the pulpit and then put on trial seven bishops who refused. His creation of a standing army with Catholic officers reminded people of Oliver Cromwell. During the same period, he issued warrants for a new Parliament designed to pass a religious toleration law. In the summer of 1688, a few powerful nobles, joined by Anglicans bishops, issued an invitation to William of Orange (whose wife, Mary, was James's daughter) to invade England. That they wanted William to rein James in was clear, but not all wanted a new king. After James's army deserted him, he fled to France. Parliament named William and Mary joint monarchs, and in 1691 Parliament, at William's request, granted toleration for worship to orthodox Protestants, preserved Anglican power by continuing tithes and refusing to allow dissenters in Parliament or universities, and made Roman Catholic worship illegal. Penn, in disgrace as a confidant of James, and Quakers played little role in shaping these laws but welcomed their new liberty and affirmed allegiance to the new monarchs.[46]

Penn's significance in the history of religious toleration stems not from his activities in England but from his success in Pennsylvania. To paraphrase the language Penn would later employ, in England, even under James, it was necessary to walk, but in Pennsylvania, Quakers could run.

RELIGIOUS LIBERTY IN EARLY PENNSYLVANIA

The honor of establishing religious liberty in England's North American colonies belongs to Roger Williams, who founded Rhode Island as a refuge from intolerant Puritan Massachusetts, and Charles, Lord Baltimore, who desired to protect his fellow Roman Catholics and reassure Maryland's Protestant settlers. Both colonies predate the English Civil War. The post-1660 proprietary colonies of New York, East and West Jersey, and North and South Carolina promoted toleration because of the diversity of their populations and as good business, as they wished to attract dissenters from England, Scotland, and Ireland, Huguenots from France, and Germans from the Palatinate. In 1678, as a meeting-appointed arbitrator for East and West Jersey, and later as one of the proprietors of those colonies, Penn approved of the freedom of conscience guaranteed there.

As a promoter of religious liberty for England and America, Penn could have made this policy a selling point for prospective settlers of Pennsylvania. It is surprising that after he received the charter in June 1682, he did not mention liberty of conscience in private letters, advertising tracts, or the "First Frame of Government." When he called together the investors and prospective settlers in England to make laws, religious liberty was addressed only after land rights, government institutions, courts, prisons, debts, marriages, and servants in section 35, almost as if toleration were an afterthought. "That all Persons living in this Province, who confess and acknowledge the One Almighty and Eternal God, to be the Creator, Upholder and Ruler of the World, and that hold themselves obliged in conscience to live peaceably and justly in Civil Society, shall in no ways be molested or prejudiced for their Religious Perswasion or Practice in matters of Faith and Worship, nor shall they be compelled at any time to frequent or maintain any Religious Worship, Place or Ministry, whatever."[47] This language would be repeated in an expanded law in Pennsylvania.

Penn's lack of stress on religious liberty in recruiting settlers was a conscious decision, because the concept earlier appeared in an unpublished draft of his essay "Fundamentals of Government." He composed and sent multiple drafts of the Frame of Government for comments and consulted with prominent Friends, including Robert Barclay and Benjamin Furly, and with the prominent politician Algernon Sidney. (John Locke voiced his negative opinion later.) There are alternative explanations for Penn's silence on toleration as contrasted with his emphasis on morality. Before all major decisions, including deciding to leave England for America, Quakers needed to seek "clearness" from the Inward Light, that is, assurance of the rightness of their decision. After rationally considering the pros and cons, they had to examine their motives. Friends approved of those who sought to escape from an immoral England, to live and raise their children in a Quaker community, and to improve their station by amassing wealth, in moderation, through hard work. But migrating merely to escape persecution was wrong. Jesus, the disciples, the early Christians, and the first Friends had not sought martyrdom, but neither had they run away in fear. If a person's motive for emigrating was freedom of conscience, then he or she should stay home and endure the persecution. In addition, emphasizing religious liberty might attract the wrong kind of settlers—those who wanted wealth without work and religion without discipline. Penn wanted morally strong Christians, not those looking for an easy life.

In 1681 Penn published *A Brief Examination, and the State of Liberty Spiritual*, which addressed an ongoing schism in the Society of Friends in which one issue was whether Friends could avoid persecution. During the Wilkinson-Story controversy, LYM condemned those who sought to worship in secret so as to avoid paying penalties or being imprisoned (fig. 2). Penn, who helped formulate that decision, realized that it would look bad if he now supported religious liberty as an escape from suffering. Even so, he insisted that Quakerism allowed no persecution for dissent within or outside the meeting. *A Brief Examination* informed Quakers that religious anarchy would not prevail in America, but neither would colonial government inflict hardship on those who dissented from within Quakerism or opposed it from without.

Section 37 of the laws agreed upon in England followed the toleration section, listing thirty-one moral offenses, but deferred specifying any penalties

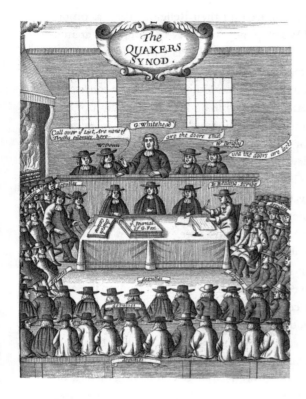

FIG. 2 | *The Quakers Synod*. From Francis Bugg, *The Pilgrim's Progress from Quakerism to Christianity* [. . .] (London: W. Kettleby, 1698), 108. This is a satirical portrait of London Yearly Meeting. Note Penn's prominent position next to Whitehead and that there are no women present. © Britain Yearly Meeting of the Religious Society of Friends (Quakers).

until the settlers arrived in Pennsylvania.[48] Penn knew that if moral legislation were to be effective, he would need the consent of Quakers who migrated and also that of the existing, religiously diverse settlers in Delaware. He may have feared attracting colonists who assumed that spiritual liberty would allow moral laxity. To his mind, toleration would foster a more ethical society by ending the advantages of hypocrisy, or outward conformity. His relative silence on toleration stemmed from his desire to deal with both issues in Pennsylvania.

In prefaces to the laws passed in England and in Pennsylvania in 1682, Penn insisted upon the sacredness of government as instituted by God after the Fall and its power to restrain evil and cherish the good. The "coercive," or lesser, function of government was to "crush the effects of evil," as contrasted with the "Care and Regulation of other Affairs more soft and daily necessary to show . . . Kindness, Goodness, Charity." In parallel phrases that show his belief in balance and moderation, he promised that the purpose of the laws would be "true Christian and Civil Liberty" against "UnChristian licentious and Unjust Practices," so that "God may have his Due," "Caesar his Due," "the People their Due" "from Tyranny and Oppression," on one side, and "Insolency and Licentiousness on the other for the Present and Future Happiness."[49]

Article 1 in the laws agreed upon in Chester summarized Penn's theological reason for liberty of conscience. God was the "only Lord of Conscience... Author as well as Object of all divine Knowledge, Faith and Worship, who only can Enlighten the Mind and perswade and Convince the Understanding." The word "only" meant that any human-made intermediary between human conscience and God, including penal laws, the Book of Common Prayer, and confessions of faith, would have no legal standing in Pennsylvania. For Quakers, the word "convince" had a special meaning; a "convinced Friend" was an outsider who converted and became a member. Religious authority here was both mental and individual, the product of an enlightened mind, or, as Quakers called it, the Inward Light.

The actual statute reaffirmed what had been law 35, agreed upon in England. Anyone living in the province "now or at any time" who confessed "God to be the Creator Upholder and Ruler of the World," and who lived "Peacefully and Justly under the Civil Government," would not be "Molested or Prejudiced for his or her Conscientious Perswasion and practice" or forced to maintain or attend any religious worship "place or Ministry." Governor Benjamin Fletcher and the Pennsylvania General Assembly confirmed this law with no changes in 1693, and in the 1701 Frame of Government Penn guaranteed that it "should be kept and remain, without any alternation, invioliably for ever." Toleration in Pennsylvania and Delaware in 1701 went beyond what Penn had advocated in England under King James—a Magna Carta for Christian freedom that would endure.[50]

Under the theory of synteresis that Penn upheld, all thinking individuals could affirm this confession, given originally in Noah's seven principles[51] and confirmed by revelation in the Ten Commandments and later by the teachings of Jesus. In keeping with the Quaker practice of having women speak during worship and travel in the ministry, the law protected "his and her" rights. In theory at least, a Jew, Muslim, Protestant, Catholic, or Native American could make this declaration and have freedom of worship and "Practice." Practice allowed a significant expansion of what Penn had sought in England and was now guaranteed in Pennsylvania; it meant no compulsion to swear oaths, pay tithes, or serve in a militia. In the eighteenth century it protected the legal existence of two Roman Catholic churches in Philadelphia.

The law contained two additional sections: one, perhaps derived from the earlier statute on religious liberty in Maryland, provided that any person who "shall abuse or deride any other for his or her Diferant Perswasion and Practice in matters of Religions" would be punished as a "disturber of the Peace."[52] Penn may have been concerned about social stability, but this clause was never invoked and it was omitted in the 1701 Frame of Government. Quakers never observed such a restriction in either England or Pennsylvania; it could have been a significant limit on the practice of Christian liberty. The second section required no labor on the Sabbath (or "First Day"), not because the day was holy but because of the "Example of Primitive Christians for the Ease of Creation," so that masters, parents, children, and servants could attend services on Sunday and read the Bible. This clause was also dropped in 1701 but was then reenacted as a distinct law.

Penn never wavered in his advocacy of religious liberty and always coupled it with demands for government enforcement of strict morality, because he saw no contradiction between the two. The next law restricted government service to men who declared that Jesus was the Son of God and savior of the world and had not been "convicted of ill fame or unsober and dishonest Conversation." "Convicted" in this context meant more than "of a crime" and referred to reputation, just as "unsober" meant more than drunk, referring to clothing, speech, or behavior that departed from the Quaker emphasis on plain style. Likewise, "Conversation" referred to general behavior, not just speech. Any good Protestant or Catholic could qualify, but a Unitarian probably could not—and a Jew definitely could not. The loyalty affirmations to the king and the proprietor required by Pennsylvania could have been taken by Catholics even after the Glorious Revolution.[53] Penn believed that if his new colony were to combine liberty and morality and be an example to the world, its governors, whether Quaker or not, must be men of the highest moral character, and this the law attempted to guarantee in fact. After the two first laws on toleration and Christian legislators, the next twenty-seven laid out the moral legislation. Penn probably wrote these laws, and both he and the colonists approved them in 1682 and 1683. With minor changes, all were reaffirmed under Governor Fletcher in 1693 and passed again under the 1701 Frame of Government. Only then did Penn notice a requirement in the charter that laws be submitted to England every five years. Now, after the Crown vetoed many such laws, the Assembly repassed similar laws but made them expire before the five-year period was up.

In England, Penn had worried that immorality might provoke God's judgment. Now he could demonstrate in Pennsylvania that his government would combine religious liberty with Christian moral rigor. The new laws governing the colony provided a fine of either five shillings or five days at hard labor in the "house of Correction" with a diet of bread and water for anyone who swore by God or Christ; spoke "loosely" of God, Christ, the Holy Spirit, or scripture; cursed oneself or others; was drunk in public; allowed excess drink in a home; or played cards, dice, or lotteries. Justices had discretion to enforce the fine or the hard labor. Drinking to someone's health was slightly less bad and carried the same monetary fine but no hard labor. Disturbing the peace, staging plays, bullbaiting, cock fighting, and May Day celebrations cost the miscreant twenty shillings. More serious was selling liquor to the Indians, for which the fine was £5.[54]

Quakers had years of experience with English trials, penalties, and jails, and Pennsylvania lawmakers sought reform in the colony. Only murder carried the death penalty in Pennsylvania, although under English common law treason was also a capital offense. New York had ten capital crimes, Massachusetts, sixteen, and Connecticut, seventeen. Both New York and Massachusetts decreed the death penalty for a child who threatened a parent, but Pennsylvania confined the child to jail for as long as the parents desired. The criminal code of Massachusetts listed 123 crimes, twice as many as Pennsylvania; New York had one-third more. Whereas other colonies made such offenses as rape, sodomy, and incest capital crimes, Pennsylvania punished these offenses with "forfeitures, corporal punishments, and imprisonment." For example, assaulting a magistrate brought one month's confinement, incest, one year.[55]

Whether Pennsylvania ever embodied Penn's moral commonwealth is debatable. Some who complained about scandalous deeds and loose living nevertheless sought to undermine Quaker rule and what they saw as too lenient a criminal code and excessively strict moral laws.[56] Penn returned to England after two years to defend his title against Lord Baltimore. As a result, he was dependent on information furnished by his supporters and enemies and soon began lamenting the reports of bad behavior. In epistles, Philadelphia Friends complained about the profane behavior of youths, and the caves along the Delaware River where some settlers lived during the first winter later became notorious for prostitution and the unlicensed sale of alcohol. Philadelphia became a port, and sailors had their own codes of behavior, as did the non-Quaker population of Delaware and Pennsylvania, which including earlier settlers, indentured servants, and slaves. Two studies of Pennsylvania courts conclude that in the early years there was little violent crime, extensive use of arbitration and appointed "Peace Makers," and some enforcement of the moral laws.[57] After 1701, in response to vetoes by royal officials, the Assembly revised many distinctive laws, and by 1720 Pennsylvania's criminal law codes had become much harsher and more like the laws of England and other American colonies.

CONCLUSIONS

When William Penn returned to England in 1683, he could take satisfaction in knowing that what George Fox and the first Friends had advocated in 1652 had been accomplished in the Delaware River colonies of West Jersey, Pennsylvania, and Delaware. Christian liberty meant freedom from an established church, tithes, church courts, militia duty, and invoking God's name in business and in civil and criminal courts. Legislation required that inhabitants were not to drink to one another's health, swear, use heathen names for days of the week and months, stage plays, or play cards, and there were no special privileges for clergy. The government sought by legislation to foster strict moral standards and instituted reforms of criminal and civil law designed to simplify court procedures and guarantee justice through trial by jury. Financial support of churches came from voluntary contributions, and any Catholic or Protestant Christian (even Quaker ministers) of good character could occupy any position in government. Perhaps Penn had been right that Quakers and Pennsylvania could provide the religious and moral leadership needed for a new English reformation. But this was not to be.

Instead, the period from 1685 to 1688 marked the highest achievement of religious liberty in England until the nineteenth century, as a Roman Catholic king and Quaker politician worked to guarantee toleration by suspending penal laws, freeing religious prisoners, and seeking parliamentary sanction for toleration. Penn lobbied the king and nobles, wrote pamphlets using familiar arguments in favor of toleration, sought to enlist Friends in James's political campaigns to influence Parliament, and accompanied the king and made speeches for religious liberty in royal visits intended to influence public opinion. The failure of these efforts, and the reaction after the so-called Glorious Revolution, meant no Roman Catholic religious liberty, continued suppression of Ireland, the continuation of tithes and church courts of the Church of

England, and a privilege (not a right) for dissenters to worship but not to hold political office or attend university. The arguments of Penn, other dissenters, and a few Anglicans were factors in achieving toleration, but the insecurity of the new regime, fear of Catholic France, William III's support for easing restrictions, and a general revulsion against persecution prompted Parliament to pass a law that many hoped would be only temporary.

In England and in most of its colonies in North America, toleration, now defined as allowing liberty of conscience with an established church, became the norm. Freedom of conscience meant a plural establishment in New York, mandatory tithes for Congregational and/or other churches in New England, and an established church with tithes in Maryland and the two Carolinas. Virginians begrudged even toleration of Presbyterians. The English government forced anti-Catholic loyalty oaths on officeholders in every colony, but Rhode Island, New Jersey, Delaware, and Pennsylvania remained free from an established church. In those places, many denominations flourished, and the people maintained their own standards for worship and governance and learned to adjust to religious liberty. In Pennsylvania from its inception and years later in the new United States, Penn's plans for freedom of conscience with no taxes for any church, along with allowing affirmations instead of swearing oaths, became the law, but still fell short of his vision for a strictly regulated godly, moral, and peaceful people.

Chapter 6

MORALIST

Penn's conversion to Quakerism in 1667 brought an inward transformation made visible to others though his failure to observe what most Englishmen saw as polite behavior. He refused to doff his hat, bow respectfully, address his superiors with a deferential "your grace" or "my Lord," or sign letters "your humble servant" or "sincerely." He would not dance, attend plays or musical concerts, read romances, or participate in bowling or other sports. He showed no appreciation for any visual art, including painting, architecture, and fine furniture.[1] His clothes exemplified "plainness" by having no lace or frills. In his speech, manners, and appearance, Penn showed the world that he lived as a Quaker. No one could be saved by external actions, but these manners were mandatory in a life transformed by the Inward Light of Christ. Observing Quaker testimonies became a religious necessity, a sign of self-surrender to the will of God. Exhorting others to practice what he saw as Christian morality remained a constant theme in Penn's writings.

In 1669, while confined in the Tower of London for allegedly denying the Trinity, the twenty-six-year-old Penn finished writing the 110-page treatise *No Cross, No Crown*. In 1682, at age thirty-eight, after receiving the charter for Pennsylvania and while planning his new colony, he finished a second edition, expanded to five hundred pages—essentially a new book with the same title. Created at the request of the MFS, *NCNC* has remained in print for centuries and is considered a minor Christian classic. In 1693, at age forty-nine, in hiding, accused of treason, his colony lost, and facing the lingering decline of his wife, who would die in a matter of months, Penn composed *Some Fruits of Solitude in Reflections and Maxims* (which went through seven editions before

1718)—in content and tone so different from his earlier ethical treatises that one might assume it was the work of another man. He would expand its contents in a final publication on ethics titled *More Fruits of Solitude* (1702) after regaining his colony and acquiring a second wife, but with the same ethical tone as the 1693 work. Friends read these three works on morality, even though they were ostensibly directed at outsiders, as devotional tracts designed to foster self-examination. Penn's theme was ethical living, but salvation was his goal.

An examination of these three works reveals what remained constant in Penn's ethical thought and what evolved owing to changing circumstances. Although he exhorted others to become true Christians, in drawing upon his own religious experiences Penn was, perhaps unconsciously, preaching to himself, thinking about his own need to reform himself on his Quaker pilgrimage. His primary authority in ethics was his knowledge of the Inward Christ, but, as always, he also invoked the Bible, reason, the early church fathers, and heathen divinities.[2] Penn's ethics were in a sense only a slightly more extreme version of the moral code derived by Christians for centuries from the Ten Commandments, the teachings of Jesus, and church tradition. Penn sought obedience to these ethics, not originality, and gave no indication that he thought sententiousness a danger.

Differences in approach and style in the three treatises illustrate Penn's evolution in his relationship with the outside world, for his primary audience was non-Quakers. The second edition of *No Cross, No Crown* was approved by the MMM and published with the imprimatur of the MFS.[3] Penn published it in the same period in which he was seeking a charter, busy preparing the Frame of Government and laws for the new colony, and recruiting settlers. It can be seen as a justification for Penn's political activities on behalf religious toleration and an end to government persecution, an address to Friends in England, and a guide for all who would migrate to Pennsylvania. Theological differences could be tolerated there, but moral laxity would be against the law. If Pennsylvania were to become a model commonwealth, a light to the nations, all settlers needed to practice a self-denying Christian ethic.

NO CROSS, NO CROWN (1669)

Although an openly professed Quaker for only two years, Penn, already a public defender of Friends, wrote two treatises while imprisoned for denying the Trinity. In *NCNC*, he ignored the reasons for his incarceration and did not emphasize the major themes of Quakerism: the authority of the Inward Light of Christ, the spiritual nature of sacraments, perfection, silent worship, true ministry, and the right of women to preach. Penn's goal was not to convert people to Quakerism but to persuade them of the reasonableness and biblical basis of Friends' ethics. On the title page, Penn portrayed himself as a "humble Disciple, and patient Bearer of the Cross of Jesus," although to outsiders he seemed neither humble nor patient.

Exactly when in 1669 Penn wrote *No Cross, No Crown* is uncertain, but he was in prison. The printer was responsible for forty-three errors in the first edition. Penn probably wrote the manuscript in the Tower and sent it to the printer, but he only saw the completed text, which he then corrected, after his release. The title, which sounds scriptural, comes from the dying words (addressed to and transcribed by Penn) of William Loe, the minister whose preaching converted Penn: "Dear Heart, bear thy cross, stand faithfull for God & bear thy testimony in thy days & generation & God will give thee an eternal crown of glory that none shall ever take from thee."[4]

The treatise was dedicated to eight "ancient Friends" referred to with initials; scholars have tentatively identified a few with whom Penn had earlier contact.[5] His sister and brother-in-law are two of the eight. Because Quakers already observed singular customs, Penn's primary audience consisted of those who could not understand why a rich young man had joined a sect with such odd practices. The preface claimed that Penn's "matter stile and method speak not the least premeditation or singularity."[6] What exactly he meant by "premeditation" is not clear, since the tract is organized into chapters with subheadings like "Reason 1" and has four distinct sections: covering the head, using "you" as a form of address, recreation, and testimony. Perhaps Penn intended to show that the contents came to him spontaneously, as in speaking in meeting. An alternative explanation is that Penn recognized that his tract started as a defense of Quaker practices but that this aim was soon eclipsed by a plea for moral principles basic to many sectarian Christians. The style was "plain," containing no rhetorical gimmicks or elaborate metaphors, and was not "singular," that is, it strove not for originality but to represent the Quaker community.

In the first two sections, Penn sought to educate outsiders in the rationale for Quakers' rejection of outward deference and use of plain speech, practices that most people in the seventeenth century saw as good manners. Friends also rejected the normal practices of using the second-person plural "you" for social "superiors" and addressed all people in the second-person singular, as "thee" or "thou." Penn's defense of these Quaker peculiarities took up only fourteen pages of a one-hundred-ten-page book. He sought to employ reason (i.e., intelligence), scripture, and ancient Greek, Roman, and early Christian authors to demonstrate that these supposedly innocent practices fostered sin. In this way he sought to make Quakerism respectable and, whether he intended it or not, show that he was a reasonable and cultured man. For example, he argued (with no proof) that the Romans "Brutus, Valerius, Cato, Marcellus, Scipio, Pompius, Cicero" never had a title other than magistrate,[7] and that no titles were given to sixteen biblical figures, including the four Gospel writers, Jesus, Paul, and a variety of Christians, including the theologians and emperors "Irenaens, Tertullian, Justin, Alexander, Constantine, Justinianus, Maximinian, Theodosius, Jerom, Barnard, Luther, Sarania, Calvin, Beza, Grotius, Vossius, Amiraldus and the like."[8] We might see this as name dropping; Penn insisted that it showed the "practice" of wise men in all ages. As a rhetorical device, the names might be impressive, but only the highly educated would know these men. In a society in which most people were illiterate and few men had a classical or theological education, a small audience could understand and assess the validity of Penn's arguments. In short, Penn wrote for men like himself and assumed that the common reader would be awed by the names of these authorities—whether or not they knew who they were.

NCNC began by listing fifteen reasonable reasons for rejecting the "hat honor." Bible verses were listed by number, but not by content, in the margins; the reader would have needed to be extremely conversant to know where the passages came from in order to grasp their applicability. Not until reason eleven did Penn actually quote a biblical verse—the stories of Mordecai in the book of Esther and the centurion in Matthew. (Esther's role was not mentioned.) Penn wrote in a tone of calm rationality, with no threat of apocalyptic doom. In actuality, the many reasons he adduced could be boiled down to one sin, pride. Pride was the origin of honorific titles and the cause of complaints against those who would not use them and refused to doff their hat. If a true Christian actually merited praise, he would not need superfluous titles. The only hint of social radicalism or class leveling in Penn's argument was indirect and lay in Penn's complaint that when plowmen who obeyed their superiors went to market and tried to show respect, they were then esteemed, he said, by a "Court Crittic so ill-favoured, as only fit to make a jest, or be laugh'd at." Penn confessed that previously "none hath been more prodigal and expensive in those vanities (call'd Civilities) than my self," but he avowed that "the certain sense I had of their contrariety to the meek and self-denying Life of holy Jesus" had changed his mind. Though such titles might be innocent in themselves, because of "the esteem and value the vain minds of men do put upon them (who must be stript and crucified)," Friends had learned to testify against them from "the infallible sense of the Eternal Spirit."[9]

The second section defended the Quaker practice of using the second-person singular "thee" and "thou" rather than "you" for all people, regardless of social rank. Penn's task here was difficult, because using bad or incorrect grammar as test of morality was even then considered absurd. Penn could draw upon George Fox, John Stubs, and Benjamin Furly's *Battle-Door*, which demonstrated that ancient and modern languages differentiated between the second-person singular and plural. Penn listed seventeen of these languages without giving those authors credit, but, although he regularly cited non-Quaker sources in footnotes, he never cited other Friends' books or mentioned any other Quakers in either edition of *NCNC*.[10] His strategy was to determine the reason for the custom of referring to kings as "you" and, again, it was pride. Social superiors wanted to be addressed as the plural "you" by their inferiors but would use the singular when talking to common people. Christians talked to God using "thee" and "thou" but could not do so when addressing nobles. Addressing them as "thou" was a rebuke to their arrogance. As in the first section, Penn's tone was of moderate rationality.

RECREATIONS AND FRIVOLITY

Two New Testament passages sum up the essence of the third section: "they [who] would live to pleasure are dead to God" (1 Tim. 5:6), and "Do not love the world or anything in the world. If anyone loves the world, love for the Father is not in them. For everything in the world—the lust of the flesh, the lust of the eyes, and the pride of life—comes not from the Father but from the world" (1 John 2:15–16). Penn used the term "lust" not primarily as sexual but as referring to any earthly or sensual pleasure. His argument here was based in part on Stoic or "heathen" rationality, but more important were prophetic denunciations from both testaments, which he quoted at length. Penn contrasted the dress and customs of biblical fathers and mothers with those of Restoration England and used the story of Lazarus and Dives as a rebuke to the wealthy. Unlike the earlier sections, in which Penn confessed his earlier transgressions, here he expressed only disapproval and the fervor of a new convert condemning his former life. If reason failed to persuade, Penn now proclaimed apocalyptic hellfire and damnation.

The list of earthly pleasures that Penn condemned was extensive: the "vain Apparel and usual Recreations of the Age as Gold, Silver, Embroyderies, Pearls, precious Stones, Lockets, Rings, Pendents, breaded and curl'd Locks, Painting, Patching, Laces, Points, Ribonds, unnecessary change of Cloaths, superfluous Provision out of state, costly and useless Attendence, Rich Furnitures, Plays, Parts, Mulbery and Spring-Gardens, Treats, Balls, Masks, Cards, Dice, Bowls, Chess, Romances, Comedies, Poets, Riddles, Drolery and unnecessary Visits, &c."[11] And in case anyone failed to find his own infractions in this list, Penn repeated most of these sins and added more. (One of Penn's less appealing writing techniques was to compile long lists of virtues, sins, great men, etc.) At times, he used utility as the test: clothes came in after Adam's sin. At first, their function was to protect the body from cold, cover nakedness, and distinguish the sexes. Now costly fabrics and ornaments signaled status and worldly pride. Drunkenness, not mentioned in the list above, resulted in wasted estates and led to the abuse of women and children and defiling the marriage bed. "Wanton women" beautified their outward appearance, played cards, and read romances while neglecting their children and their housewifely duties of cooking, cleaning, and sewing. Checkers, chess, bowls, cards, and other diversions killed time to no constructive purpose.

Humans, who enjoyed only a short time on earth, should be working out their salvation in "fear and trembling" (Phil. 2:12). Instead, they sought pleasure in the fantastic plots of romances and the immoral conduct in plays. Even if the reader believed that some of these practices were innocent or indifferent (for example, some ancient Greek tragedies praised virtue), the wise man would refrain from going to the theater in order to discourage attendance at the many ancient and modern comedies that condoned vices. Against the argument that many games and diversions were "indifferent," that is, not immoral in themselves, Penn claimed that no one could justify a need to engage in them.[12] A virtuous person would refrain so as not to set a bad example for his neighbors. The test for leisure was utilitarian: would it do good for the society and the person involved? Good Christian pastimes included helping the sick, visiting prisoners, reading pious historians, studying geometry and natural history, gardening, and meditating.

Against the argument that providing luxuries gave work to the poor, Penn countered that money could be more directly spent on better projects. Now, he said, nineteen men out of twenty labored to support the luxuries of one rich man. However, "if the Landlords had less lust to satisfie, the Tennants might have less Rent to pay, and turn from poor to rich, whereby they might be able to find more honest and domestique employment for their Children . . . and were more hands about more lawful and serviceable Manufactuers, they would be cheaper and greater vent might be made, by which a benefit should redound to the World in general."[13]

In the final section of *NCNC*, Penn used sixty-eight stories of exemplars from ancient Greece and Rome, early Christians, modern Christians, and political leaders. His footnotes provide an indication of the many books Penn had read or knew about. Only two of the exemplars were women: a Roman wife known for her chastity and modesty, and the wife of the ancient Greek philosopher Crates of Thebes. Hugh Barbour has demonstrated that sixteen of the names on Penn's list came from Sir Thomas Stanley's *History of Philosophy* (1655), and that others probably came from a commonplace book Penn kept.[14] So there are deathbed confessions, stories about the virtues of the early Christians from Machiavelli, quotations from Calvin, Luther, Grotius, Erasmus, and Charles V (of Spain), and a long account of the Waldensians—later identified by Penn as a forerunner of Friends.

The 1669 *NCNC* shows both Penn's fervor and his limitations as a writer. It is repetitious and assumes too much knowledge on the part of readers, and its message could easily be refuted by those who had read extensively in the church fathers and more modern reformers. The rational tone of the first two sections was vitiated in the third by scorn for the worldly and threats of hellfire. Why the difference? Penn's former life of worldly pleasures was fresh in his mind; as suggested above, he was probably preaching to himself.[15] He had been redeemed, and now, through self-denial, could envision an eternal crown. Penn was a young convert whose denunciations were unlikely to persuade dissenters or those who took their guidance from the court of Charles II.

NO CROSS, NO CROWN (1682)

By 1682, Penn was in a prestigious position. He was a supporter of King Charles, who had given him the ownership of Pennsylvania and the authority to govern it. He could rely upon the favor of James, Duke of York, the man to whom Admiral Penn had entrusted the care of his son and whose claim to the throne had survived an exclusion crisis in 1679. Penn had married well, to a devout Quaker with a substantial dowry, and now had two surviving sons and a daughter and landed estates in England and Ireland. Although in debt, he hoped the new colony would aid him financially. At the same time, he was busy issuing advertisements for settlers, selling land, and drawing up Frames of Government and laws.

He had also become a leading Friend, the writer of sixty-two tracts defending Quaker beliefs and practices and advocating religious toleration. He lobbied powerful members of the aristocracy, Parliament, and the king, dealt with those who threatened schisms, and helped shape policy decisions in important organizations of Friends. His journeys to preach in England, Wales, and on the Continent brought him many contacts that he could draw upon in populating the new colony.

Historians have often commented on Penn's omission, in his tracts recruiting settlers to Pennsylvania, of any discussion of his religious motivation, and his almost exclusive focus on the business side of colonization. He did address his religious motives in a few personal letters that show how easily he could move from what we might call secular concerns into religious questions, because he believed that God's Providence ruled all facets of life.[16] He could also publish a new edition of *NCNC* and a tract on Quaker church discipline with no direct discussion of colonization. All of his writings were designed to attract the right kind of settlers, moral Christians who would be hardworking, peaceful, and obedient to government.[17] As Penn announced in the preface to the 1682 edition of *NCNC*, his goal was to win readers to Christian discipline and pay his debt "to my Country and to the World of Christians."

Friends were one audience for the new edition, and Penn submitted the manuscript to the MFS and MMM to make sure that they approved. Quakerism indirectly flavored the contents, and Penn could not resist attacking Anglican clergy.[18] Yet Friends were mentioned only once in the five hundred pages, and except for brief sections on the hat and speech (essentially unchanged from the 1669 work), were ignored in more than 90 percent of the book. No Quaker writings or authors were cited. Friends reading the book would see their essential beliefs confirmed, but outsiders would find advocacy of a spiritually based imitation of Christ requiring mortification and strict morality. A Baptist or Mennonite debating whether to migrate to West Jersey or Pennsylvania would find no religious reason for staying in Europe.

Penn's method of composition in the second iteration of *NCNC* was similar to that of the first, with insights grouped into chapters but no logical progression of subjects. There is duplication, many digressions from the subject at hand, personal anecdotes (for example, one about disarming a man in France who had challenged the young Penn to a duel), short sermons, and exemplars from classical Greece and Rome, early and modern Christians, and deathbed sayings. All the contents of the first edition appear in the second. The aim was not to produce an original philosophical or theological treatise but to encourage the reader to meditate, "to Retire into Thy Self," as Penn put it in the preface, "and view the condition of thy Soul."[19] *NCNC* was a devotional guide to Christian practice in which Penn, as in his earlier tracts advocating religious liberty, argued that moral living benefited the body politic.

In the 1662 *NCNC*, heathen and Christian exemplars gave advice on moral living, plain speech and dress, avarice, and politics. In the 1682 edition, by contrast, Penn also cited kings, emperors, and statesmen from ancient Greece and Rome on how best to rule. Philip of Macedon "refused to oppress the Greeks with his Garrisons, saying, I had rather retain them by kindness than fear." Lycurgus, in order to prevent luxury, "disbanded many TRADES; no MERCHANT, no COOK, no LAWYER, no FLATTERER, no DIVINE, no ASTROLOGER." Marcus Aurelius wanted "an equal Commonwealth, administered by Justice and Equality; and of a Kingdom, wherein should be regarded nothing more than the good and welfare, or liberty, of subjects."[20] Penn had government on his mind and sought to learn from successful rulers in planning his colony.

Penn addressed the nature of true worship, the ethics required in taking up the cross and their political implications, and exemplars of virtue. The 1669 edition of *NCNC* began with a defense of Quakers; in 1682 the subject was Christian morality, and Penn, who had recounted his spiritual awakening twenty-two years earlier, now advocated that others follow the same path. "Christ's cross is Christ's way to Christ's crown," he wrote in the preface. New Bible verses like "Deny himself, and take up his CROSS daily and follow me" (Luke 9:23) and "laid up for me a CROWN of Righteousness" (2 Tim. 4:7–8) established the theme as an exhortation to take up the "Self-denying religion of Jesus." Bible verses and stories were integrated into the text as well as being identified in the margins. Penn used gentle persuasion rather than stringent denunciation, being mournful and distressed but not furious at the surrounding immorality. He still assumed that a wayward sinner would end up in hell and made sure the reader knew this: "'Tis Tophet, 'tis Hell, the Eternal Anguish of the damned." "Sin is of one Nature all the World over; for though a Lyar is not Drunkard, nor a swearer a Whoremonger; nor either properly a Murder; yet they all of a Church . . . one Father, the Devil."[21]

Superficial Christians were the target audience. The initial pages were a sermon contrasting conventional Christianity, allowing surrender to worldly pleasure, with a meditation upon the meaning and power of the cross. The cross became a metaphor for what Quakers termed the Inward Light, taking its power from the life, death, and resurrection of Jesus that now was experienced as an "inward mystical cross." The "mystical cross" is "Divine Grace and Power, . . . an Inward submission of the soul to the will of God, as it is manifested by the Light of Christ in the conscience of man."[22]

In describing prayer and worship, Penn became a quietist Quaker: "Tis the Language of the Soul, God hears; nor can that Speak but by the Spirit, that cannot Groan aright to Almighty God, without the Assistance of it." A Christian does not prepare by study or rely upon ability or thinking about forms of speech. "In the Light of Jesus they ever Wait to be prepared, recluse from all Thoughts that cause the least Distraction or Discomposure in the Mind, till they see the Angel *move*, till their Beloved please to *wake*, nor dare they call him before his time." "Worship is the Supreme Act of Man's Life."[23]

Penn contrasted the first Christians, whose religion came from "experience," with contemporary believers, who relied upon "tradition." In the early church, "not a vain Thought, nor an idle Word, nor an unseemly Action was permitted." There were no immodest looks or courtly dress, "much less the lewd Immoralities and scandalous Vices now in vogue with Christians." The contrast was with the English, who now worshipped "a dull and insipid Formality, made up of corporal bowings and Cringings, Garments and Furnitures, Perfumes, Voices and Musick." All true worship was spiritual, that is, like that of the Quakers. True godliness required surrendering the "lawful self" and denying "conveniency, ease, enjoyment, and plenty," and lay in being prepared to sacrifice husband, wife, child, house, land, reputation, liberty, and life itself. "What thy Wife dearer to thee than thy Saviour? And thy land and Oxen prefer'd before thy Souls Salvation?" Authority for a life of self-denial came from Penn's own life: "I speak my Experience, the way to keep our Enjoyments, is to resign them."[24]

Penn incorporated his earlier thoughts on the hat honor and plain speech into a long discussion of pride. Here again he continued a tradition at least as old as Saint Augustine, but he wrote of the particular temptations of a man better educated and wealthier than his Quakers peers and also one with governing power. After all, Penn was in a sense a new Adam, creating a new society, and he knew what had happened to the first Adam. Pride was the most basic sin, that from which all others stemmed. The first responsibility in a ruler or magistrate was to set a good example, to know one's limitations. Pride in rulers destroyed reason and law, resulting in tyranny and war and in insubordinate and rebellious subjects. From the "lusts" of pride flowed avarice and luxury. Pride, defined as an "Excess of Self-love, joyn'd with an Undervalue of others, and desire of Domination over them," planted in men an ambition to "exceed their station, an inordinate pursuit of knowledge, ambition and craving power, extreme desires of Personal Respect and Deference," and an appetite for luxury in food, household furniture, dress, etc.[25]

Pride resulted in an "ill Child, Servant, and Subject," and in an adult man who makes a "Wife a Servant and the Children and Servants Slaves" and "turns Love into Fear." A proud man cannot be a true friend because he "values other men as we do Cattel, for their Service only."[26] The worst form of pride was in religion, because it led to theological disputes on "doubtful and dubious Questions" and ended in persecution. Even worse, "when the Clergy has been most in Power and Authority, and has had the greatest influence upon Princes and States, then has been most Confusions, Wrangles, of Bloodshed," an example being the past sixty years of wars of religion.[27]

Avarice was kin "to pride and defined as desiring of unlawful things, unlawfully desiring of lawful things, and withholding the benefits of them from private and private." The goal here was moderation. Penn quoted a proverb on loving "Money for Moneys sake" and another that Benjamin Franklin later reversed on signs of avarice: "Do we not see how Early they rise; how late they go to bed." A wise master will set a "Standard both as to the Quantity and the Time of Traffick."[28] All trades were good if pursued in moderation, but a wise merchant would share his wealth with his workers and not forget that prosperity could be followed by lean years. Love of money in government led to corruption whereby the rich got richer and by hoarding money kept it from circulating, which harmed their inferiors. Avarice tempted merchants to cheat on customs and to trade beyond their needs.

Luxury, an "Excessive Indulgence of Self in Ease and Pleasure," could affect all ranks of society, with the poor desiring beyond their abilities and the rich wallowing in sumptuous clothing, ornate furniture, and gluttony. Luxury weakened the realm, because it diverted workers from producing more and led to importing French goods. In both the 1669 and 1682 editions of *NCNC*, Penn made same social diagnosis of the ills of society caused by overconsumption by the rich. He told civil magistrates that if all the money spent on fashions, costly furniture, taverns, theaters, feasts, and gaming were put into public stock, there would be "Reparations to broken Tenants, Work-Houses for the Able, and Alms-Houses for the Aged and Impotent." There would be "no Beggars in the Land, the Cry of the Widdow and Orphan would cease." The surplus allowed the redemption of "Poor Captives" (those taken by Barbary rulers, not Negro slaves) and aid for "Distressed Protestants" persecuted in other countries. Even the exchequer could draw upon this fund, as a bank does in cases of emergency.[29]

Occasionally, we can follow Penn's train of thought as topics evolve. For example, an often-quoted passage was that Christians should keep to the "Helm and guide the Vessel to its Port, not meanly steal out of the Stern of the World, and leave those that are in it, without a Pilot to be driven by the Fury of Evil Times upon the Rock or Sand of Ruin." Obviously, this was Penn justifying his own political activities and founding of a colony. However, the theme of this section was not politics but the "unlawful self," or pride in religion. After contrasting the virtues of the first Christians, Penn proceeded to denounce man's inventions in religion whereby the cross had become an "Ensign" and God was pictured as an old man and Jesus as a little boy, and worship consisted of music and liturgy. Such vanity and superstition resulted in unprofitable self-denial and created "religious Bedlams," that is, monasticism, under which believers secluded themselves from "Conversation with the world." By contrast, true monasticism took place within, where the inward cross gave the power to overcome the world. "The Perfections of the Christian Life extends to every honest Labour or Traffick used among men. . . . So True Godliness don't turn men out of the World, but enables them to live better in it, and excites their Endeavours to mend it." Now they can be at the "Helm" as "Pilot." After what can be labeled a self-justifying digression, Penn returned to his theme of true worship.[30]

Insisting that those who resisted "reason" and "argument" might be persuaded to virtue by good examples, he contrasted good heathens and dissolute present-day Christians. He quoted 130 men and 12 women, 75 from the classical period, 20 from the Christian past, and 37 from the modern period. His good heathens were lawgivers (Solon and Lycurgus) and philosophers—among them many Stoics who emphasized reason, following nature, God's presence within man, and simple living. Marcus Aurelius's sayings and ascetic living while emperor occupied many pages. Socrates and Heraclitus merited substantial entries as moral men, but Greek metaphysics did not interest Penn. Aristotle had one paragraph and Plato a little more, although his writings were frequently cited. Christian exemplars included Jesus Christ, with an emphasis on the Sermon on the Mount, John the Baptist, and Paul, and brief

Moralist | 117

mention of a few other disciples and various patristic theologians. As in 1662, the Waldensians, whom Penn saw as forerunners of Friends, received the longest section. Here we encounter Penn's strong misogyny: after listing several women who had led men to sin in dancing, he quoted the French theologian Peter Waldo: "The Devil tempt Men by Women three manner of Ways: that is by the Touch, by the Eye, By the Ear. . . . The Woman that Singest in the Dance, is the Prioress (or Chiefest) of the Devil."[31] Penn cited thirty-seven moderns, including Walter Raleigh, Michel de Montaigne (whose essays he praised), Hugo Grotius, Cardinals Richelieu and Mazarin, and Charles V of Spain. Four poets provided deathbed advice: Sir Philip Sidney, who repented in *Arcadia*; the Earl of Rochester, "inferior to no Body in Wit and no Body ever used it worse"; John Dunne, "a great poet"; and Abraham Cowley, whose pious, undistinguished verse Penn quoted.[32] Departing from the 1669 edition, Penn now included figures he had known, namely, Princess Elizabeth (granddaughter to James I), Bulstrode Whitelocke, and three relatives: his father, a paternal aunt, and Anthony Lowther. The distinctive personality traits of these paradigmatic figures disappeared as Penn showed them advocating self-denial and a frugal life of simplicity and virtue through actions, writings, and deathbed scenes.

Considering the crucial roles that women had played in early Quakerism, it is surprising how few comments (even fewer of them favorable) Penn made about them in either edition of *NCNC*. He made no mention of strong biblical women and quoted no women as exemplars of Christianity. Women who wore modest dress included Eve (whose garments were made by God), Sarah, Susanna, and the Virgin Mary. Saint Jerome persuaded Celantia, a noble matron, not to marry a wealthy banker, and she died a virgin. Penn cited four heathen women as models: Penelope (who, although wealthy, worked at her loom), Lucretia (a paragon of chastity), Cornelia (who wore sober apparel), and Portia (known for her modesty). But twice as many were evil: "Infamous Clytemnestra, painted Jezebel, the Lascivius Campaspe, immodest Posthumia, the costly Corinthian Lais, the most impudent Flora, the wanton Aegyeptian Cleopattia, and the most insatiable Messalina: Persons whose Memories have Stunk through all Ages."[33]

A section added in 1682 told of eleven admirable heathen women (including the four mentioned above), six of whom committed suicide after their husbands died or to resist being raped. After the philosopher Seneca committed suicide before Nero could have him killed, his wife was stopped from killing herself by the emperor, but she lived in mourning for the rest of her life. Even Penn recognized that suicide after rape was not recommended; in discussing Lucretia, who killed herself after being raped, he wrote, "I praise the Virtue, and not the Fact."[34] Only two women exemplars appeared in the section of pious deathbed sayings: Princess Elizabeth, whom Penn had visited and now quoted extensively, specifically her pious sayings and farewell to him (even though he had no knowledge of how she approached death), and his aunt, who repented of her frivolous ways on her deathbed. There are no examples of women of outstanding intellectual ability or accomplishments outside the home. Penn permitted a large range of activities to both men and women but expressed the traditional view when it came to women's tasks, which were to "Spin, Sow, Knit, Weave, Garden, Preserve, and the like Housewife and Honest Employments . . . helping others, who for Want are unable to keep Servants, to Ease them in their Necessary Affairs: Often and private Retirements from all Worldly Objects, to enjoy the Lord; Secret and Steady Meditations on the Divine Life and Heavenly Inheritance."[35] There was no mention of women's preaching or traveling in the ministry, publishing, separate women's meetings, or any role for women in church governance.

Penn made a strong differentiation between male and female virtues and expressed a clear distrust of effeminacy. A man who liked luxurious clothes, indulged excessively in food and drink, and attended the theater ended with a "Mind effeminate"; by engaging in these vices, "a Man is made Unactive, and so Unuseful in Civil Society." Penn praised manly virtues as different from Christian ethics without being specific. Cato, he said, opposed "Poetical Fancies (much less open Stages) as being too effeminate and apt to withdraw the Minds of Youth, from more Noble, more Manly as well as more heavenly Exercises."[36] Idle recreation lead to "looseness, idleness, ignorance, and effeminacy, the grand Cankers, and bane of all States and Empires."

The self-denial, humility, service to others, and simplicity that Penn advocated for both sexes had traditionally been associated with Christian women, not men. An English gentleman was to be polite but also courageous, ready to be adventurous and serve as an officer in the military. Penn grew up surrounded by military virtue. His father was a war hero, and young William had visited a warship preparing for battle against the Dutch. In all probability he had observed the rigorous discipline observed on English ships. In the 1669 edition of *NCNC* he contrasted soldiers' obedience to the Roman centurion as "is practiced now amongst Souldiers, as being an effeminate Custom, unworthy of Masculine Gravity." In France at Saumur, he had learned about and may have seen a pattern for his future life in Duplessis de Mornay, a statesman and soldier who had built the castle that dominated the town, won battles for Henry IV, supported the Edict of Nantes granting toleration to French Calvinists, and wrote theological books defending rational Christianity. In Ireland, Penn showed courage in helping to put down a rebellion and would have obtained a military command had his father not intervened. Perhaps subconsciously, Penn must have feared that opponents would see his willingness to suffer, advocacy of plain living, unconcern with social status and genealogy, opposition to war, and stress upon service as feminine.[37] Historians of Friends have noted that the MMM severely censored and restricted women's publications in the late seventeenth century. The evidence in *NCNC* suggests that Penn did not resist and may have supported this trend.

Finally, Penn summed up his theme: "No Cross, No Crown, No Temperance, No Happiness, No Virtue, No Reward, No Mortification, No Glorification."[38] The book instantly became popular, being reprinted in English three times (in 1694, 1700, and 1702), with a Dutch edition in 1687. Copies of *NCNC* and Robert Barclay's *Apology* are found in most eighteenth-century Quaker meetings' book collections. Barclay summarized Quaker theology, and Penn, Quaker ethics.

SOME FRUITS OF SOLITUDE (1693)

Compared with 1682, when Charles II was vigorously persecuting Friends and ruling without Parliament, the perspective of Quakers in 1693 had markedly improved. The so-called Act of Toleration permitted freedom of worship, although imprisonment for refusal to pay tithes continued, and those who refused to take oaths suffered many liabilities. Still, Friends had been allowed to affirm their loyalty to William and Mary, and the king and many members of Parliament showed sympathy and gave partial legislative relief in the Quakers Act of 1695.

Penn's prospects, however, seemed bleak. He was in hiding, charged with treason, had lost the power to govern Pennsylvania, and was blamed by many Friends for being too sympathetic to King James before the Revolution of 1688. His beloved wife, Gulielma, died in February 1694. He was in debt, Pennsylvania had proved ungovernable (a religious schism there had discredited him and Quakers in general), and his prospects for regaining influence were uncertain. In the preface to *FOS*, he "blessed God for his retirement and kisse[d] the gentle hand which led him to it." Praising God for sending adversity is good Christian doctrine and conforms to Stoicism's detachment from worldly affairs, but Penn also interceded with nobles to persuade the king to exonerate him and restore his colony. His *Essay on the Present and Future Peace of Europe*, also not submitted to the meeting for approval, offered King William a solution to a future of perennial war with France. Penn employed his forced leisure to write several defenses of Quakers, including "A Brief Account of the Rise and Progress of the People called Quakers," as a preface to George Fox's *Journal*, and *A Key to the Scriptures*. Penn's intended audience for *FOS* was not Quakers, and he did not submit the manuscript to the MMM, perhaps because they would have made major changes or rejected it.[39] Quakers had long been suspicious of politeness as being untruthful, but here Penn stressed behavior that might a conceal a person's real motives in a desire for success. *FOS* provided advice useful to a Friend seeking to blend into English society and to others who sought to live according to the postulates of natural law or Christianity.

FOS is unlike any other seventeenth-century Quaker writing and shows Penn as a rationalist and humanist using nature, reason, balance, moderation, and love as a guide to ethics. It contains no biblical citations (though much biblical influence), no pious Christian or heathen exemplars, no apocalyptic judgments, no expressions of self-denial or mortification.[40] The passages in *NCNC* on lawful actions that become unlawful when practiced in excess, including those regarding eating, dress, money, and family, are the main themes of *FOS*. However, the reward for controlling pride, luxury, and avarice in *FOS* is not salvation but good manners and social success. The tract assumed Christianity, but reverence was derived from contemplating the works of God in nature rather than from scripture or inward revelation. Penn still relied on knowledge of impending death as a motive for action, but not as a reason to take up the cross or imitate Christ.

Two long sections reflected Penn's changed circumstances and provided advice on subjects ignored in the two editions of *NCNC*. As a widower, Penn had sole responsibility for his three children, Springett (age eighteen), Letetia (fifteen), and Billy (thirteen). Education, marriage, and family life now were his immediate concerns, and the first section of *FOS* offered guidance on how to deal with people and success in society. The other long section included maxims for the prince and his advisers. It may seem a bit presumptuous for a man charged with treason, whose administration of a colony had failed, to instruct government officials. But Penn was conscious of his innocence even if others were not, and in *FOS* he provided lessons he had learned in the courts of Charles and James and presented himself to King William as a moral, disinterested man.

The terms "reflections" and "maxims" in the title of *FOS* refer to the origin of the advice Penn presumed to offer. Reflections came from Penn's thinking or meditation in solitude; his maxims were derived from proverbs.[41] There is no direct evidence that Penn read François de La Rochefoucauld's very popular *Réflexions ou Sentences et Maximes morales*, which had gone through multiple editions in French and English since it was first published in 1665. Although both books advocated morality and dealt with "interest" and "self," Penn's tone was very different from that of the French nobleman, who combined Stoicism, Catholicism, cynicism, and humor, writing, for example, "Our self-love is sure to prevent the person who flatters us from ever being the one who flatters us most"; "The reader's best policy is to start with the premise that none of these maxims is directed at him, and that he is the sole exception to them, even though they seem to be generally applicable"; and "The reason why lovers are never bored with each other's company is because they are always talking about themselves."[42] In any case, Penn was the very opposite of Rochefoucauld—earnest, humorless, and devout—just as he was the opposite of Machiavelli in his political advice.[43]

As in many writings about morality, Penn's creativity lay not in originality in content but in style and wording. Whereas Penn's other tracts do not survive in draft form, a draft of part of *FOS* survives and shows him making changes in wording to improve the individual sayings. The preface asserts that his sources were sudden insights or deep reflection, rather than study. In answer to a request for a list of books for the library of Sir John Rhodes, a young Quaker, in 1693, Penn listed ninety titles.[44] If we assume that Penn not only knew about but had read all of these books, it is possible to see likely influences for *FOS*. These include Plutarch's *Lives* and *Morals*, Erasmus's *Colloquies* and *Adages*, Seneca's *Letters*, Marcus Aurelius's *Meditations*, and Epictetus's *Enchiridion* (in the preface, Penn calls *FOS* an "Enchiridion"). Books of advice that Penn might have read include Montaigne's *Essays*, Francis Bacon's *Adages*, Jeremy Taylor's *Of Holy Living*, and George Herbert's *Jacula Prudentum*. Except for Herbert, these books contained essays, not apothegms. We know that Penn read Thomas Stanley's *History of Philosophy*, which contains the apothegms of the various Greek philosophers, particularly those of Pythagoras, and in style and subject resembles Penn's work here—for example, "Temperance is the strength of the Soul, for it is the light of the soul, clear from Passion"; "It is impossible he can be free, who serves the passions and is governed by them"; "Comprehend not few things in many words, but many things in few words."[45]

Penn often relied upon the wisdom books of the Old Testament. A comparison of the number of Penn's citations of Proverbs with the number quoted by Fox and Barclay shows that Penn used Proverbs much more frequently, second only to the Gospel of John, with Matthew slightly behind.[46] Proverbs, of course, is about seeking Wisdom, a female personification of God, with short sayings attributed to Solomon. "Train up a child in the way he should go: and when he is old, he will not depart from it" (22:6); "Answer a fool according to his folly, lest he be wise in his own conceit" (26:5). Like *FOS*, Proverbs offers many kinds of advice in no particular order. One contrast between *FOS* and Proverbs is that Penn never suggests that moral conduct will yield worldly success, though both texts insist that lending money and being lazy will lead to poverty.

The subject headings in Joseph Besse's 1726 edition of *FOS* and all later editions were added after the first printings and at times seem arbitrary. Some sayings stand alone, while others are short essays divided into maxims on different subjects. There are four major subjects: the first on family and domestic issues, including education, marriage, obedience to parents, servants, friends; the second on proper social behavior, including business, conversation, wit, and passions; the third on government; and the fourth, the longest, on religion. Although *FOS* was directed at "Parent or Child, Prince or Subject, Master or Servant, Single or Married . . . Rich or Poor," Penn did not mention housewives, mothers, maids or any other female occupation.[47] Perhaps because he believed that the soul had no sex, Penn wrote for men.

In his earlier writings, Penn had not gone much beyond biblical clichés in dealing with women (Prov. 31:23–31), education ("Education has a mighty Influence and strong Byass upon the Affections and Actions of men"), and children ("A Wise Parent even withdraws those Objects, however innocent in themselves, which are too prevalent upon the weak Senses of Children, on purpose that they might be weaned").[48] Penn was not unique in his comparative neglect of children. When Plutarch,[49] the Stoics, Erasmus, Francis Bacon, Montaigne, George Herbert, and others gave advice on the subject of raising and educating children, they assumed male children (the only children to which education applied); the only important topics were discipline, education, and marriage; and the father was in control: "Fire, Sea, Woman, Three Evils" (Erasmus); "Woman is the woe of man," "Woman as necessary evil," "Marry your sonne when you will, your daughter when you can," "Advise none to marry or go to war," "The more women looke in their glasse, the lesse to their house" (Herbert); "Chastity is not for men, but women" (Montaigne). Plutarch insisted that the love of a woman was no better than that of a boy. On marriage, he wrote, "govern with the eye to the merit of a woman, as much as to the size of a horse," and a "well managed household is done by mutual consent, but the husband's supremacy is exhibited." Rochefoucauld averred, "If love is judged by most of its results, it is more like hatred than friendship."[50] Like these authors, Penn did not question male supremacy, but unlike them he expressed no misogyny or mixed messages. In his view, the proper household was governed by mutual respect and love between husband and wife.

Penn's vision of the family reflects a humanist view of Quaker teachings. Penn reinforced a new emphasis upon the right education of children among postrevolutionary Quakers who recognized that the survival of their faith depended upon their children's adopting a distinctive way of life. He fused two primary emphases: that knowledge of the world was useful and that nature provided rules for life. Friends had decried the traditional emphasis on studying Latin and Greek, partially because these languages were requisite for the professions of divinity and law. Penn knew and used Latin, French, and some Greek, but the first laws of Pennsylvania required that statutes be in English and that all children be "instructed in Reading and writing. So that they be able to read the Scriptures, and to write" by age twelve and to learn a "useful trade or skill." In *FOS*, Penn opposed schooling that taught grammar and a "strange Tongue or two," that taught children to talk rather than to know.[51] Instead, he argued, teaching should be adapted to the child. Children liked to "make tools and instruments of play; shaping, drawing, framing and building things." Latin should be taught in a book about mechanics and nature. Pupils should learn about nature so that if they later became gardeners or farmers, they would understand "the reason of their calling," just as artisans knew the rules of mechanics. An additional ethical benefit of this approach to education was that the rules of nature were "few, plain, and most reasonable." Knowledge of nature would make adults less likely to abuse it and would lead people to the Creator, "whose stamp is everywhere visible."[52]

All of the evidence suggests that Penn's marriage to Gulielma was a happy one, and he drew upon his experience and Quaker teachings in describing family life.[53] In both editions of *NCNC*, Penn condemned choosing a wife for her wealth. "Never marry but for love, but sees that what thou lov'st is lovely"; love was to be "thy chiefest Motive." And love, for Penn, meant a "union of souls" that transcended all "lusts"—beauty, money, social status, etc. "In marriage ... prefer the Person before money, Vertue before Beauty, the Mind before the body."[54] Penn downplayed physical attributes that could give only short-term pleasure. (He never discussed the physical pleasures involved in marriage, but he sired seven or eight children by Gulielma and another seven by his second wife, Hannah, who was twenty-seven years younger and whom he married when he was fifty-two.) Quakers insisted that husband and wife should be of equal status, and, the "union of souls" notwithstanding, both of Penn's wives had considerable property. Penn later complained that his son Billy's wife had brought neither money nor sense to that marriage.[55]

The relationship between husband and wife was later referred to as companionate, and Penn wrote that a man's partner in marriage should be "a wife, a friend, companion, a second self." A wife incapable of being a friend was only half a wife. Between husband and wife, love must rule; authority was for children and servants, though even there it should not be without "sweetness." A wife and husband in love who valued each other would show their children that this was the way to behave to each other. "They are best loved of those that love most"; "nothing can be more contented and constant, than such a couple."[56]

Penn says little about rearing children, except that discipline in the household is required and that children must obey their parents as a natural right: "He that begets thee, ownes thee, and has a natural right over thee." Preserving "nature in children" will in time create an affectionate relationship between parents and children that can be nurtured by visits, letters, and presents.[57] Disobedience of parents amounted to rebellion against God. Perhaps remembering his own disobedience to his father, Penn allowed an exemption: "If we must not disobey God to obey them, at least we must let them see, there is nothing else in our refusal."[58] Children should not dominate servants or vice versa, because there is but one master and mistress in the house. Servants were part of the family and were to be treated with respect and to comply with the master's desires. They should neither "Indulge" the "Master's Children" nor refuse what was "fitting," and because servants' behavior influenced children, they must be chosen carefully.[59]

Friends often used the terms "Brother" and "Sister" to refer to the close relationships among members in meetings. *FOS* describes relationships among friends as nearly equal to that between husband and wife, defined by a "Union of Spirits, a Marriage of Hearts, and the Bond thereof Virtue." One should choose a friend "as thou dost a wife" because they are "Twins in Soul" and guided by the same principles of "Love and Aversion." A striking omission in

Penn's advice on family and friends was any mention of the division of authority between father and mother in rearing children, and he seemed to assume that his thoughts on friendship applied only among men.[60]

The second section in *FOS* on personal conduct recommended prudence, moderation, and balance in dealing with business, charity, detractors, temporal happiness, and jealousy or wit. Penn, who often used many words when a few would have sufficed, was direct and concise on these subjects. A few of the briefer maxims convey Penn's vision of wisdom in conduct: "All Excess is ill," he attested, particularly drunkenness. "Seek not to be rich, but happy: The one lies in Bags, the other in content; which wealth can never give." "Passion is a sort of fever in the mind, which ever leaves us weaker than it found us." "Affect not to be seen, and men will less see thy weaknesses." "Only trust thyself, and another shall not betray thee." "Silence is wisdom; where speaking is folly, and always safe." "If thou thinkest twice, before thou speakest once, thou wilt speak twice the better for it." The maxim that best summarized Penn's worldly ethical advice (and notice the "we" rather than "thou"): "We must not be concerned above the Value of the thing that engages us; Nor raised above Reason in maintaining what we think reasonable."[61]

Penn's political advice should be understood in its post-1688 context. It took nerve to discuss politics and give advice to William and Mary and their advisers. After all, Penn had counseled and supported James II, was suspected of supporting him even now, and was rumored to be a Roman Catholic. His political suggestions served to justify his past actions and, he hoped, pave the way to his exoneration. The advice can be understood as explaining in abstract terms why James had fallen and how William and Mary could prevent another revolution. Penn began by distinguishing between a legitimate king, who ruled by laws to which the people gave their consent ("freedom") and one who used "absolute Will and Power" ("Tyranny"). A king ruling by law could be strict so long as he was also just, and his real security lay in the people's thinking that they ruled. He could indulge them in little things while being firm in great matters. However, weakness was as dangerous as tyranny, because a people's ambition "shakes" the constitution and, if indulged, could lead to idleness and effeminacy. A tyrant's "ill administration" threatened the tyrant and his family. A ruler should have no passion, "nor resent beyond interest and religion." He should not create fear, for that would provide no security, and "service upon inclination is like to go further than obedience upon compunction." Penn's triumvirate for good government was law, moderation, and justice against "looseness, oppression, and envy."⁶² Penn's advice to the king risked being nothing more than pious clichés.

Penn, no longer an adviser, still insisted that the "Public must and will be served" and that those who advised deserved a salary. A good officer should have "ability, clean hands, dispatch, patience, and impartiality," receive a sufficient salary, take no bribes, and be "governed neither by compassion, fear, profit, or prejudices." He should be prepared to provide the king with instruction in the law and to forfeit favor by giving sound legal advice. The people should understand that the king's impact on them would come through his servants, and his advisers should be prepared to be judged and criticized for their actions, but not unfairly.⁶³

There were omissions in Penn advice. He never mentioned war, assumed that laws created by Parliament would be just (though he knew better), allowed the king's interest and religion to be dominant, and said nothing about what would happen if the people's interest or religion diverged from the king's or the statutes'. Penn's belief that counselors should be unconcerned with their own gain or interest did not reflect his father's or his own status as the recipients of enormous tracts of land from Charles and James, and he continued lobbying on behalf of the colony of Pennsylvania. Although he had created constitutions and laws for West New Jersey and Pennsylvania, his view of law in *FOS*, as in his discussions of common law, was that it was a static entity that guaranteed justice.⁶⁴ Although Penn regained his colony and appeared as a Quaker petitioner and a defender of proprietary rights before William and Anne, he never again served as a counselor to a monarch.

In discussing religion, Penn wanted to influence those who remained suspicious of a man whom many considered either a sectarian fanatic or a devious Roman Catholic. Yet he aimed to be ambiguous enough that his fellow Quakers would believe he was endorsing their faith. He began with a warning about the inadequacy of believing oneself virtuous in general while in fact neglecting one's flaws. As in *NCNC*, he stressed the need to conquer one's evil inclinations. Religion "was the Fear of God" based not upon knowledge but upon faith and shown in the imitation of Christ. Penn was most Quaker in discussing the value of silence in worship, the necessity of religious experience for ministers and in worship, and the congruence of a preacher's life with his teaching, but he presented these virtues in a way that might appeal to, or at least not irritate, other Protestants who believed that Christian piety was more important than doctrine. "It is a rule with me, that man is truly religious, that [he] loves the persuasion he is of, for the piety rather than the ceremony of it."⁶⁵

The religion Penn commended in *FOS* brought harmony. "A good end cannot sanctify evil means; nor must we ever do evil, that good may come of it." Reason and nature reinforced religious observance, for the wonders of God's mercies in creation should make all grateful and create "a resolution to alter our course and mend our manners." "Grace perfects but never spoils nature," he insisted. "To be unnatural in defense of grace is unnatural." Although he did not mention hell, Penn invoked death and eternal life as everyone's ultimate end. "The truest end of life is to know the life that never ends." "The humble, meek, merciful, just, pious and devout souls are everywhere of one religion; and when death has taken off the mask, they will know one another, though the diverse liveries they wear here, make them strangers."⁶⁶

FOS ends with a paeon to Christian love. "What we Love, we'll Hear; what we love, we'll trust; and what we love, we'll serve, ay, and suffer for it to." "Love is above all; and when it prevails in us all, we shall all be lovely, and in love with God and one with another."⁶⁷ Advising Christians to love one another and focusing on God's love through Christ's sacrifice had been standard exhortations for centuries, but Penn had not made a point of them in the two editions of *NCNC*.⁶⁸ Why not, and why did he do so now? One answer is that in *NCNC* Penn was primarily interested in morality as a sign of self-denial, the end, as always, being salvation, but in *FOS* he had expanded his vision to encompass the whole society. He now focused on the ill effects on society of partiality, argument for the sake of achieving victory rather than truth, and pride and greed. Unlike in 1669, he accepted that Friends would be a minority, and if Pennsylvania provided any lessons, it was that Quakerism did not guarantee social harmony or stable government. Now, in *FOS*, he aimed for a lower common denominator of natural or heathen morality that might bring about moderation, justice, and Christian piety. As he phrased it, "Let us see what love can do."⁶⁹

Equally important, he was now less secure in his vision of Pennsylvania and his own role in English society. He was experiencing the secluded country life of retirement that he had recommended for others. His social circle was now made up of Friends, family, and acquaintances, not kings and aristocrats. He was probably depressed after the death of his wife and fearful of the life-threatening decline in the health of his eldest son. He did not doubt the authenticity of his religious experience but had come to realize that wisdom, reason, nature, and morality needed to be supplemented by Christian charity and love.

CONCLUSIONS

Life as a pilgrimage, behavior in the short term leading to eternal bliss or never-ending hellfire, was a major theme in the first two editions of *NCNC*, but this theme was muted almost to nonexistence in *FOS*, except in the preface. In *NCNC*, revealed Christianity dominated; in *FOS*, a kind of Stoicism, humanism, and ethical Christianity prevailed. Penn was a prophet in the first edition of *NCNC*, a preacher in the second, and a moralist in *FOS*. In 1669 he hoped to change people by Quaker Christianity; in the 1682 *NCNC* he sought to reform England by a model Quaker colony; in 1693, no longer optimistic, he provided a means for an individual to survive in an unpredictable society. True belief, which led to self-denial and thus salvation, evolved into reasonable behavior that brought domestic tranquility. In all three treatises, however, Penn's eclecticism, his willingness to meld Quakerism, Christian traditions, Stoicism, reason, and nature, makes it difficult to say where final ethical authority resided.

In evaluating these treatises, it is reasonable to ask whether Penn followed his own advice. The answer is: not always. He suggested reading few books carefully, but he owned, recommended, and cited many. He wanted to stay out of debt, but he overspent his income for years. He advised that one conceal his opinions and remain silent, but he did just the opposite—perhaps to a fault. Moderation in food, drink, and housing? Perhaps, but his standards allowed for differences in rank; his house at Worminghurst was a "grand gentleman's country seat," and Pennsbury was an impressive estate befitting the proprietor of a vast colony.[70] He disdained pride in family, but the monument erected to his father was militaristic and elaborate, and he was proud of the family coat of arms. In early life a rebel against authority, he was very aware of his status as a gentleman and his authority as a proprietor. For a model father, his surviving sons turned out badly, leaving the Society of Friends; one became an alcoholic and the others were greedy and self-serving. In choosing his second wife, he ignored the opposition of Friends and married a much younger woman. But his letters to Hannah before and after the marriage conform to the advice he gave in *NCNC* and *FOS*.[71] Penn exalted friendship, but his letters suggest that he had no close personal friends, and Mary Maples Dunn suggests that he "was not capable of a continuous relationship."[72] The one constant in Penn's adult life was his commitment to Friends, and surviving evidence shows that, with some exceptions, they esteemed him greatly. In 1702, Falls Monthly Meeting in Pennsylvania said of him, "his Conversation deportment [and exemplary life] well [agreed] with his Doctrine to the Comfort & edification of the honest hearted. . . . As our Governor he hath Chosen rather to rule as an elder not with rigour but in much love & brotherly kindness. . . . Some of his Chiefest opposits having said [that he is too good a man to be a governor, and there are others] that wold never desire a better Governor were he not a Quaker." Penn's memorial minute from Reading Quarterly Meeting described him as a man of "great Abilities," "Excellent Sweetness of Disposition," "full of the Qualification of True Discipleship, Even Love without Dissimulation, as extensive in Charity, as comprehensive in Knowledge," and said that he "may justly be rank'd among the Learned, Good, and Great."[73] These encomia suggest that he tried to live by the principles he espoused in *NCNC* and *FOS*.

The differences in tone in Penn's three major ethical treatises show how external circumstances influenced his advocacy of moral precepts for the whole society. In the 1669 tract we meet the belligerent, arrogant, aristocratic Penn, newly converted and ready to pronounce apocalyptic judgment, confident that his exhortations will persuade others that those willing to practice self-denial in this life will reap eternal rewards. In 1682, Penn saw himself as God's instrument in defending religious liberty in England and creating a Christian society, a Philadelphia where people would do God's will. *NCNC* proclaimed a Quaker-inflected Christian morality designed to attract serious, hardworking, disciplined, pious people from many denominations. The Bible, nature, and reason buttressed Penn's inward certainty that the practice of these virtues would yield an orderly society. Penn laid out in 250 pages his critique of nominal Christians and the requirements for an ethical life, and, in case this was insufficient, he added another 250 pages to the second edition of *NCNC* citing heathen and Christian exemplars. The early laws of Pennsylvania could not create moral people, but they forbade the recreations and luxuries that Penn decried. In 1693, when Penn addressed the world in *FOS*, he was no longer confident that God intended him to build a Christian society or that religious experience alone would suffice. Now he wanted a peaceful society governed by a common morality based upon natural religion, justice, and common sense. Religion was still important, but he confined it to the preface and final sections. Only in a concluding invocation of the power of love did Penn write with his old mystical fervor.

Whether these treatises influenced the moral choices and behavior of the inhabitants of the American colonies or the people of England cannot be determined, but the fourteen editions of *FOS* before 1726 and the forty-two of *NCNC* in Britain and America by the mid-nineteenth century must mean that many people, even outside the Society of Friends, found help in reading and silently reflecting on Penn's moral advice and exemplary life. A modernized edition of the second version of *NCNC* is still in print, and quotations from it are esteemed by many who do not know or care about their original context.

Chapter 7

PREACHER

As a graduate student in 1965, I took a course in Reconstruction history from Avery Craven (b. 1885), who at that time was as old as I am now. He told how as a young man he had heard the great American historian Charles Beard (whose parents and wife were raised as Quakers) caution that "history is a damn dark hole and we have a damn dim candle." I have often used this quotation with my own students to convey the limits of our ability to reconstruct the past. For the student of early Quakerism, one of the dark holes is what went on in the meeting for worship. That meeting was Friends' central focus, what kept their conviction steady. We have a copious amount of writing advocating Quaker beliefs, accounts of disputes with opponents, and comments by outsiders, invariably negative, about Quaker preaching.[1] Today's Friends often recall Robert Barclay's assessment of early Quaker preaching, in which he downplayed the importance of the spoken word. After attending his first meeting, Barclay claimed that it was not the strength of the defense of Quaker beliefs that moved him but something more ineffable. "When I came into the secret assemblies of God's people," he wrote, "I felt a secret power among them, which reached my heart." Barclay's defense of inward revelation and disregard of systematic thought did not stop him from writing a thousand pages of theology, the most famous being his *Apology for the True Christian Divinity.*[2]

Necessity may be the mother of invention, but in scholarship it can make for misleading, simplistic, or wrong history. Because Friends did not write down their sermons, Michael Graves, in his study of early Quaker preaching, could find only one sermon before 1670, during the formative period of Quakerism (by George Fox in 1653), a few others by Fox, delivered in the

1670s, and none by anyone else before 1680.³ Those who seek to understand early Friends must extrapolate from tracts and epistles the content of worship, and such a method invariably leads to disagreements. Epistles addressed to Friends are probably the best source for understanding Quaker preaching to members, but beginning in 1673 all printed materials had to be approved by the MMM in London, whose members read and edited the contents.⁴ Any spontaneity or deviation from Quaker norms would disappear in the process. Consequently, we have some idea of Fox's preaching from a few sermons, but there are none from Isaac Penington, Edward Burrough, or James Nayler, and only one each from William Dewsbury and Robert Barclay.

In 1694 a non-Friend wrote down in shorthand and published several of Penn's sermons. The tone and content of Penn's messages differ significantly from those of his other writings published earlier on, even in the same decade.⁵ An analysis of Penn's sermons, the theme of this chapter, is useful for understanding his ideas and roles in Quaker meetings, but it also serves as a caution about inferences made about the preaching of others in meetings for worship.

Preaching to Friends became a significant activity for Penn two years after his convincement in 1667 and remained important for more than forty years. Penn's account of his trip to Holland indicates that he preached frequently, sometimes for several hours at a time.⁶ He preached so often, in fact—and other members of the team were also notable speakers—that there must have been very little silence in meeting, and his listeners may have resented that a young aristocrat was assuming dominance. A Friend criticized Penn in 1677 for wearing a wig. As noted in the introductory chapter, Penn was bald because of childhood smallpox and his time in prison. Fox, to whom the Friend had complained, defended Penn by saying that the wig was small and was needed to protect his health, because he became "in danger of his life after violent heats in meeting."⁷ Because silent meeting should not cause "violent heats," Penn probably became excited while preaching. His voice was loud enough that he could be heard in court during Bushel's case even after being confined in the bail dock, and he had been arrested for attempting to preach in the open air on a London street after soldiers locked the meeting house in enforcing the Conventicle Act. Yet witnesses could not testify as to what Penn said because the noise of the soldiers and the crowd was too great.⁸ In November 1694 Penn took a preaching tour to the western counties and spoke to "large meetings." There were so many attendees in Wells that, rather than stay in the Market House, they adjourned to adjacent fields, "and a great Gathering there was."⁹

Our best account of Penn's abilities as a public speaker appears in a 1675 anti-Quaker tract about a four-day debate at the Baptist Barbican and Quaker Wheeler Street meeting houses. George Keith, George Whitehead, Stephen Crisp, and Penn defended Friends' beliefs, but only Penn was singled out—probably because he was seen as a leader. Penn had a "Voluble Tongue, a strong Voice and clear, a grateful utterance, and I believe good Lungs that thou art to be commended for an excellent Rhetorican and a Fluent Tongue," "partly acquired at Our Schools," schools that Penn criticized—i.e., Oxford and the Inns of Court. His eloquence was as "plausible as a Jesuit's oration" and consisted of incessant "Railing" instead of "Reasoning," "unchristian Carriage," and long answers that lasted "about a whole hour."[10] From this we can conclude that Penn's education and upper class showed.

Penn appears to have been a popular preacher for Friends and outsiders.[11] He attracted large crowds as a traveling minister in the west of England and Ireland in 1698. The MMM advised Southwark Friends in 1688–69 to attend their regular local meeting rather than overcrowding Grace Church Street Meeting during the time that Penn, George Whitehead, and Stephen Crisp also attended there.[12]

WHO PRESERVED PENN'S SERMONS?

The most significant collections of early Quaker sermons, more than two-thirds of the surviving seventy-nine from the seventeenth century, date from the 1690s and were preached in London, most in Grace Church but enough from a wide variety of London meetings to give a sense of what Friends heard in worship, at least in the capital. A person identified only as "A Lover of that People" but not as a Friend took down in "short hand" thirty-two sermons by Stephen Crisp between 1687 and 1693. These were popular enough to have had a second edition in 1696 and a third in 1707. The response to Crisp's sermons seems to have encouraged the same man to write down a series of fourteen messages and concluding prayers preached in London, including two by Penn, one by Robert Barclay, and another by William Dewsbury, along with ten by less well known Quaker ministers. Though published in 1694, three of the sermons, including Penn's (delivered at the funeral of Rebecca Travers), date from 1688, but most date from 1693–94. Most important for our purposes was a collection of ten sermons that Penn delivered in London meetings in 1694, plus one each by Benjamin Coale, Samuel Waldenfield, and George Whitehead given the same year.¹³ The transcriber of the sermons titled each one and included one prayer by Penn and another by Whitehead. Either the publisher omitted other prayers or Penn intended his benedictions, taken from the Bible or the Book of Common Prayer, as final prayers. In a separate category are two farewell addresses: a last sermon preached by Penn at Westminster Meeting in London that is not included in Joseph Besse's *Works of William Penn*, and a farewell epistle when he was preparing to return to America that Friends published with the approval of the MMM.¹⁴

The MMM did not authorize the publication of these volumes of sermons, and Penn's discourses are not included in Besse's 1726 works of Penn. However, Edwin Bronner and David Fraser suggest in their bibliography that there was Quaker collaboration and even approval of these publications.¹⁵ Several arguments support their conclusion. For example, it would have been fairly easy to stop a non-Quaker, sitting with paper, ink, and quill in Grace Church meetings over the course of many weeks, from taking notes. Additionally, the sermons show careful editing by someone with an excellent knowledge of the Bible, someone who put the scripture citations, most of which were not identified as biblical, in italics in the printed version. The biblical citations needed to be checked to make sure the male preacher (there were no females in these collections) had spoken accurately. In the late eighteenth century, Friends called verses that sounded biblical but were not in scripture "Quaker texts."¹⁶ There are many of these in the sermons, but they are not in italics. Finally, although fifteen individuals delivered these sermons using no notes or Bibles and with no preparation, the transcriptions suggest that the preachers spoke in complete sentences and seem never to have stumbled into incoherence. My conclusion is that someone spent a considerable length of time preparing these discourses for the public and did so with at least the tacit consent of Friends. The non-Quaker who published them claimed that they were "for the information of those, who, by reason of ignorance, may have received a prejudice against them." He argued that the sermons showed that Quakers unanimously approved of the main Protestant doctrines and contained "many Gospel Truths, delivered with such Plainness, Zeal, and Demonstration, and generally agreeable to the Known Doctrines of Christianity."¹⁷ Nathaniel Crouch, who was not a Quaker, printed the Crisp sermons and those in *Concurrence and Unanimity*, but Jane Sowle, who was a Friend, published the Penn sermons. So there was at least an unofficial authorization of his messages, and the reprinting of all three collections by T. and J. Sowle in 1707 shows that Friends still found these sermons acceptable.¹⁸

There are plausible reasons why these sermon collections were at first not officially approved. The first concerned the testimony for truth. A carefully edited sermon with any mistakes corrected is not a spontaneously delivered message, which is what these sermons purported to be: "he has not in the least altered or imposed upon the Preacher's Sense, either in taking or transcribing of them."[19] Second, Friends believed that messages should be tailored to a specific audience and that a speaker, in the middle of his sermon, might be led to change the subject because of his or her sense that individuals present might benefit from different counsel. There was a crucial difference between a carefully worded epistle or tract edited and published by the MMM and a sermon taken down in shorthand. Third, a person writing down the sermon would be more interested in his task than in listening to the speaker and thus would not be actually worshipping. The very act of writing destroyed the spiritual essence of a meeting for worship, bad enough in a sermon but worse during a prayer. Also, sermons recorded in shorthand did not have the imprimatur of the MMM or MFS and had not been edited by Friends for content. Approving them officially would have established a bad precedent.[20] Finally, and most important, Nathaniel Crouch, who seems to have viewed printing Quaker sermons as a way to make money, printed sermons by Thomas Budd and George Keith delivered in Quaker meetings in 1694. Budd and Keith, though still officially Quakers, were under discipline by LYM and should not have been preaching or airing their differences in print.

Friends could have welcomed those of Penn's sermons that espoused a unique form that Protestantism that agreed with other churches on the status of Jesus, the power of his atoning death, the pervasiveness of sin, the necessity of salvation, and need for sanctification. Quakers were not Roman Catholics and therefore qualified for freedom of worship under the so-called Act of Toleration, which applied only to orthodox Protestants. The sermons supported the Friends' stance that they agreed with the Church of England, and also with other dissenters, on Christian fundamentals, but suspicion of Friends' motives remained strong, particularly among high Anglicans, and the tracts of Francis Bugg, an apostate Quaker, and later of Charles Leslie, insisted that Quakers were double-dealing heretics who could not be trusted. However, an outsider reading these sermons might be persuaded that Friends were respectable people who could be trusted.

Their own schism directly threatened Friends' status under the Toleration Act. In Pennsylvania in 1691, a theological and political controversy involving George Keith had resulted in the creation of a separate meeting of self-described

"Christian Friends," in Keith's disownment by Philadelphia Yearly Meeting, in the use of the courts to silence Keith's advocates by arresting the only printer in the colony and seizing his type, and in a bitter pamphlet war.[21] In spite of efforts by London Friends to conceal the controversy in England by buying up all copies of the pro-Keithian tracts opposing the main body of Philadelphia Friends, the bishop of London had obtained copies and republished them.[22] Keith accused American Friends of preaching exclusively about the Inward Light and denying the efficacy of the atonement of the historical Christ, the resurrection of the body, and religious persecution. If he were right, then Friends were not orthodox and did not qualify for toleration. In 1694 both sides appealed to LYM, which rebuked them both and instructed Keith, who insisted he wanted to remain a member, to call in his pamphlets and clear Friends of heresy.[23] Afterward, Keith spoke against the decision and complained of his persecution by the leaders of LYM, including Penn, continued to publish critiques, and created a separate meeting in London with the support of dissident Quakers and ministers from the Church of England. The result was a pamphlet war in London in which prominent Friends issued tracts attacking Keith. In 1695 LYM disowned him. Friends surely welcomed the publication of Penn's sermons counteracting Keith's charges. Virtually all of the 1694 sermons affirm belief in the indwelling Christ and the historical Jesus as necessary for salvation.

Penn had his own reasons for being pleased with the publication of his sermons. Though he was often accused of being a Jesuit, the sermons showed Penn as definitely Protestant.[24] After the Revolution of 1688, Penn had been accused of treason and had gone into hiding, although he emerged to attend the funeral of George Fox in 1691. The Crown had seized the government of Pennsylvania from Penn and the continuing troubles in that colony reflected badly on him.[25] It is uncertain how widespread the animosity to Penn was in Quaker circles, but some Friends blamed him for the disrepute that afflicted the sect after the 1688 revolution. As if the external troubles were not enough, Gulielma Maria, Penn's wife, died in February 1694 after a long and debilitating illness, during the same period in which these sermons were delivered. Given the earlier deaths of four of his children, his mother, and now his wife, Penn's preoccupation with death in these sermons is understandable. That Penn could remain intellectually productive and spiritually affirmative during this time of trouble speaks to his psychological and spiritual fortitude. In 1693 Penn emerged again as a leader of British Friends, serving on the epistle committee of LYM and making speeches about George Keith. Although George

Whitehead was the unofficial leader of LYM, Penn was the more famous and controversial Quaker, and the anonymous compiler included ten of his sermons and only one of Whitehead's.[26]

THE PENN SERMONS

A few cautions are in order when considering Penn's sermons. First, as already noted, Penn did not seek to be original. Quakerism was early Christianity rediscovered, and the purpose of preaching was to reinforce subjects that were perennial topics. Michael Graves has analyzed the content of all extant seventeenth-century Quaker sermons and identifies five key themes in most of them: light versus darkness; the voice of God versus the voice of Satan; the seed as a metaphor for growth and the indwelling Christ; hunger/thirst; and life as a journey or pilgrimage. Penn addressed all five of these themes in various ways.[27] Graves stresses that the use of familiar metaphors from the Bible, agriculture, and daily life could be useful in extemporaneous discourse and a helpful method of communication to an audience. Penn preached to congregations steeped in biblical stories and imagery, and he could assume a basic knowledge of Christian beliefs. Unlike Puritan sermons that announced a text and then in logical order explicated its meaning and relevance, Quakers normally (but not always) did not begin with a single text. In the course of Penn's sermons, he sometimes identified specific Bible verses but he usually did not. Sometimes he even strung Bible verses from various books and both testaments together. Unless he departed from a text extemporaneously (which we cannot know), a listener would have to be an expert in both familiar and esoteric scriptural passages to know when Penn was quoting, when paraphrasing, when using biblical metaphors, and when just sounding biblical. Penn concluded his sermons with a benediction, based in scripture but found also in the Book of Common Prayer. Most sermons ended with a prayer that was—in Robert Barclay's case—longer than the message but generally only a couple of pages long. However, the editor omitted many of Penn's prayers.[28]

Penn's sermons varied greatly in length: the shortest (five pages) was the funeral sermon printed in *Concurrence and Unanimity*. The average length of the sermons in this collection, which were by many ministers, was fewer than ten pages; the average length of Penn's ten sermons in *Harmony of Divine and Heavenly Doctrines* was twelve pages.[29] We can gain a sense of how long it took

Penn to deliver an average sermon by reading one aloud with short pauses for emphasis. If Penn spoke quickly, with few pauses for emphases, it would take thirty to thirty-five minutes. If he stopped to wait for inspiration, however, an extra five or ten minutes could be added. Stephen Crisp's sermons also show considerable variation but with essentially the same approximate time for delivery. Other sermons in the 1694 collection—for example, those by Benjamin Coale (an average of nine pages), Samuel Waldenfield (fifteen pages), and George Whitehead (twenty-six pages)—were more than twice as long as Penn's on average. Whitehead evidently liked long sermons; he spoke in LYM in 1716 for two hours.[30] When Penn was young, he could preach for more than an hour. When the MMM rebuked women ministers for speaking so long that it hindered the men from speaking, one wonders whether the reprimand might more easily have applied to weighty male Friends.[31]

There are surprising omissions in Penn's sermons. He did not discuss the importance of plain style in speech, dress, furnishings, or the education of children—themes prominent in LYM epistles.[32] Although England was at war with France at this time, no pacifist advice appears. The Yearly Meeting was seeking an affirmation law from Parliament, but he ignored this subject. The Quaker testimonies on tithes and religious liberty were also omitted, though Penn did refer to the recent end of suffering when gathering for worship and thanked God for preserving Friends through many tribulations.[33] Despite the 1694 pamphlet war with Keith and with Anglicans, Penn emphasized that following Christ transcended denominational boundaries and that all churches had followers who knew the teachings of the Bible but were not true Christians. However, all churches and religions included some who submitted to the Inward Light and would be saved. The only exception to his irenic spirit was a brief statement that the doctrine of transubstantiation went against common sense. He made no mention of a hireling ministry, predestination, Anglican liturgy, or the forced payment of tithes. The Quaker assumption that Friends were the only true church was stressed by other ministers, but not by Penn.[34]

In *No Cross, No Crown* and his *Treatise of Oaths*, Penn displayed impressive erudition, quoting ancient Greeks and Romans and early and later Christian writers. There are no similar signs of scholarship in these sermons, nor do they praise or quote any Quaker. In the 1690s Penn issued *Some Fruits of Solitude* and his *Essay on the Present and Future Peace of Europe*, which were filled with wise sayings and recommended a life of moderation and reason. Reason is rarely mentioned in the sermons, invoked only to make the point that given the alternatives of eternal life in heaven or hell, a reasonable person would opt to be saved by Christ.[35] Clearly, Penn tailored his remarks to his audience and stayed within Friends' expectations of meeting for worship.

Penn also differed in style from other Quaker ministers of the 1690s. The most striking contrast was the impersonal tone of his sermons. Here, for example, is William Dewsbury: "I stand here as a Witness for the God of Heaven, I never heard the Voice of Christ (as his follower) till I was slain, and Baptized and lay as a little Child under his Heavenly Chastisements; as soon as ever my Soul was brought to this in my Humiliation, O then the dreadful Judgment was taken aaway [sic], and the Book of Life was opened unto me; and the Lord spake comfortably to me."[36] By contrast, here is Penn: "I would not have you gathered to a Notion of my Experience, or others' Experience," but, instead turn your minds from "all visible things" and have the Lord's "experience in you."[37] Penn made very few references to himself or his personal experience; one exception is the statement "I remember such a time." Most of his personal references show concern: "Friends I would have you"; "It is my Hearts desire and prayer"; "It is the desire of my soul"; "may a sincere and humble soul say."[38]

Even more remarkable is Penn's omission of the source of his inspiration in speaking. The closest he came were his statements "This is that which did spring up in my soul this morning, as I sat here among you," and "I testify to you from the Lord, that God is with you and will be with you as faithful."[39] By contrast, here are the remarks of his contemporaries: Charles Marshall, "The testimony which lives in my Soul," "This is that which hath opened upon my Soul this Morning," "So that now my Friends, That which opens and lives in my Soul, and that which I have to say"; William Bingly, "It is weighty upon my Spirit this Day";[40] Whitehead, "I bless God he hath made me, and many more," "My Friends, I could say many things, but the time would fail me to mention what the Lord hath opened to me"; Stephen Crisp, "It is in my heart at this time," "That which lies upon my mind to speak to you at this time," "I would not have you think that I am judging," "I do not doubt but that most of you can say them *all*" (the Ten Commandments), "I would put one question to you." Crisp's sermons are very personal compared with Penn's, strewn with *I*'s and *we*'s and even containing the inner dialogue of a sinner.[41] None of these sermons were ever attributed to anything the speaker himself had thought or read. In keeping with Quaker dogma, Whitehead called ministers "oracles of God" and affirmed that Quaker sermons were not human-derived intellectual discourses but the Word of God flowing through a human conduit.[42]

Quaker belief in extemporaneous speaking under the guidance of the Holy Spirit made preaching an awesome experience for listeners and endowed ministers with enormous responsibility.

Penn's sermons on special occasions, which included a marriage, a funeral, and another possible funeral (although the deceased was not named or mentioned), were also impersonal. In the marriage sermon, Penn spent eight pages talking of the fear of God and the final judgment; his only mention of marriage comes in a quotation from Paul warning husbands to "be as they had none"—i.e., as if they had no wives—and reminding Friends that "our superlative love [is to] be set on the Lord Jesus Christ, who should be our husband and lord." Penn generally affirmed at weddings that "We are now present at the Solemnity of a Marriage, which is a thing of itself Joyous, Let us Rejoice in Christ Jesus."[43] The institution of marriage was blessed by God, who created Adam and Eve; the couple were to be helpmates to each other, and marriage should not be based on natural affection, worldly interest or advantage, or carnal finery. He concluded with a defense of Quaker practices in marriage and cited the biblical example of Ruth and Boaz. Penn never described what a loving relationship should look like—in fact, he never mentioned the word "love" in the sermon, provided no information about the couple, and spent more time talking of death than of marriage.

At Rebecca Travers's funeral, Penn provided no insights into the personality, family, ministry, travels, or contributions to Friends of the deceased except to say that she had suffered, endured, and completed her journey in obedience to God and could now enjoy immortality. The assigned task for hearers was a "Heavenly Pilgrimage: They set their Faces Sion ward, and go on not Fainting, not Doubting, not desponding" in faith. And faith was "a pure resolution of Living to God, in a Holy Dependence on him, and a committing our selves intirely to him."[44] Penn often used the pilgrimage metaphor in stressing the need for steady faithfulness, given the briefness of life here and the eternity of life after death.

Because Friends believed that scripture expressed the mind of God, quoting the Bible and applying its teachings to contemporary life guaranteed infallibility. Consequently, all Quaker ministers stayed close to the scriptures, either consciously or unconsciously, because listeners gained assurance that the words conveyed truth. The quoted Bible verses fit the context of the themes and could come from either testament and be used ahistorically, but in the understanding that the teachings of the New Testament fulfilled and superseded the Hebrew Bible. Time was telescoped in that the counsel delivered from the

Bible was contemporary, so Penn could mix Luke and the Psalms, the prophets and the Acts. Penn most frequently cited verses from Paul, John, Hebrews, Genesis, Psalms, and Isaiah, but on occasion he turned to Revelation and Deuteronomy and sometimes quoted half a page of verses, one after another, and relied heavily on biblical metaphors: "Wait upon the Lord, and improve that measure of Light, and Grace bestowed upon thee, and thou shalt grow as a Tree planted by the Rivers of Water, that bringest forth fruit in Season; then thy Leaf shall not wither, and whatsoever thou dost shall prosper. The Dew of Heaven shall be upon thy Root, and thou shalt grow and Flourish in the Courts of the Lord. Exercise self-denial, and take up the cross of Christ (for NO CROSS, NO CROWN), Follow Christ the Captain of our Salvation."[45]

The Old Testament was read typologically as foretelling Jesus; Penn cited "holy" King David as a type of Christ and the Isaiah passages, which later appeared in *The Messiah (Wonderful Counselor, Mighty God, the Prince of Peace)*, as foretelling of Jesus. Unlike the other ministers, Penn retold Bible stories: David and Goliath, Adam and Eve, Mary and Martha, Nicodemus. He quoted the Beatitudes, threatened his listeners with the stories of Sodom and Gomorrah and the house built upon sand, pled that Jesus was the Good Shepherd, and warned about the wise and foolish virgins and the prodigal son. However, he rarely referred to Christ's miracles (no loaves and fishes, no walking on water, no raising Lazarus) and did not discuss Palm Sunday, Christ's resurrection or crucifixion or sayings on the cross—though he did often stress Jesus's suffering. Penn mentioned Moses as leading the Israelites to Canaan (a type of the Christian pilgrimage to Zion), and he held up Joshua as an example of obedience, but he did not discuss the conquest of the Holy Land or judges or various kings, except King David. Christian triumphalism is a basic theme in Penn's sermons and those of other Friends, and he depicted the Jews as having forfeited the blessing of God because of their legalism and their rejection of Jesus as the Messiah. Quakers were to become the new Jews.[46]

PENN'S BASIC SERMON

P. Linwood Urban, a professor in Swarthmore's Religion Department, once observed that most ministers have one basic sermon that they present in various forms. The best minsters have two sermons. Penn had one message, which he presented with varying emphases. Quaker sermons were not logically organized discourses. They addressed the major themes, then circled back, using different verses from the Bible, and always came to the same conclusion. Penn insisted upon the necessity of an "experimental" knowledge—by which he meant firsthand knowledge based on personal experience—of the inward dwelling Christ. This experience was more than intellectual assent; it involved a reorientation of the whole being of a person that, through surrender of the will, provided the power to overcome sin, take up the cross, and embark on a new life in conformity to God's will. Penn consistently stressed the power of the Holy Spirit, which gave one the ability to resist the enticements of the visible world and to conform one's will to God. The purpose of preaching was to promote "Conversion to God; *Regeneration and Holiness*," not to teach "doctrines, Verbal Creeds or new Forms of Worship."[47]

Penn's sermons all invoked the familiar Protestant Christian framework of sin and redemption. God created Adam and Eve perfect in the Garden of Eden, but they fell from grace and were driven out of that earthly paradise, though Penn did not discuss how the Fall occurred or Eve's role in it. He stressed the end product, the alienation of humans from God, rather than how original sin was transmitted. The goal of human life was to reach heavenly paradise, but sin made this goal impossible to reach by our own, unaided efforts. Penn and the other preachers often mentioned Satan, but it is unclear whether the devil was the symbol of the realm of sin or a being who existed to subvert God's purposes for humans. "Your Adversary, the Devil," Penn wrote, "goes about like a roaring Lion, continually seeking whom he may devour." Satan was a "Spirit of World, or Prince of Power of the Air, that rules in children of Disobedience." "Have a care that your Adversary the Devil, does not prevail over you," Penn warned, because he "can seduce you from your duty to God or your Neighbor."[48] The devil's power lay in tempting humans with the allure of worldly things and exploiting our desire for pleasure in the here and now. Note that for Penn and most preachers in the 1690s, sin was a pervasive but abstract power. Seventeenth-century ministers often ticked off serious individual sins: drunkenness, greed, illicit sex, gambling, gossip, lying, and seeking power, as well as more prosaic failings like sleeping or nonattendance at meeting, violating Quaker testimonies on plainness, or marriage out of unity. But Penn, like most preachers, never gave specific examples of particular sins. The closest he came was in admonitions such as "Do not Indulge your selves in any Sin; Do not gratify your Lusts and Passions, and Appetites, but keep them under Government"; "Blessed is he that overcometh his Lusts, his concupiscence, and all Ungodliness and Unrighteousness." Sin was the enemy, to be overcome by the power of God, and Penn identified the visible world as the realm of sin, which could be transcended only by concentrating on the spiritual realm. "What is this world but an empty bubble, a shadow that flies away?"[49]

Because God loved humanity even under the dominion of sin, he sent his only son, Jesus of Nazareth, who by his life overcame the power of sin. The only power that could overcome sin was the inward Jesus in each of us, who gained his victory by dying on the cross and who could purify us, enabling in us a kind of internal death on the cross, so that we could stand in the presence of God on judgment day. Jesus entered history and lived as a perfect, sinless man; his suffering on the cross and atoning blood allowed humans to be cleansed of sin and presented before the throne of God after death. No moral life, no good works, nothing purely human in origin could wipe away the power of sin and bring salvation. For Penn, Jesus's role was cosmic; he came to redeem Moses and the prophets in his earthly life, and now, postresurrection, he could do the same for all Christians who went beyond a historic or intellectual faith and surrendered to the Inward Christ.

Just as the devil was real but abstract, so was the final judgment. All people of true faith would stand before God, and through the intercession of Jesus the saints would be saved and enjoy eternal life. Penn, unlike some Quaker minsters, did not dwell upon the fate of the unredeemed sinner in hell, but he clearly believed in this outcome for the unredeemed and often reminded his listeners of the stark alternatives they faced. Penn's sermons did not attempt to frighten people with images of hellfire and brimstone, but he wanted all to be aware of the contrasting fates of saints and sinners. "O That will be a Trying Day indeed," he wrote, "when the Lord Jesus Christ shall be Revealed from Heaven with his Mighty Angels in flaming fire, taking Vengeance on them that know not God, and obey not the Gospel of our Lord Jesus Christ, who shall be punished with Everlasting Destruction from the presence of the Lord."[50]

Within this basic seventeenth-century Christian worldview, Penn strove to convince his listeners of their choice and stressed the doctrine of visitation. All people at some time would be visited by the Light of Christ, but this would not occur constantly. Visitation allowed a preaching strategy very similar to later revival sermons. Now was the time to hearken to the visitation of Christ within, because delay might mean dying apart from Christ's mercy. Penn did not offer "cheap grace" or suggest that salvation was as easy as deciding in favor of Christ. Instead, he focused on the difficult process of purging sin, using biblical language that Friends had employed from their beginnings.

Understanding the risk of being found wanting before God caused turmoil, despondency, and suffering, but this would eventually lead to convincement. "The word of the Lord is as a fire, and as a hammer, and a circumcising Knife, the instrument of our purification, which takes away every thing unclean."[51]

The joy and peace that came after the initial surrender to Christ was only the beginning. In one sermon, Penn reminded listeners of Jacob's ladder—that is, of life as a series of steps toward full surrender of our will to God. Penn's preaching strategy was to persuade his audience of the need to go beyond their current status and condition, to accept the cross now so as to receive the crown later:

> The Lord Calls from Heaven . . . My Son, give me thine Heart. Let the Answer be, Lord take my Heart, Purify and Cleanse it; Break it, and make it New, make it fit for thy acceptance. . . . Open your Hearts to him and he will come in and sup with thee. Consider, my Friends, where are your Hearts and Affections this day? Do you love God above all? Do you love him with all your Hearts, with all your Souls, and with all your Strength. . . . Examine now, whether God hath your Hearts this day: I exhort and beseech you all to give up your hearts to God, give the Crown and Diadem to him; let him be your Lord, and Lawgiver, and King, and he will save You.[52]

The third peroration falls on the second page of a sixteen-page sermon, and there are several similar pleas in the course of this sermon. Every Penn sermon is a prayer that Friends surrender to the Light of Christ and become more disciplined, even though, theologically, all the power to do so comes from God.

CONCLUSIONS

All of the sermons in these collections stress the historical Jesus of Nazareth. If this emphasis was a reaction to George Keith, then we would have to conclude that although Keith was disowned, he prevailed on the major issue. Unfortunately, too few early sermons survive to support the conclusion that there was major adjustment in content (or even to determine whether the anonymous scribe took a representative sample of sermons). Their opponents had long accused Friends of undervaluing Jesus's death on the cross by stressing the Inward Light of Christ. Theologically sophisticated Friends like Robert

Barclay and William Penn accepted the paradoxical nature of Christian belief: God's omnipotence and the existence of evil, Jesus as both fully divine and fully human, the necessity but at the same time the ultimate irrelevance of good works for salvation, the Inward Christ and the historical Jesus. By the 1690s, after the death of most first-generation leaders, Friends had matured, had seen the easing of persecution, defined the faith, and compiled their history. They still saw themselves as a visible embodiment of the true church, but they realized that they were a minority, even among English dissenters, and saw their task as to survive and to come to terms with Protestant thought. Penn's surviving sermons show how Friends could proclaim their distinctive witness and also affirm their links to Protestant Christianity.

Penn's sermons add another dimension to our view of this very complicated man. Penn was a humanist who wanted to be a soldier, an apocalyptic radical Friend who judged all churches harshly, a defender of authority in Quaker meeting, a courtier who served two authoritarian kings, a pragmatic defender of religious toleration, a colonial proprietor who wanted popular assent so long as it did not infringe his power, and even a precursor of liberal Protestants in his view of the Bible and religious creeds. In 1694 Penn was a conservative Quaker preacher who demanded radical submission to God but at the same time defended an ethic based upon reason and moderation. How did he live with such contradictions?

Now that we have reviewed the content of Penn's sermons, it is time to see what we can conclude about the impact of hearing him in a meeting for worship in 1694 at Grace Church Street Meeting. There is a late eighteenth-century drawing of the interior of this meeting house showing a large room with a facing bench in front where the ministers would sit underneath a curved sounding board that projected their voices. Men and women sat separately (no children are depicted in this drawing), and some outsiders, identified as such by their fashionable attire, are shown in the balcony.

The Friends attending in 1694 did not know which ministers would be present, because the MMM made sure that all London meetings were attended by some ministers, but not too many at any given meeting.[53] Penn's ten extant sermons were preached at three different meeting houses. When Penn came in, he would have been wearing a hat and good-quality clothes, plain in Quaker fashion but also showing his status as a gentleman. He would have stood out from other ministers on the facing bench because of his reputation. After all, he was the son of a war hero and had conversed with kings, socialized with powerful nobles, suffered in prison, written devotional works and defenses of Quakerism, and was the proprietor of Pennsylvania. His political activities caused controversy, but there was no question of his commitment to Friends.

After a period of silence, he would have risen and begun preaching, but he would not have removed his hat until he began to pray. If descriptions of later eighteenth-century ministry apply earlier, Penn might have begun slowly but gained fervor when he came to compassionate pleading to accept God's mercy and avoid his wrath.[54] His sermons were not unusual in content but were more eloquent than most given his mastery of scripture and his ability to apply its lessons to daily life. Penn saw himself and was seen by Friends as declaring the mind of God. Throughout the sermon, he would aim for balance among the themes of guilt for having fallen short, fear of death and judgment, hope and faith in the power of Christ to overcome sin, and assurance of a final home in heaven. His hearers would be forced to examine their lives from God's perspective and acknowledge their weaknesses. However, in advising his listeners never to despair, Penn emphasized Christ's power to overcome evil, the pleasure of surrendering to God's will, and the joy that came when one accepted the cross, which brought a form of peace that could be glimpsed here and fulfilled in eternal life. Christ's visitation took place in the here and now, and his gracious love overcame the devil's temptations. All one had to do was accept Jesus the Good Shepherd, who knocked at the door, inviting a sinner to repent and follow the Light. Even though Penn did not dwell on his own religious experience, he stood as an exemplar of a man who had surrendered to the Light. So his life became congruent with his message and inspired his hearers to dedicate themselves once again to follow the Inward Light. Friends felt the presence of God in meeting, and as they left they gave thanks that they had heard the words of a Christian disciple.

Is this the way it was? Our dim candle does not provide enough illumination to know for sure, but it is possible.

Chapter 8

WILLIAM PENN IN MYTH AND HISTORY

Many years ago, I walked through Hamleys, London's most famous toy store. One section featured dolls of famous historical figures: Queen Elizabeth I, Queen Victoria, Henry VIII and his wives, and one Quaker—the Victorian prison reformer Elizabeth Fry. There was no William Penn doll. In England, Fry remains famous and instantly identifiable, even appearing on the £5 note from 2002 to 2016, but Penn is little remembered. The opposite is true in America, especially in Pennsylvania, where a Penn doll, particularly if it is dressed to look like the man on the Quaker Oats canister, can be recognized immediately. Penn remains the most famous seventeenth-century founding father. Having a prominent subject eases the historian's task of finding an interested audience, but it also complicates his research, because he must consider whether what the reader thinks she knows about Penn is true. For example, the style of dress of the figure on the Quaker Oats box belongs more to the Revolution than to the late seventeenth century, and there is no evidence that Penn normally wore black clothes.

Thomas Clarkson, who published the first real biography of Penn in 1813, encountered a problem that has faced all later writers—what to do with the legends and myths surrounding William Penn. This chapter examines the documentary evidence for three traditions about Penn—the sword story, which is often retold in the Quaker community, the treaty with the Native Americans commemorated in Benjamin West's painting, and Pennsylvania's "holy experiment," with Philadelphia as the city of brotherly love, an image used by historians and journalists. The issue here is Penn in historical memory, and the means used by Friends, biographers, historians, journalists, Pennsylvanians, and the general public to maintain his fame. The topic is the heroic William Penn, or Penn as a symbol, bearing in mind that people create myths to capture and preserve what they regard as important truths.

In July 1940, before America entered World War II, Harold Evans of the American Friends Service Committee testified before the US Senate seeking to justify the Quaker claim of conscientious objectors who would not serve in the military but would provide alternative public service. Evans told the senators the story of young William Penn and his sword.[1] According to this anecdote, Penn, who had shortly before become a Quaker, approached George Fox with the question whether he could continue to wear a sword. Fox told Penn to wear the sword "as long as thou canst." The next time Fox met Penn, he had no sword. The story has long been popular among Friends, but for Quakers, who have a testimony for truth telling, the issue is whether Evans was speaking fiction to power.

The sword anecdote does not appear in any eighteenth or early nineteenth-century biography of Penn and was not cited in the four volumes of Penn's writings, including his letters, compiled by the Dunns. Its first appearance in print occurs in Samuel Janney's *Life of William Penn*, published in 1851. Janney's account provided a context for Penn's question to Fox. Penn knew that carrying a sword in Paris had saved his life, because he disarmed an opponent who challenged him to a late-night duel. The story also shows Penn worrying about adhering to a scriptural command: "Christ has said, 'He that hath no sword, let him sell his garment and buy one.'" In Janney's account, when Fox next met Penn after their exchange and saw that Penn had no sword, he asked him, "'William, where is thy sword?' 'Oh!' said he, 'I have taken thy advice; I wore it as long as I could.'" Janney, who sought to be a careful scholar, provided a footnote saying that the story was related to him by one "I. P." of Montgomery County, Pennsylvania, who learned it from one "Simpson, b. 1743."[2] Janney does not identity I. P. The story's authenticity rests upon oral tradition.

Now, there were certainly early oral traditions surrounding Penn. William Sewel, in his 1722 history of the Quakers, says that he has not included everything he knows.[3] That comment comes shortly after a story about the king, a Quaker, and the hat honor, in which the Quaker comes to court wearing his hat. He encounters the king, whose head is bare (normally, only the king wore his hat at court; all others doffed their hats as a sign of respect). When the Quaker asks why his majesty wears no hat, the king replies that only one person's head can be covered in the presence of the king. The story appears in both Gerald Croese's 1696 (critical) and Sewel's 1722 (favorable) histories of

Friends—the two earliest published histories. Neither account says that the Quaker in this story was Penn, whom they discuss in the pages that follow. By 1851 the story was recounted as involving Penn and Charles, an instance of the tendency of good stories to attach themselves to significant figures.[4]

There are other oral traditions involving King James II. There is a supposed dialogue between him and Penn on religion in which the king asks Penn the difference between his religion and Catholicism. Penn asks for James's beribboned headpiece and compares it to his plain hat to suggest that Quakerism is a plain, unornamented religion without unnecessary trappings. Clarkson's biography says that King James came to Quaker meetings twice to hear Penn speak.[5]

Since Sewel cited oral tradition, one cannot dismiss the sword story merely because no early written record survives. And it should be noted that there are variations in the story; in one version, Penn gives up his sword in a flamboyant gesture at his first imprisonment in Ireland—the time when he announced he was a Quaker. It is easy to imagine the radical young convert making such a gesture; recall that after his second arrest, for publishing *The Sandy Foundation Shaken*, Penn wrote his father (and the bishop of London and the king) announcing dramatically that he was prepared to make his prison his grave rather than recant.[6]

Another version of the sword story is based on what is known as the Harvey manuscript, dated 1729. Penn had been arrested in Ireland. "As he went to prison," the Harvey manuscript reads, "he gave his sword to his man & never wore one after."[7] The Harvey manuscript is the only source for another story, which says that on the same day as Penn's arrest, when a soldier broke into the meeting to arrest him, "W. P. go's to him takes him by ye collar and would have throw'd him down stairs but a friend or two come to him desireing to let him alone for they was a peaceable people." Since the two events seemingly happened together, the Harvey manuscript has Penn learning the antiwar testimony very quickly.

At first glance, Harvey's account would seem definitively to refute the other sword story. But things are not quite so simple. The Harvey manuscript was also based on oral tradition. It was titled "An account of ye Convincement of Wm Pen deliver'd by himself to Thom Harvey related to me in a brief manner as well as his memory would serve after such a distance of time." Neither Thomas Harvey nor the first-person narrator ("me") has ever been identified.[8] Most of Harvey's account of Penn's conversion cannot be confirmed because it is the only source for that event, but it contains at least one questionable assertion—that Penn was "sent to Oxford where he continued till he was expell'd for writing a book ye Preists did not like." There is no evidence elsewhere of a book that Penn wrote at Oxford, and there are alternative stories of why Penn was banished. Although the Harvey manuscript discredits Janney's story of the sword, it is not absolutely conclusive.[9]

To prove the authenticity of the Fox-Penn dialogue on the sword, it would be helpful to have accounts of an early meeting between Penn and Fox, but there is no record of when the young convert and older leader first met. Again, the negative proves nothing decisively. The question is whether the other actions of the two men are congruent with the story. Joseph Besse's 1726 biography, attached to his edition of Penn's works, told of the evolution of newly converted Billy Penn's thinking through the implications of the hat honor. After a family friend in Ireland sent news of his son's conversion, Admiral Sir William Penn summoned the young man home. After several stormy scenes, the father asked William at a minimum to agree to uncover his head in the presence of the king, the Duke of York, and himself. William asked to retire for a time of "Fasting and Supplication" to know the will of God and soon returned to announce that he could not agree.[10] The father then turned the young man out of the house with blows, although his mother gave him money.[11] Besse's account is intriguing for the sympathetic way in which it treats the admiral; one can almost imagine Besse worrying that young Quaker boys might find in Penn's behavior justification for their own rebellions.

Besse's account of the hat incident shows that young William Penn, who did not observe the hat honor on his first return home, seems to have made a complete acceptance of all the Quaker testimonies at his conversion; at least there is no historical record of any gradual growth. And while converted Quakers who had served in the army might have continued to wear swords in the 1650s, certainly by 1667, when Penn declared himself a Friend, the peace testimony was well established and the Quaker testimony on suffering for faith would seem to preclude such a practice. In conclusion, Harvey's account of Penn's giving up his sword seems more likely.

Fox's advice also seems out of character. It is difficult to imagine Fox, for example, saying to Penn, "Swear an oath as long as thou canst." Now, it might be reasonable to expect Fox to handle Penn, a prestigious potential convert, with care. Quakers did expect growth in grace, but they also demanded that all follow the Light in their consciences. Fox rarely acted so indirectly on a matter of Truth. Yet there are exceptions. Rosemary Moore has discovered that Friends allowed a great deal of latitude to Isaac Penington, another prestigious convert. Larry Ingle notes that Fox wavered on whether Friends should accept judicial confiscation of estates as a rationale for refusing to pay tithes, concluding "that on balance Fox was more attuned to compromise than he has normally been depicted, especially when it came to status and wealth."[12] Still, Friends' normal practice was to insist upon the totality of Quaker practices. Fox's standing and influence among Friends came because he so unyieldingly resisted the demands of the Church of England.

Janney's version of the sword story seems out of place in seventeenth-century Quakerism, but it certainly fits the mindset of mid-nineteenth-century American Hicksites like Janney who sought to legitimize themselves by history. Hicksites published thousands of pages of the writings of early Friends, named their college Swarthmore to show that they preserved the seventeenth-century faith, objected strenuously to external authority or credal statements in religion, and saw religion as a search for truth in which verification came from the individual conscience. Hicksites like Lucretia Mott flirted with Transcendentalism and Unitarianism and esteemed Penn as an exemplar of reason in religion who broke with priestcraft and evangelical orthodoxy. For Hicksites, the Penn and Fox of the sword story represented the earlier Friends as they wished to remember them: as tolerant and arriving at community consensus through free growth in grace rather than under pressure from external authority.

Thomas Clarkson's 1813 biography of Penn popularized other stories based on oral tradition in order to humanize his subject. These stories first appeared in Robert Sutcliff's *Travels in Some Parts of North America* (1811). Sutcliff, an Englishman who came to the newly independent country in 1804, told two stories about Penn in America. In one, a boy in Merion, Pennsylvania, crept up the stairs one night in a house where Penn was staying, peeked through a crack in the wood, and saw Penn at prayer. Sutcliff provided a source: the sister of "O. J.," someone exiled to Virginia during the Revolution. This was probably Owen Jones Jr., who was exiled to Virginia.[13] The boy who told this story was Jones's sister's grandfather, probably Jonathan Jones of Merion. In another story, Penn, while riding through the woods to a meeting in Haverford, encountered a barefoot girl named Rebecca Wood from Darby en route to the same place. He offered the little girl a ride and together they rode into town, he being unconcerned about a lack of dignified appearance. The moral was explicit: Penn "did not think it beneath him thus to help along a poor bare-footed girl on her way to meeting."[14] Again, we have no verification of these accounts, which rest on oral tradition. In Sutcliff's version, the girl is not named; Sutcliff writes that Penn, on the way to meeting, "would occasionally take up a little-bare-footed girl behind him, to relieve her when tired." Like the sword story, these tales are designed to humanize Penn and engage the reader's sympathy. But unlike the sword tradition, which distorts what we know of Fox and fits the needs of nineteenth-century Hicksite Friends, these other two stories, because they have not made the leap from England to America and seem less significant, may be true. A child who had ridden with Penn, or a naughty boy who had spied on the proprietor at night, would remember the incident and tell their stories. But one must be skeptical of the Rebecca Wood story; it seems doubtful that seventeenth-century parents would allow a little girl to walk alone through the woods for several miles when Darby meeting was close by. These two Penn stories can be retold if they are understood as appearing in print only a hundred years after the fact, in that some provenance can be established.

When I mentioned my skepticism about Janney's account to a responsible Quaker lady, she wailed, "But it's my favorite anecdote. Can I still tell it as a story?" I suggested that she continue to tell it as an example of Quaker traditions that are more revealing about the faith of Hicksite and modern Friends than about William Penn and George Fox. Perhaps I should have replied, "Tell it as long as thou canst."

PENN'S TREATY

In 1869, President Ulysses S. Grant sought to reform the US government's treatment of the Native Americans west of the Mississippi. Having heard stories of Quakers' long tradition of work on behalf of the Indians and believing that they would be honest agents, he entrusted the implementation of government policy to Friends.[15] Quakers, who recalled not only the initial seventy years of harmony but their history of advocacy for Indian rights since 1755, also believed that they would be effective in working with Native Americans. (One Quaker Indian agent took an engraving of Benjamin West's painting *Penn's Treaty with the Indians* with him to the West.) Quakers traditionally attribute the beginning of American Quaker concern with the Indians to William Penn.[16] The visible symbol of this tradition is Penn's treaty with the Indians, an event which supposedly took place in 1682, on Penn's first visit to America.

The first pictorial representation of Penn and an Indian was a medallion made in England in 1731; in 1755, American Friends created a medal with a picture of King George II on one side and a Quaker, presumably Penn, and a

FIG. 3 | *William Penn's Treaty with the Indians.* Engraving by David Hall from the painting by Benjamin West, 1775. Courtesy of the Historical Society of Pennsylvania.

native on the other. The Pennsylvania government also commissioned a gorget, a piece of armor worn around the neck, with a picture of Penn and an Indian, their hands extended in friendship.[17] The coin and the gorget, created during Pennsylvania's first Indian war, were probably given to Indians during negotiations as a way of rebuilding confidence. In 1771, with a commission from the Penn family in England, Benjamin West painted the famous picture of the treaty (fig. 3). Thomas Clarkson, in his three-volume *Portraiture of Quakerism* (1806), said that an engraving of West's painting was the only work of art to be found in most Friends' houses.

Long before the American Revolution, Philadelphians revered an elm tree under which the treaty was signed. When this elm blew down in a storm in 1810, pieces of the wood were saved, and descendants of the "treaty elm" were planted at a few places in the Philadelphia area. (Most of these trees died in the Dutch elm disease epidemic of the 1970s, but in 2010 a seedling allegedly descended from the original tree was planted in Penn Treaty Park.) In the

1850s, Granville Penn donated a wampum belt to the Historical Society of Pennsylvania that he claimed was given to his great-grandfather at the time of the first treaty under the elm tree at Shackamaxon Creek. As with the sword story, it is possible to date the first written account of Penn's treaty. In his *Letters Concerning the English Nation* (1733), Voltaire described the event as "the only Treaty between these people and the Christians that was not ratified by an oath, and that was never infringed."[18] He could have read about the good results of Penn's and the Friends' policies on Indians in several sources. Before he visited Pennsylvania, Penn wrote an eloquent letter to the native kings in which he stressed his desire for good relations, justice, fair dealing, redress of any grievances, and peace. "The Concessions and Agreements of West New Jersey" also show a desire to conciliate and live in peace with the Lenape tribes. Penn's 1683 "Letter to the Free Society of Traders" contained a long and sympathetic description of native culture and peoples and praised their conduct in negotiations over land.[19]

Early accounts of Pennsylvania, both published and in manuscript, emphasized the harmony in Lenape-colonist relations that prevailed in the colony, which contrasted with events elsewhere in America. John Oldmixon's 1708 history of the British Empire stressed that the peace between Quakers and Native people was the result of just land dealings, and Oldmixon mentioned that no Friend had ever been killed by an Indian.[20] (This may be the origin of the legend that no Indian ever killed a Quaker.) Caleb Pusey, an early settler who was a Quaker elder, a business associate of Penn's, and defender of Friends against George Keith, wrote a history of Pennsylvania before 1725 in which he idealized Penn and praised him for achieving peaceful relations with the Indians.[21] Pusey mentioned the Indians and a governor in negotiations in 1721, referring to a "league" and "treaties" of friendship and peace between Penn and the Indians. His account would later be drawn upon by Samuel Smith of New Jersey and Robert Proud of Pennsylvania, who composed the first published histories of Pennsylvania.[22] Though they attributed good relations with Native Americans to Penn's policies, neither mentioned a specific treaty, though the tradition was established by the time they wrote. Their descriptions of the meetings between Penn and the Lenape also did not mention the elm and did not put the treaty signing at Shackamaxon Creek.

The most likely source for Voltaire's statement about the treaty is Joseph Besse's 1726 biography—essentially the first biography of Penn, though it consisted mainly of Penn's letters, with little narrative to tie them together; his very brief account of Pennsylvania included Penn's 1683 letter to the chiefs. Penn announced in that letter that before his arrival, he would send over commissioners to negotiate over land and enter into a firm "league of peace." Note that it was not Penn who was to create this league. Besse added, "His friendly and pacifick manner of treating the Indians begat in them extraordinary love and regard to him and his people, so that they maintained a perfect amity with the English of Pennsylvania ever since."[23] Besse also mentioned negotiations between the Indians and Governor William Keith in 1723, in which the Native Americans evoked the memory of Penn and his covenant of friendship. Voltaire could have learned of these negotiations from Penn's laudatory description of a ceremonial meeting included in his "Letter to the Free Society of Traders," favorably mentioned and also reprinted in Besse's collection of Penn's works. Not unreasonably, Voltaire concluded that these negotiations had resulted in a formal peace treaty based on a written document signed by Penn and the Native Americans.

Throughout the eighteenth century, the Lenape recalled Penn's just treatment and the covenant of friendship he had established. In 1720 the tribe reminded Governor Keith that at their first council Penn had promised "so much Love and Friendship, that he would not call them Brothers, because Brothers might differ; nor Children, because they might offend and require Correction; but he would reckon them as one Body, one Blood, one Heart, and one Head."[24] A colonial governor in 1717 reminded the Native Americans of nine policies affirmed by Penn in a league or covenant of friendship.[25] Stressing the covenant established between the proprietor and the Indians was a useful negotiating tool for both sides. Because Pennsylvania had no militia and the Quaker-dominated General Assembly did not intend to establish one, keeping the peace was imperative. The goal of maintaining harmony with the Indians justified the Quaker reluctance to provide military defense and served as a pragmatic reason for Friends' pacifism. For the Lenape, who did not wish to be attacked and wanted to preserve their lands, citing Penn's just treatment would remind the proprietor's governors, sons, and the Assembly to honor their heritage. The Native Americans and Pennsylvanians reaffirmed their covenant, and soon both sides acted as if there had been a formal treaty, even when each side violated its spirit.

Before the American Revolution, the oral tradition of "Penn's treaty" was well established. When Thomas Penn commissioned the American-born Benjamin West to create the picture, the painter was aware of this tradition and, in the belief that Thomas's ancestors had been present, put his father and brother into the picture, although in the painting there is no treaty elm and the place is not Shackamaxon.²⁶ Almost immediately, those who knew history saw West's anachronistic touches in making Penn too old, in dressing him in a later style of clothes, in the houses that were not yet built, and in having the Indians carry weapons at a treaty negotiation. West's picture, probably commissioned out of familial pride, also served to remind the colonists of the benevolence of proprietary government and the necessity of peaceful adjustments of disputes with the Penn family and the British government. During the Revolution, the painting lost any immediate political context, but in the form of the Hall engraving it remained popular in Britain and America. Its appeal may have resided in its exotic content in creating harmony between savage Indians and placid Quakers in primitive America. In the nineteenth century, Friends saw it as a tribute to the practicality of justice and pacifism in preserving tranquility. The picture also glorified the past in a new nation seeking historical roots. West's painting became an icon in contrasting the results of Penn's justice with the incessant Indian wars fought by the United States.

The difficulty with Penn's treaty was that neither members of the Penn family in England nor antiquarians in postrevolutionary Philadelphia, seeking to write biographies of William Penn and the history of Pennsylvania, could find any written record of the treaty. Why, they wondered, would such an important treaty not be preserved when land deeds were kept? Thomas Clarkson, who wrote his biography of Penn to show that Christians could be statesmen, admitted that he could find no documents pertaining to the treaty, but he was certain of its existence. After all, Pennsylvanians revered the "treaty elm" and the Indians recalled the covenant. Clarkson learned that Joseph Kett, who lived near Norwich, had in his possession the blue sash worn by Penn at the signing of the treaty—so Clarkson created a scene in which Penn, a few other Quakers, and many Lenape signed a parchment treaty.²⁷

Because they believed that an event so important must have merited a documentary record, the Philadelphia gentlemen who created the Historical Society of Pennsylvania in the 1820s investigated thoroughly. John Watson's *Annals of Philadelphia and Pennsylvania* used the recollections of Mary Preston, a hundred-year-old woman of sharp intellect who died in 1774 and who avowed that she distinctly remembered Penn's arrival. Penn was the handsomest man she had ever seen, and he had engaged the Native Americans in a jumping contest, which he had won.²⁸ She did not mention the treaty, but later biographers used her account of Penn's eating Indian food and competing with them as events that occurred at the treaty negotiations. Of course, Preston's memory is open to question. After all, Penn may not have been a handsome man. He had lost his hair from the smallpox, a disease that often left scars on the face. He does not appear to have engaged in regular exercise and had just completed a two-month voyage on a cramped ship in which he nursed passengers during a smallpox outbreak. In any athletic contest, he would have been competing against Native Americans who did not spend most of their time in reading, writing, and attending Quaker meetings. If Penn outperformed the Lenape men, they probably let him win. So, unlike Watson, modern historians will not find the woman's memory credible.

Watson, Roberts Vaux, and other Philadelphia gentlemen learned from many good sources that Penn met with the Indians several times on both his first and second visits, and it is quite possible that one of those meetings took place at Shackamaxon under an elm. The issue was not whether Penn sought peace with the Lenape but whether a treaty took place in 1682. Does the elm story authenticate the treaty? Our first written source comes from Richard Peters Jr. Peters, an old man in 1822, recalled an incident as a child swimming in Shackamaxon Creek. Benjamin Lay, an eccentric Quaker hunchback who lived in a cave (he entertained his friend Benjamin Franklin there) and whose strident antislavery tactics were long remembered, used to remind the boys that they were swimming beneath the "treaty elm."[29] But Lay migrated to Pennsylvania in 1733. A second source used to authenticate the treaty is the wampum belt given to the Historical Society of Pennsylvania, which the Penn family claimed in the nineteenth century Penn was given at the first treaty signing. Unfortunately, there is no documentary evidence connecting this or the other belts preserved by the Penn family with the first treaty, and ethnographers are not even sure that the belts originated with the Lenape.[30] Relying upon oral traditions of the treaty and the Indians' testimonials, and later on the Penn family's wampum belt, one member of the Historical Society concluded that there was a Penn's treaty and that it was not a land sale, but that the promises were verbal, not written, as was the custom with illiterate Indians. An investigation by two other Philadelphia gentlemen came to an opposite conclusion because Governor Patrick Gordon referred to it in 1728 as an agreement "in writing on record." The treaty now became either "the only treaty never written, signed, nor broken," as the Frenchman Jean de Marsillac insisted, or a document that was once extant but no longer survives.[31]

Qualms about the existence of the treaty did not hamper nineteenth-century biographers of Penn or historians of Pennsylvania.[32] The most reliable admit that there is no documentary evidence; not until 1900 did Sydney Fisher argue that there was no such treaty and that Penn and the Indians followed normal colonial American negotiation patterns of making rhetorical promises before getting down to the business of land sales. He concluded that the significance lay not in the promises Penn made, which were not particularly original, but in the fact that Penn and the Quakers kept them.[33] Throughout the nineteenth century, historians of Quakers and Pennsylvania and biographers of Penn continued to discuss the treaty, basing their remarks on Voltaire's assertion, oral traditions, and West's picture. Penn and Indians appeared on tablecloths, dishes, playing cards, puzzles, and advertisements.[34] Part of the appeal was the romanticism of the story: in an America plagued by constant wars over land with Native Americans, the Lenape were unthreatening noble savages. For non-Quakers, the meaning of West's tableau, and its many reproductions, changed from peace to trustworthiness, and the Indians became mere background.[35] For merchants, Penn represented honesty, a willingness not to take advantage. The customer, in some strange sense now analogous to the natives, would not be cheated, because the product was of good quality. Representations of the treaty were used on bank notes, insurance policies, and the labels of a wide variety of products. When two Philadelphia Quaker merchants (one Orthodox and one Hicksite) established the Strawbridge and Clothier department store, they used a medallion of Penn and the Indians as their logo. The reputation of Friends for probity, rather than any personal commitment to Quakerism, led a new company of cereal makers to style themselves the Quaker Oats Company and to use as a symbol a broad-brimmed hat similar to that worn by Penn in West's painting. In America, such symbolism continued until the 1930s but then declined, either because Friends were no longer seen as honest, or even known, or because Quaker Oats had by then become more famous than the Society of Friends.

The image of Penn's peace treaty with the Indians most familiar to Americans today comes not from Benjamin West but from the rediscovery after 1950 of the early nineteenth-century American primitive painter and Quaker Edward Hicks.[36] Hicks's sixty-two paintings titled *The Peaceable Kingdom* make religious use of the image of Penn's treaty (fig. 4). Hicks's pictures have a dual focus: one side of the canvas features the lion, the lamb, and the little child, and the other depicts the signing of Penn's treaty with the Indians. The border has lettering from Isaiah about the future reign of peace, which the church had for centuries interpreted as foretelling the birth of Christ and the eternal peace that would follow Christ's return and the battle of Armageddon. Hicks's paintings link Isaiah's prophecy of a peaceable kingdom with Penn's treaty. Just as the lion and the lamb would coexist in peace during the future

FIG. 4 | Edward Hicks, *The Peaceable Kingdom*, ca. 1827–35. Courtesy of the Friends Historical Library, Swarthmore College.

reign of Christ, Quakers and Native Americans in early Pennsylvania prefigured the coming of Christ's peaceable kingdom. In West's painting, the central focus was William Penn, virtue belonged to the Friends, and the Indians were armed savages who were tamed by the Quakers.[37] In West's justification for peaceful imperialism, the emotion evoked in viewers was nostalgia, even complacency. For Hicks, the virtue originated with God and transformed both groups, and even animals; the emotion he hoped to provoke was a prayerful kind of hope, symbolized by the origins of Pennsylvania. Most strikingly, Hicks had a better understanding of Penn's intentions for this "holy experiment" than any historian ever has.

The myth of Penn's treaty had both a positive and a negative impact on later history. For Friends, it served as a goal to keep their meetings aware of Indian rights and the abuses of British and American government policies. Friends consciously set out to make sure the US government did not take Indian lands by force. Yet the myth also precluded a careful evaluation of whether Penn's treaty and policies really had brought justice in Pennsylvania.[38] Did honesty, the sanctity of land-sale contracts, and unlimited European immigration actually impede the theft of Native American land? Or did Penn's policy merely ease the American conscience, including that of Quakers? Until the 1930s, Quakers supported Native American assimilation to European cultural Christian norms, though it should have been apparent that this policy led to cultural erasure, demoralization, and the appropriation of tribal lands. Penn, whose knowledge of the Lenape was rudimentary, seems to have respected Native American culture; later American Friends had not much more accurate information and less respect. When President Grant turned to American Friends to carry out a policy of forced assimilation, the experiment failed miserably. The Quakers could not escape the blinders imposed by their uncritical acceptance of the Penn treaty story; captives of a myth, they failed to realize that what had seemed noble in 1682 was irresponsible at best in 1870.

"AN HOLY EXPERIMENT"

Penn's most famous phrase in connection with the founding of Pennsylvania appeared in a letter to James Harrison in August 1681. "For my Country [I see?] the lord in the obtaineing & mor[e was] I drawn inward to looke to him, & to o [i.e., to owe it?] to his hand & powr then to any ot[her way?]. I have so obtained it & des[ire] that I may not be unworthy of his love, but do that wch may answear his Kind providence & serve his truth & people: that an example be Sett up to the nations, there may be room there, tho not here, for such an holy experiment."[39] Many historians and biographers have used the concept of a "holy experiment" to capture the essence of Penn's intentions for his colony.[40] Besse did not mention the letter containing the phrase, but Robert Proud included that letter in his *History of Pennsylvania* (1797), italicizing the phrase "holy experiment" in a footnote, and it is given pride of place in Clarkson's two-volume biography. Since then, the phrase has appeared in most serious biographies and in shorter sketches designed for children. It was the theme of Benjamin Trueblood's 1894 speech, given at the dedication of the statue of Penn atop Philadelphia City Hall. The "holy experiment" served as the organizing theme of the artist Violet Oakley's 1927 murals in the State Capitol Complex in Harrisburg, and it appears in the titles of many histories of early Pennsylvania and in a book calling for Quaker spiritual awakening.[41] Countless American undergraduates have read the phrase in textbooks, often as the heading for sections on the early history of Pennsylvania. Unlike the legitimacy of the sword story and the Indian treaty, the authenticity of the source is not in question—the original letter exists—the issue is its significance for understanding Quaker Pennsylvania.

Virtually all scholarly and popular references assume that the meaning of the phrase "holy experiment" is the first meaning listed in dictionaries: "experiment" is understood as a test or trial, that is, a kind of scientific or empirical experiment. Just what Penn was experimenting with is open to debate, the most common assertions being self-government, religious liberty, individual freedoms, pacifism, fair treatment of the Indians, and refuge for persecuted religious minorities—all of which were features of early Pennsylvania. On occasion, the term has been taken to refer to Penn's experimenting with democracy, separating church and state, or reforming of the criminal code and abolishing capital punishment for most crimes. Again, all of these endeavors were pursued in the colony to some degree. Almost no one asks whether the riskiest experiment was entrusting Quakers with the power to govern, though that clearly was new, and in later life Penn might not have judged that aspect of early Pennsylvania a success. All of these interpretations have in common the assumption that the experiment involved creating political arrangements that would allow Quakers to practice true Christianity; even the goal of religious liberty was to prove whether such freedom would create anarchy. Unfortunately for the political interpretation, there is little evidence that Penn thought that government by assembly, the rule of law, religious liberty, or pacifism needed a trial or test to prove its value, or that a government that upheld those principles would have a decisive impact on true piety. After all, Quakerism was flourishing in Britain, which had none of them. If Penn were referring to a scientific experiment, why would he use the word "holy"?

The common mistake of the mythmakers is to overlook what the *Oxford English Dictionary* refers to as the second meaning of "experiment," which is "to have experience of." In one of the phrases that occurs most often in his *Journal*, George Fox, writing about authenticating knowledge gained through inward revelation, commented, "That I know and know experimentally." Penn often referred to the experience of the Inward Light as "experimental."[42] As a student of nature, Penn understood both the "trial" and the "experience" meanings of the term. At issue is whether Penn's holy experiment was a trial of principles of government or a sign of grace. Everything we know about Penn suggests the latter, for it is clear that in 1681 he saw his receiving the charter as a testament of God's providential gift and a sign of the approach of the millennium.

Just before Penn referred to the "holy experiment" in his letter to Harrison, he acknowledged that the Pennsylvania charter came from "the lord" and that he "owe[d] it to his hand & pow[e]r then to any ot[her] way." Since the land was a gift from God, Penn, like the biblical people of Israel, had to "serve his truth & people: that an example be Sett up to the nations." The same day, Penn wrote a letter to Robert Turner in which he used essentially the same phrase: "that an example, a standard [be] Sett up the Nations."[43] The scriptural reference for both passages is Isaiah 11:10: "In that day the root of Jesse shall stand as an ensign to the peoples; him shall nations seek, and his dwellings shall be glorious." The Isaiah prophecy had originally been applied to the indestructible Mount Zion, the dwelling place of the Lord. The Christian church had reinterpreted the prophecy as referring to the coming of Jesus and also to the return of Christ at the end of time and the creation of a new Jerusalem.

That Penn was not just using the verses metaphorically is shown in a letter written to Thomas Janney four days earlier. Again he referred to England as too crowded a land and contrasted it with Pennsylvania. "God will plan[t] Americha & it shall have its day; [the fifth kingdom] or Gloryous day of Christ in us Reserved to the last days, may have the last part of the world, the setting of the son or western world to shine in."[44] Notice that it is God, not Penn, who is planting America. The fifth kingdom is a reference to the book of Daniel, in which the prophet tells the king that the first four kingdoms will end because of flaws in their composition, but the fifth, its foundation laid by God, will endure. Penn testifies in several letters, using terms still current in the Quaker community, to the religious clearness of his actions in obtaining the charter. Penn's careful waiting and his pure motives allowed God to be "over all," that is, to show his power in creating the colony. The "Gloryous day of Christ in us Reserved to the last days" is a reference to the book of Revelation, in which Christ returns at the end of time, making way for a new Jerusalem that will need neither sun nor moon because "the glory of God is its light," and there will be no night. Penn's metaphor joins the sun's setting in the west (i.e., America) and the Light of Christ, conflating the "son" Jesus and the light of the "sun."

The example to the nations, the fifth monarchy, the last days—these terms refer to the biblical language of the apocalypse, the end of time. Additional evidence of the millennial significance of Penn's "holy experiment" is seen in the name and prayer Penn gave to the colony's chief city, Philadelphia. Virtually everyone comments on the Greek derivation of the term "brotherly love." One biographer, ignorant of the fact that there was a religious group of Philadelphians in England, gave Penn the credit for inventing the phrase. Only Sydney Fisher, in 1900, noticed that Philadelphia is mentioned in the book of Revelation, but he misunderstood the significance of the biblical passage.[45] In Revelation 3:7–8, Christ tells the "angel of the church in Philadelphia," "I know thy works: behold, I have set before thee an open door, and no man can shut it: for thou hast a little strength, and hast kept my word," and prophesies that the town will become "the city of my God, the New Jerusalem, which cometh down out of heaven from my God" (3:12).

The messianic utopianism that Penn manifested before coming to Pennsylvania he continued to express during his first visit there. In 1684, just before he returned to England, Penn wrote a farewell letter to prominent Friends in the government in which he included what has become known as the prayer for Philadelphia:

> And thou, Philadelphia, the virgin [settlement] of this province, named before thou wert born, wt love, wt care, wt service, and wt travil, have there been to bring thee forth & preserve thee from such as would [abuse] and defile thee. O that thou mayest be kept from the evil that would overwhelm thee; that, faithful to the God of thy mercies in the life of righteousness thou mayest be preserved to the end. My soul prays to God for thee that thou mayest stand in the day of trial, that thy children may be blessed of the Lord and thy people saved by His power.[46]

Four passages in this prayer are important for our purposes; two of them have a double meaning: the "virgin [settlement]" and the significance of being "named before thou wert born." Philadelphia was a virgin, a new and unsoiled town that Penn had named in England and founded in Pennsylvania. Yet the prayer also links the city with a virgin birth, recalling the purity of Penn's motives in founding the colony. "Before thou wert born," what love, what care, what service, what travail "have there been to bring thee forth & preserve thee." Philadelphia, like the land of Israel in both Isaiah and Jeremiah, is a virgin; and the city, before its birth, was not only named by Penn but was named and described by John, the author of Revelation. In Revelation 12:1–2 a woman "robed with the sun" was "with child, in anguish for delivery." After the red dragon comes, "her child was snatched up to God . . . and the woman fled into the wilderness, to a place prepared for her by God" (Rev. 12:5–6). Another significant phrase in Penn's prayer: "that . . . thou mayest be preserved to the end." The end of what? We think of individual death as the end; but cities endure virtually forever—but all cities except Jerusalem will cease at the eschaton. And what accompanies the end of time: the four horseman of the apocalypse and the war between Christ and the Antichrist—a period of stress and trial. Penn prays "that thou mayst stand in the day of trial"; the day of trial could refer either to the series of trials at the end of the world (1 Pet. 4:12), "concerning the fiery trial which is to come," or to Revelation 3:10 in which Philadelphia is preserved from the trial, or to the trial before God at the last judgment, with the separation of the good from the bad. On this occasion, it is crucial that the children of Philadelphia be "blessed."

Penn's vision of godly Pennsylvania was not unique. It was echoed in Philadelphia Yearly Meeting's epistle to London Friends in 1683: "o[u]r god hath engaged us, yea he hath over Come us wth his Antient glory, the Desert sounds, the wildernesse rejoices A Visitation & outwardly is Come to America, God is Lord of all the Earth & at the setting of the sun will his name be famous."[47] Notice that the founding of Pennsylvania is equated with the spread of the lordship of God over all the earth. One would have thought that God's name was already famous, but invoking the "setting of the sun" to the west of Europe (i.e., in America) is another reference to the apocalypse as described in Revelation.

The conclusion is clear: the idea that Pennsylvania was conceived as a "holy experiment" in free government and religious liberty is wrong, because Penn thought such political arrangements neither new nor holy. Instead, he prayerfully believed that his colony had the potential to become a holy experience, a meeting in the wilderness in which pure worship and righteous behavior might lead God to inaugurate his new Jerusalem there.

It is easy to understand why the "holy experiment" was later reshaped into a secular myth. Penn's new province proved extraordinarily difficult to govern; even the devout Quaker colonists proved obstinate. The caves along the Delaware where settlers lived the first winter were, before 1700, rumored to be houses of ill repute. Penn soon dropped the eschatological language. After all, at the same time that he was anticipating the end times he was also writing multiple Frames of Government, approving laws, establishing a legislature, and selling land. He, his sons, and the colonists soon began depicting Pennsylvania as a land of political and religious freedom and economic opportunity, "the best poor man's country." In the eighteenth century, Pennsylvania could be thought of as an experiment in religious liberty, representative government, the rule of law, and Quaker political power—all of which made the land prosperous, but not holy. Still, Penn's success in creating the colony and its later history could be viewed as providential, as if God had particular care for a Quaker colony.

The late eighteenth-century Quaker historian Robert Proud thought Penn's aim was to provide as much freedom as was compatible with godly moral conduct.[48] So when Isaac Norris II, Speaker of the Pennsylvania Assembly, chose an inscription for the statehouse bell in 1752, he picked Leviticus 25:10: "Proclaim liberty throughout all the land and to the inhabitants thereof." Perhaps this was a conscious tribute to Penn's 1701 Frame of Government, but in the nineteenth century the Liberty Bell became a symbol of American democracy. The making of that myth belongs to American, not Quaker, history.

FAME

English Quakers, American Quakers, the Penn family, nineteenth-century American antiquarians, and American and English Whig historians created and preserved oral traditions about Penn because his memory served a purpose. All biographers of Penn need to determine why different groups preserved traditions about him and how this collective memory captures or distorts the man. The first and most obvious group wanting to define the memory of William Penn was the Society of Friends in Great Britain. For English Quakers, Penn was one of the Friends who had created and transformed their faith, and it was his religious beliefs and work on behalf of Quakers that mattered to them. Penn received the same treatment that other important early leaders did, among them Penington, Burrough, Barclay, and Fox—namely, a folio edition (in 1726) of about half of his published works, a few letters arranged in a biography, and tributes from his meeting and important Quakers. Little is known about the editorial processes Joseph Besse used in selecting what to include, but the normal procedure was for weighty Friends in the MMM to read all of a person's letters, tracts, and books and select the most relevant. The MFS would select a printer, finance publication, and issue an appeal for subscriptions.

West New Jersey, Pennsylvania, and Delaware were of limited interest to English Quakers, except insofar as they exemplified religious liberty and were populated by Friends. Besse ignored all of Penn's printed works about Pennsylvania and New Jersey except for the "Letter to the Free Society of Traders."

None of the Frames of Government appeared, but Besse did publish the laws on religious toleration and an address Penn made to the General Assembly during his second visit. No other political events in Pennsylvania were mentioned, including the temporary loss of the charter, debates over the power of the Assembly and Council, and controversies over quitrents and tax support for the government. Besse also omitted some of Penn's political pamphlets, but he included those involving subjects still of interest to the English Quaker community: religious toleration, oaths, the blasphemy bill, and the future peace of Europe.

By contrast, Besse's 1726 compilation included more than seven hundred pages of writings about religious disputes, subjects that all biographers, including Quakers like Samuel Janney, found uninteresting and unimportant. There was not even a scholarly analysis of Penn's theology until 1973.[49] Thomas Harvey's recollection, which is dated three years after Besse published the collected works, was a response to what he saw as Besse's inadequate account of Penn's conversion, a subject of great interest to Quakers. The English Quaker community valued Penn also for his devotional and advice-giving writings: *A Key to the Scriptures*; *No Cross, No Crown*; *Some Fruits of Solitude*; and "A Brief Account of the Rise and Progress of the People called Quakers" (his preface to George Fox's *Journal*). Unlike Penn's political and controversial writings, editions of these tracts, along with *Fruits of a Father's Love*, stayed in print well into the twentieth century.

Eighteenth-century London Friends remembered that Penn had often lobbied the English government, a practice continued by members of the MFS. They could also use his treatise on oaths to support acceptance of the limited form of affirmation allowed Friends. Victorian Quakers who participated in politics and engaged in a wide variety of charitable enterprises claimed to be following Penn's example.

Quakers in colonial Pennsylvania must be distinguished from British Friends, because they preserved memories reflecting their unique position. They saw Penn as the man who legitimized their role in governing and sought to preserve his policies. Religious liberty, no religious oaths, reforming laws, the lack of a militia, and the role of the Assembly as spelled out in the Frames of Government had been instrumental in allowing Quakers to gain and retain power. For example, Penn had compromised on military matters and had recommended that the Assembly provide money to the Crown for relief, while supporting its refusal to create a militia. This remained the colony's policy, except for one brief break in 1755, until the Revolution. Few in the colonies had access to Besse's edition of the collected works before the Revolution; they could not even have read the tracts on toleration or blasphemy law, issues of little importance to them. Penn had also established the parameters of Pennsylvania policies relating to Native Americans. For Quakers, Pennsylvania governors, and the Native Americans, an oral tradition of harmony was politically useful and fostered mutual trust, which was more important than the details of treaties. So Penn's treaty with the Indians, which later generations invested with great importance, would have been seen in the eighteenth century as just another part of the first proprietor's political legacy. His legacy sanctified the policies of the colonial Assembly. Against the non-Quaker majority in the colony, Pennsylvania's Quaker politicians insisted that Penn had bestowed a "birthright" on Friends that meant they could not become dissenters in their own land.[50]

Because Penn remained an exemplar of the faith, his practices legitimated the nineteenth-century American Quaker practice of petitioning government but not holding office themselves, support for higher education, and works on behalf of Native Americans. After 1827, as Friends experienced a whole series of schisms, each group sought to reclaim Penn as exemplifying the faith of Hicksites, Orthodox Friends, Wilburites, Evangelical Holiness Friends, and Liberal Friends. Because Penn wrote so much about religion over such a long period of time, often changing his emphases, each group could make a credible claim that Penn endorsed its views. Penn, who in the seventeenth century was cited by conservative Quakers who opposed the abolition of slavery but were willing to convert Africans to the faith, became in the nineteenth century a Christian abolitionist. He also became the patron saint of Quaker prison reformers and of Quaker Indian agents. In the first decades of the twentieth century, Friends redefined their peace testimony in an effort to reform the international political system. Again, Penn's example was useful, and a reprint of his *Essay on the Present and Future Peace of Europe*, with its call for a European parliament, seemed to prefigure the League of Nations. Penn's role as a defender of liberty gave American Quakers a prominence far out of proportion to their numbers, as they tried to make Pennsylvania live up to the founder's expectations.

A third group interested in controlling the memory of William Penn was his family. After all, Thomas and Richard Penn's claim to control the government and lands of the colony derived from their father. The Penn family had a vested interest in playing down the history of repeated conflict with Quakers over politics and in minimizing skeptical views of Penn's competence in running the colony. Such doubts might have raised questions about the advisability of a single family's hereditary claim to own huge tracts of land, to veto any legislation, to appoint governors, and to derive a profit. Instead, Penn's heirs romanticized early Pennsylvania, because it would not do to say that Penn had better relations with the Indians than with his fellow Quakers. The sons continued to wrap themselves in William Penn's cloak. Colonial governors gave thanks to the religious and political liberty inaugurated by Penn and expressed their gratitude for his bringing peace and prosperity to the colony. For the Penn family, even preserving William Penn's letters was an act of filial piety, and it was also politically useful in the boundary dispute with Lord Baltimore that would not be settled until the Mason-Dixon line was drawn in the mid-eighteenth century. Because Penn's sons left the Society of Friends, the later proprietors had little reason to stress his faith, except as a way of reminding American Quakers of their vulnerability to royal and Anglican rule. Thomas Penn wanted to create a militia and to use an oath to prevent Friends from sitting in the Assembly after 1755, positions absolutely contrary to his father's wishes. Thomas's resistance to any taxation of his estates during the French and Indian War so disgusted Benjamin Franklin that Franklin sought to make Pennsylvania a royal colony after 1763. Before the Revolution, for the Penn family, praising Penn was a political maneuver.

After 1783, when the Commonwealth of Pennsylvania bought the rights to the Penn descendants' land, the family's interest was in preserving the memory of their famous ancestor. In England, John Penn of Stoke created a society to commemorate William Penn that held public lectures on subjects of general importance and allowed Thomas Clarkson access to the Penn letters for his biography. Penn's great-grandson Granville Penn gave a wampum belt and Penn's letters to the Pennsylvania Historical Society and wrote a hagiographic biography of Admiral Penn, a man more in sympathy with Granville's ideals. A nineteenth-century copy of a portrait of a man in armor that the Historical Society says is young William is probably in fact the admiral, but most Philadelphia gentlemen were happy not to think about pacifism.

Finally, there is the influence of a group that I know little about: those in eighteenth-century England and later who were simply curious about a man who could be devout as well as rich and famous. Brief sketches of Penn by various European authors appeared in the eighteenth century. He was also included in John Aubrey's *Brief Lives*, Francis Dashwood's (1708–1781) sculpture garden, and Lord Cobham's Temple of British Worthies, because he was an anomaly in late seventeenth-century England—the son of a naval war hero who became a pacifist, a Whig who consorted with Stuart kings, a rich man who spent time in debtors' prison, a Quaker who became the proprietor of the largest grant of land ever given to an individual.[51] People wanted to know what made this very public yet also very private man tick, and that is still the case.

During the American Revolution, Quaker pacifism discredited William Penn. Even Jonathan Dickinson, whose wife was a Quaker, does not appear to have read Penn's political works. But the new American Republic needed historical heroes, and in many ways Penn fit the bill. The direct influence of Penn's ideas on the US Constitution remains difficult to prove, but popular legend gave Penn significance as an influence on the two births of Pennsylvania, in 1681 and 1776.[52] Penn's rehabilitation into an American hero came in the election of 1800, when the Democratic-Republicans identified Thomas Jefferson and William Penn as heroes of religious liberty who suffered the attacks of persecuting clergy.[53] Linking Jefferson and Penn helped both men. In 1824, Philadelphia gentlemen like the Quakers Roberts Vaux and Samuel Bettle joined with many whose ancestors had once been Friends in creating the Historical Society of Pennsylvania. These antiquarian historians exalted William Penn as a man who combined legal acumen, love of liberty, strict morality, and deep piety—traits they thought were needed in industrializing Philadelphia. By 1829, when Parson Weems wrote his biography of Penn, trying to duplicate his success with Washington, Penn had become a republican whose dedication to political and religious liberty paved the way to American independence.

The republican Penn exalted by American patriots was a friend to Algernon Sidney and John Locke and was deeply committed to a philosophy of natural rights. He was also alleged to be the author of the "Concessions and Agreements of West New Jersey." Penn's conduct in the Bushel trial exemplified his defense of the rights of Englishmen to rule by law, trial by jury, and religious liberty. Penn the lawgiver and defender of political and religious liberty picked up other endorsements: Montesquieu wrote of him, "William Penn is a real Lycurgus. And though the former made peace his principal aim as the latter did war, yet they resemble one another in the singular way of living to which they reduced their people—in the astonishing ascendance they gained over freeman, and in the strong passions which they subdued." Jefferson described Penn as "the greatest lawgiver the world has produced; the first, either in ancient or modern times, who has laid the foundation of government in the pure and unadulterated principles, of reason and right." And Lord Acton called him "the greatest historical figure of the age."[54]

Some Whig historians found Penn's Quakerism an embarrassment. William Dixon could not decide whether Penn's Quakerism was "a reasonable conviction or mere madness," but he distinguished between Fox's enthusiasm and Penn's sensibility and claimed (as did George Bancroft) that the Quaker belief in the Inward Light provided an intellectual basis for democracy.[55] For Sydney George Fisher, Quakerism was "a violent . . . and hysterical effort to return to primitive Christianity" and had only one positive belief, the "inner light." Penn really only wanted "a religion which an honest educated gentleman could follow without being a sycophantic Churchman, a shuffling, traitorous Roman Catholic, or a whining, malignant Puritan."[56] At least, unlike other Quakers, Penn had good manners. By contrast, nineteenth- and twentieth-century Quaker biographers like John W. Graham insisted that it was his religion that made Penn a democrat.[57]

Objections to what the English historian Thomas Macaulay termed the "canonization" of Penn came from historians on both sides of the Atlantic. Macaulay described Penn as "weak" and "not a man of strong sense," and, while he admired many of Penn's ideas, accused him of surrendering to "royal smiles, female blandishments, by the insinuating eloquence and delicate flattery of veteran diplomatists." Macaulay faulted Penn's pride for causing him to betray British liberty and religion by supporting James II's tyrannical designs.[58] A 1962 study by Vincent Buranelli cited the conclusions of five nineteenth- and twentieth-century historians and biographers who asserted that Penn was either a "fool or a knave" for supporting James II.[59] Recent historians who believe that James II wanted to establish Roman Catholicism and absolutism must explain why Penn supported him. In 1965, Joseph Illick called Penn "indiscreet" and a "poor judge" of character.[60] Mary Maples Dunn has argued that Penn's single-minded pursuit of religious toleration made him overlook James's flaws. Richard Dunn blames Penn's economic problems and failures in Pennsylvania on his own bad judgment.[61] Mary Geiter has contrasted Penn's "historical status" in England with his iconic status in America. She argues that his Quaker faith was less important than his membership in the "ruling elite," describes Pennsylvania as primarily a commercial and imperialistic venture, and cites the negative portraits of Penn by those who dealt with him, including Lord Baltimore, Bishop Burnet, and the fellows of Magdalen College. Like Macaulay, she argues that there is strong evidence that he remained a Jacobite after the Revolution of 1688 and violated the Quakers' peace testimony on numerous occasions.[62]

A few Quakers have recently begun to question Penn's heroic stature, not because of King James but because of his policies on slavery and Native Americans. In Washington, DC, Friends renamed the William Penn House Friends Place on Capitol Hill, and London Quakers, after a long debate about ahistorical standards of morality, removed Penn's name from a room in Friends House. *Friends Journal* has provided a detailed account of the evidence for Penn's buying and selling slaves.[63] Starting with Macaulay and continuing through both older and modern biographies, the five-volume *Papers of William Penn*, and papers given at two conferences, held in 1981 and 2015, most scholars still find Penn's failures balanced by his extraordinary accomplishments. Penn's popular acclaim has survived centuries and will endure today's notions of political correctness, because his weaknesses need to be balanced against his successes in founding a successful colony, advocating religious freedom, and writing eloquently about religious faith.

Before the Civil War, Penn's American image had become fixed, and it has endured essentially unchanged to the present. As the founder of Pennsylvania, he stands atop Philadelphia City Hall facing the direction of Shackamaxon Creek and is commemorated annually in Harrisburg. There is a shrine to him at Pennsbury and a park named after him in Philadelphia where his significant sayings are engraved on stone (a Quaker version of the Ten Commandments) at the site of the slate-roofed house where he stayed during his second visit to the colony. A second park at the site of the famous elm commemorates Penn's treaty with the Indians. In 1944, *Life* magazine did an article on the tricentennial of his birth that, while disapproving of Penn's pacifism, stressed his commitment to liberty and democracy and his advocacy of a pan-European parliament.[64] In 1947 William Wistar Comfort, the Quaker president of Haverford College, published *William Penn and Our Liberties*, which is still in print, combining the Whig and Quaker interpretations of Penn. Comfort called Penn "one of humanity's signal benefactors," a man whose achievements in colonizing Pennsylvania and securing religious liberty meant that it was "he more than anyone else who, however unconsciously, had prepared the way for American independence."[65] In 1908, during the annual Bible conference Founder's Week, fifteen leading Christian denominations (including Roman Catholics) celebrated William Penn and the American tradition of religious liberty; in 1944 and 1976, similar gatherings took place.[66] The National Institute for the Humanities and the Commonwealth of Pennsylvania provided funding for the Historical Society of Pennsylvania's Penn Papers project, which provided an annotated bibliography of his published writings, four volumes of his letters, and microfilm copies of all of his correspondence, in recognition of Penn's significance in the shaping of the American experience. Penn may be the only seventeenth-century colonizer whose life has inspired an impressive epic poem and an oratorio performed by the Philadelphia Singers.[67]

William Penn's status as the founding father of Pennsylvania has also resulted in two of the silliest commemorations: an attempt in the 1880s to bring Penn's bones from the Jordans Friends' Meeting House in England, to be placed either in Philadelphia City Hall or in an impressive monument near Independence Hall. Endorsed by the mayor of Philadelphia and the governor of the state, the effort ended in failure because English Friends objected to the whole project, adding that, since Quakers used no gravestones in 1718, it could not be determined with certainty where Penn and his two wives were interred in the Jordans graveyard. The second silliness was the US Congress's resolution in 1984 to make William and Hannah Penn honorary American citizens.[68] A 1942 movie titled *Courageous Mr. Penn* was historically inaccurate and rather dull; the highlight was Deborah Kerr as Gulielma Penn (a second wife was never mentioned). I await with bated breath a Walt Disney animated movie about Penn.

In recent times, Penn has become a symbol of good works completely divorced from his religion. The William Penn Foundation, founded by the Otto and Phoebe Haas family in 1945, now with assets of $2.2 billion, supports a wide variety of social and educational programs for the disadvantaged and aims at improving the quality of life in the Philadelphia area though grants for artistic and environmental causes. The Philadelphia Chamber of Commerce, recognizing that Penn was an "English real estate entrepreneur," bestows an annual William Penn Award to an "outstanding" businessperson. Similarly, the Historical Society of Pennsylvania gives an annual Founder's Award for exemplary service to history that includes a medal with an engraving of William Penn based on the city hall statue. The Commonwealth of Pennsylvania celebrates its founding in Harrisburg each March by showing the original charter from Charles II and with special events at the twelve sites of the Historical and Museum Commission.

The Quakers' interpretation of William Penn as one of their own continues unabated. Edwin Bronner's Everyman edition of Penn's writings, titled *The Peace of Europe, Solitude, and Other Writings* (notice the secular emphasis), contains nothing not in the 1726 Besse edition except *Fruits of a Father's Love*. Still in print are *No Cross, No Crown* and the preface to Fox's *Journal*, titled "A Brief Account of the Rise and Progress of the People called Quakers." In 1982, *Friends Journal* devoted a commemorative issue to Penn in which his example was used to justify many contemporary Friends' social concerns: city planning, environmental protection, civil liberties, racial equality, women's rights, income inequality, and peace. The theme paraphrased two famous

Penn quotes: "Our Continuing Holy Experiment: What Love Can Do in '82."[69] At present, Penn is still firmly in the Quaker pantheon, with mention of the "holy experiment," and four quotations in both the 2018 Philadelphia Yearly Meeting's *Faith and Practice* and the 2020 Britain Yearly Meeting's *Faith and Practice*, where the "sword story" is repeated.[70]

Penn's trial for holding an illegal religious meeting still commands attention. The *New York Times* cited the Penn-Mead trial, which established the precedent that an English jury could not be coerced, as the most important trial of the last thousand years. The *Philadelphia Inquirer* cited Penn's unruly behavior in this trial as similar to the disruptive behavior of the Chicago Seven in 1969 and Delbert Orr Africa's MOVE trial in 1980.[71]

When evaluating the prominence of myth in religion and history, scholars need to be careful, for in relying only on documentary evidence our enterprise can be destructive rather than informative. Without oral history, there would have been no synoptic Gospels, no hadith of Muhammad, no lives of the Buddha. In the case of those three myths, it was often historians devoted to documentary truth who helped to propagate the stories. Many of us remember that for several years, when the statue of Penn on city hall needed repair, it was imprisoned in scaffolding. A "Free William Penn" movement raised the money to restore Alexander Milne Calder's monument. One task facing all Penn biographers will be to free Billy Penn from centuries of folklore, of stories that assume that something happened because it ought to have happened. There is clearly a kernel of fact in the legends about Penn. He did stop wearing a sword; he did meet with the Lenape and seek a covenant of peace; he did attempt a "holy experiment." But long before literature professors began discoursing on deconstruction, and long before liberal, modernist theology, early Christian apologists and mystics understood the symbolism in biblical stories and warned against too literal an interpretation. Such a caution is also useful in considering the myths surrounding Penn.

Thomas Budd's 1685 account of Pennsylvania and New Jersey contains the story of a negotiation between West Jersey Lenape and Friends before Pennsylvania was settled. The Indians recited the history of Europeans' selling them alcohol. The Dutch had sold alcohol; they had, said the Lenape, "no Eyes, they did not see it was for our hurt." The Swedes had come next and also sold alcohol for profit. The Swedes also "were blind." Finally, the Quakers came, and they had "eyes." They had seen the deleterious effects of alcohol on tribal life, and by "mutual consent" had abolished its sale.[72] We should all approach William Penn in myth and history with our eyes open.

Chapter 9

AFTERTHOUGHTS

The Enigmatic Mr. Penn

Ours is an age of instant new heroes and the denigration of familiar ones: Christopher Columbus, Robert E. Lee and other Confederate generals, and four of the first five American presidents, their reputations stained by the sin of slavery. Should Penn also be reevaluated, even if the removal of his statue from Philadelphia's city hall is unlikely? Let us look at his successes, assess what we (though not his peers) see as his blind spots, examine the reasons for his controversial support of James II, and attempt to make sense of this complicated man's legacy.

In addition to his work for Friends, Penn's most important public achievements were founding the colonies of Pennsylvania and Delaware, planning the city of Philadelphia, and securing religious liberty for all Christians. Given that he was from the upper gentry but was not an aristocrat, and that he was a leading spokesman for what most Englishmen thought was a weird religious sect, Penn did amazingly well at an immoral court in an intolerant society. He obtained a charter that gave him political and economic power over an immense tract of land, attracted colonists from a variety of cultures and made naturalization very easy for them, provided for representative government and guaranteed rights, reformed criminal justice, and created an enduring pattern of religious liberty.

Among his failures, Penn did not work well with those who risked life and wealth to settle the new colony. He wanted benevolent rule, but they wanted the right to initiate legislation that they observed in other places. Settlers valued him as a Quaker minister, but in time they saw him more as a demanding absentee landlord. Pennsylvania did not become the Christian example to the nations that Penn hoped it would, a place where moral, hardworking people lived in harmony, paid their taxes, and deferred to their social superior—the proprietor. Still, Penn preserved a pacifist colony in wartime against royal officials, and in attempting to sell the right to govern in 1702 he sought to defend the distinctive liberties guaranteed in his Frames of Government.[1] Penn belongs to a long line of visionaries who failed to create their desired utopias, in his case because of his personal faults, the settlers' recalcitrance, the characteristics of the emergent English empire created by war, and human nature. In his personal life, he practiced, and advocated for others, strict moral standards.

Penn's myopia with respect to significant injustices in both England and America stemmed from his class, education, and historical context. No upper-class Englishman condemned slavery or sought to ease the oppression of the Irish peasantry by absentee landlords. He could have learned about the slave trade and the life of enslaved Africans from the 1688 Germantown Quaker Petition Against Slavery and complaints by Chester County Quakers, but he did not. (Whether he knew of the antislavery protests is uncertain.) Although he visited Ireland many times and drew wealth from twelve thousand acres there, he, unlike Jonathan Swift, never identified with the Irish. Few questioned a king's right to give Europeans title to lands the Native Americans occupied. Penn recognized that the Lenape had a government and, according to the laws of nations, owned the lands they occupied. He sought to purchase their land, as he had purchased land in England, but he also issued a map to prospective migrants that showed Pennsylvania as empty.[2] Penn spent liberally on his upper-class lifestyle, lived beyond his income, and miscalculated the cost of founding and governing a new colony. He blamed his steward and the colonists rather than his own financial carelessness for his eventual debt and was fortunate that wealthy Quakers bailed him out by taking a mortgage on Pennsylvania. When he died in 1718, he was still in debt.

Nineteenth-century Whig historians and more recent scholars have censured Penn for his close relationship with the autocratic James II. Friends and other supporters of William and Mary in 1689 also condemned this relationship, and Penn wrote (but did not publish) a letter in his own defense that also revealed, probably unconsciously, his character.[3] He began by establishing his credentials as a worker for Friends for twenty-two years, a commitment that brought "troubles and afflictions" from "neer relations, or the Governments of the world, or my neighbours, or my enemys or my fals friends." This followed a testimonial to his "experience" of the divine that had enabled him "to speak" for the "goodness" God had "chosen to my soule both in his judgments and mercy." True religion originated in a personal "revelation of this word in the soule," which had cleansed him as a "young man" and guided the "old man." He exhorted Friends "to know the convincing, converting, and redeeming power" that allowed one to forsake "self love" and the "lusts and vanities" of this world and prepare for that crown that never fades away. Before addressing the main subject of this epistle, Penn linked suffering and criticism for his faith with the opprobrium he would endure for his work with King James, blamed and blessed God for his troubles, and preached his basic sermon on religious experience, moral living, and eternal life. He could assume that he had enlisted Quakers' sympathy for his suffering and their approval for his faithful witness.

Finally, Penn got to the "tousing and revolutions" of recent times and proclaimed his innocence from the "imputation of Jesuitisme, Popery, and Plots." Quakers already knew that the first two charges were absurd, but what about "Plots"? Penn did not specify whether the alleged plots were against English liberties under James or against an insecure dynasty under William and Mary. "I have universally sought the liberty and peace" of the nation, he wrote, and done no action "that unbecomes a Christian" and an Englishman; "neither [popery,] blood, money, nor slavery can be laid at my door." Instead, he had used his "small interest" with James, who had promised liberty of conscience, to break the "Jaws of persecution" so that prisoners could be released "and the poor and widow, and the orphan [might] come forth." His conscience was clear, he proclaimed, for the achievement of religious liberty justified working for any government. Under James, the English had achieved "liberty, peace, and plenty" (in contrast to the battles in Ireland and Scotland). The "good days" under James were not a "trick to introduce evil ones." If Penn had believed otherwise, he would have opposed the king. In conclusion, Penn embraced his unjust suffering for God and country and called on Friends to "be *steadfast* and *immovable*" in every good work.

When Penn claimed that all that he had done under James he had done for the public good, he also ducked responsibility for any failures. "If some things were not done well," he said, this was not his doing. He did not specify what was "not done well" or whether his opposition might have made any difference. Rather, by linking suffering, testimony for truth, and liberty of conscience, Penn justified working with "any government." In essence, freedom of religion trumped alleged tyranny. "I wrought as well as I could, with the strength and instruments I had, for a general good." In all of Penn's letters, this statement was as close as he ever came to saying publicly that he had been wrong.

Historians trying to understand the private Penn from the remove of three centuries are often perplexed. At a conference several years ago, three eminent scholars grappled with the complexities of his personality. Professor Gary Nash declared that we needed insight into Penn as an introspective, searching man. Professor Richard Dunn countered that Penn was always busy, restless, on the go, and that he could find no evidence of his having engaged in deep self-analysis. In a later essay, Professor Mary Dunn suggested that Penn's frequent changes of address, constant travel, and incessant activity were signs of a man seeking to avoid self-knowledge.[4] At the time, I agreed with the Dunns that we have no evidence, during Penn's many years as a Quaker, of any critical self-evaluation, religious darkness, or doubt caused by other Friends' critiques of his activities in meeting, in politics or at court, and in Pennsylvania. Instead, Penn consistently gave the strong impression that he saw martyrdom as the mark of true devotion, that suffering signaled triumphant work for truth, as he proclaimed in *No Cross, No Crown*, and that he was prone to wallowing in self-pity, as so many of his letters after 1702 make clear. He seems not to have doubted the Providence of God in obtaining the charter of Pennsylvania or sailing there in 1682. For example, when smallpox broke out on the *Welcome*, killing several passengers, the Quakers on the ship did not observe a day of fasting and confession of sins, unlike the New England Puritans' response to what they saw as providential evils.

More recently, I have reconsidered my conclusion. Was it possible that Penn sat in silent meeting for two hours each Sunday and in midweek meeting, monthly business meetings, Quarterly Meeting, Yearly Meeting, MFS, and MMM, and to have endured the isolation of long imprisonments, the enforced withdrawal from society after the Dutch conquest of 1688, and a stay in debtors' prison, and still not have critically examined his life? When George Whitehead and other prominent Friends opposed his second marriage as inappropriate, how could Penn so confidently have assured Hannah Callowhill that his listening to the Light showed how blessed their union would be?[5] After all, Penn should have remembered his strenuous arguments that dissidents must accept the authority of leading London Friends. Now he ignored their counsel. How many hundreds of messages in meeting for worship must Penn have listened to requiring him to hearken to that "still small voice" within; could he really never have wondered whether it was better to withdraw from his frantic pace of life? He certainly recommended the quiet country life in *Fruits of Solitude*.

Perhaps the problem is the idiom in which Penn thought and wrote. Like George Fox and other early Friends, Penn knew the Bible intimately and used its metaphors extensively. Historians must constantly examine the context of the verses he quoted to be sure what Penn meant. In addition, religious experience and daily events were so consistently compared to biblical norms that issues not raised in scripture might not make it into print. While scattered biblical verses do demand introspection, this is not a prominent theme in the Bible in comparison with, say, trust in God or ethical behavior. For example, there are few positive references to self in the King James Bible.[6] It never says "know thyself" or "an unexamined life is not worth living." In the scriptures, knowledge and wisdom come from an encounter with God that leads to praise, prayer, and a moral life. The question is whether the Bible led seventeenth-century Quakers to religious introspection in a particular way that is difficult to discern today. For early Friends, the Bible was the source for religious language because, even though spiritual experiences came to an individual, the final authority was God, as understood within the community.

We must also ask whether in judging Penn's self-knowledge we commit the fundamental historical error of judging the past from the perspective of the present. Should Penn be judged by norms that arose one, two, or three centuries later, as exemplified, for example, by John Woolman's constant self-examination and fear of outrunning his gift? Do we know of any seventeenth-century Friend who engaged in doubt and prolonged self-examination after his or her convincement? George Fox showed no sense of sin or deep introspection after he was converted, even though he underwent a period of depression in 1659, nor do others of the First Publishers of Truth. Nor do the women portrayed in the documentary collection *Hidden in Plain Sight*.[7] Among the first generation of Friends, only James Nayler seems a divided person, and that only after he fell from grace, as evidenced by his so-called messianic entrance to Bristol in 1654.[8] Of the next generation, Isaac Penington comes closest, but there is no self-doubt in the surviving writings of Robert Barclay, George Whitehead, or George Keith.[9]

The lack of self-scrutiny can be explained not only by the kind of writings that Friends preserved but by the nature of Quaker belief itself. The primary source of authority for Friends was a religious experience that they shared with others, and they insisted that this experience was normative for all Christians. For Quakers to have confessed doubt would have been to agree with the Puritans and Anglicans that the Light of Christ within was natural, or, even worse, a sign of the devil's power. Certainty of their conversion had to be proclaimed forcefully. For Friends, there could be no acknowledgment of a "dark night of the soul," no agonized searching for a hidden God. There is no equivalent in early Quakerism to Cotton Mather, who constantly searched himself to make sure he was of the elect and looked at events to see the Providence of God. The key difference was the doctrine of assurance. Quakers believed that even one who had experienced God could fall and then encounter the Light again. Calvinists insisted that those who really were of the elect could not fall. If theology alone were the key, then the Puritans should have been less introspective after conversion than the Quakers, but the opposite is true. The Puritans remained careful of being too certain of the original experience of grace, whereas the Quakers proclaimed their absolute confidence. Penn argued that if a person did not know, or doubted a direct encounter with, the Inward God, then he had not experienced it. Never in any of his writings after 1667 did Penn evince any hesitancy in proclaiming that he had encountered the God within. This was certain knowledge, learned from spiritual senses. In his advocacy of religious toleration, Penn argued that conscience cannot be coerced, but he did not make the skeptical argument that one cannot know truth.

An additional factor came from what Friends believed should happen in silent meeting. Our age is preoccupied with the self: self-discovery, self-actualization, self-fulfillment, the authenticity of the self. In today's liberal form of Quakerism, the congregation "centers down" to contact their innermost being. Penn did not worry about his self, authentic or otherwise. To the contrary, Penn's desire in worship was to escape or negate the self, to suppress it and all self-willing, so that the earthly self did not contaminate the experience of the Inward God, which led to knowledge, prompted action, and gave one power to overcome the shallowness of worldly things. For early Friends, including Penn, when a person plunged deep into his or her self, at the core was not an id, ego, or superego, or a Jungian archetype, but the seed of God. Penn's grounding in religious experience, which he constantly renewed in silent meeting, is the key to understanding how he could deal with triumph and defeat. It may be why he never worried about or even acknowledged the evolution in his theological perspective from apocalyptic prophet to rationalist Christian. Even in his earlier writings, Penn could be distinctly Quaker, judgmental, tolerant, close to theologically orthodox, humanist, and rationalist. He affirmed many perspectives while tailoring his emphasis to his audience and to the temper of the times. Theological debate was necessary to defend the truth, but it remained a secondary activity of little ultimate significance.

The primary purpose of the human children of God in this life of trial was to be governed by the Inward Principle.

To us, Penn is an enigma because we do not understand how he could manage to be an influential Quaker Christian, Irish landlord, preacher, advocate of toleration, moralist, theologian, courtier, Whig politician, proprietor, governor, and associate of kings and nobles. He stood out as a singular man in each role, an oddity even to his contemporaries. Penn attempted to serve God in all of these roles, but he did not need to worry about consistency or a clear conscience because he was serving God, and outward success and failure were nothing in the Lord's sight. Obedience to the guidance of the Light conquered all and was all that really mattered.

Would Penn think he deserved a statue on city hall? Probably not, because a statue glorified human pride. His work on behalf of religious liberty and his founding of Pennsylvania were acts of service done in the love of Christ, but they were nothing compared to the glories of eternal life. But he would have rejoiced in those who stopped to read and contemplate his prayer for Philadelphia, displayed in the courtyard of the same city hall: "Faithful to the God of thy mercies in the life of righteousness thou mayest be preserved to the end. My soul prays to God for thee that thou mayest stand in the day of trial, that thy children may be blessed of the Lord and thy people saved by His power."

ADDITIONAL READING

On William Penn: the first four volumes of *The Papers of William Penn* (1981–87), edited by Richard S. Dunn and Mary Maples Dunn (with co-editors Richard Alan Ryerson, Scott M. Wilds, Jean R. Soderlund, Ned C. Landsman, Marianne S. Wokeck, Joy Wiltenburg, Alison Duncan Hirsch, and Craig W. Horle) contain the most important letters, with annotations and introductions. The fifth volume (1986), edited by Edwin B. Bronner and David Fraser, is a complete bibliography of Penn's published writings from 1660 to 1726. Joseph Besse's two-volume *Collection of the Works of William Penn* (1726) is the first biography with a selection of letters and publications. Melvin B. Endy Jr., *William Penn and Early Quakerism* (1973) is the best theological analysis; also valuable are Endy's articles "George Fox and William Penn: Their Relationship and Their Roles Within the Quaker Movement" (2004) and "William Penn's Political Pacifism as Seen in Pennsylvania and in His *Essay on the Present and Future Peace of Europe*" (2011). Several chapters in Jane Calvert's *Quaker Constitutionalism and the Political Thought of John Dickinson* (2008) place Penn's ideas on the basis for government in a Quaker context in England and Pennsylvania. Andrew R. Murphy's *Liberty, Conscience, and Toleration: The Political Thought of William Penn* (2016) stresses the complex relationships among Penn's theories on government, religious liberty, and morality and his attempt to institutionalize them in Pennsylvania. Articles by many scholars on a wide variety of topics relevant for understanding Penn may be found in Richard S. Dunn and Mary Maples Dunn, eds., *The World of William Penn* (1986), and *The Worlds of William Penn*, edited by Andrew R. Murphy and John Smolensky (2019). Older and more recent biographies are listed in the preface of the latter. Good bibliographies can also be found in Andrew Murphy, *William Penn: A Life* (2018) and in Murphy's *Liberty, Conscience, and Toleration*.

On Quakers: primary sources are available in Hugh Barbour and Arthur O. Roberts, eds., *Early Quaker Writings, 1650–1700* (1973) and the Digital Quaker

Collection at the Earlham School of Religion in Richmond, Indiana, which provides free access to the writings of the most important early Friends. A recent reference book is Stephen W. Angell and Pink Dandelion, eds., *The Oxford Handbook of Quaker Studies* (2013), with essays covering 350 years of Friends' history. General histories include Hugh Barbour and J. William Frost, *The Quakers* (1988, reprinted 1994) and Thomas D. Hamm, *The Quakers in America* (2003). Articles useful for understanding the changes in Quakerism during Penn's lifetime can be found in Richard C. Allen and Rosemary Moore, eds., *The Quakers, 1656–1723: The Evolution of an Alternative Community* (2018). The classic books for this period are William Charles Braithwaite, *The Beginnings of Quakerism* (1912) and *The Second Period of Quakerism* (1919; rev. eds. 1955, 1961, edited by Henry Cadbury). The best histories of early Friends include Hugh Barbour, *The Quakers in Puritan England* (1964; 2nd ed., 1985) and Rosemary Moore, *The Light in Their Consciences: Early Quakers in Britain, 1646–1666* (2000). Stephen W. Angell and Pink Dandelion, eds., *Early Quakers and Their Theological Thought, 1647–1723* (2015) contains essays on significant early Quaker thinkers, including Whitehead and Penn. On George Fox, in addition to his *Journal*, see H. Larry Ingle, *First Among Friends: George Fox and the Creation of Quakerism* (1994) and Hilary Hinds, *George Fox and Early Quaker Culture* (2011). Jordan Landes, *London Quakers in the Trans-Atlantic World: The Creation of an Early Modern Community* (2015) assesses the impact of British Friends on the colonies. Phyllis Mack, *Visionary Women: Ecstatic Prophecy in Seventeenth-Century England* (1992) and Christine Trevett, *Women and Quakerism in the Seventeenth Century* (1991) illustrate the increasing conservatism of English Quakers on women's roles during Penn's lifetime.

On early Pennsylvania: Craig W. Horle, Marianne S. Wokeck, et al., eds. *Lawmaking and Legislators in Pennsylvania: A Biographical Dictionary*, vol. 1, *1682–1709* (1991), contains essays and biographical sketches of leading Quakers in their legislative but also religious and economic roles. John Smolenski, *Friends and Strangers: The Making of a Creole Culture in Colonial Pennsylvania* (2010) is excellent but can be supplemented by Gary B. Nash, *Quakers and Politics: Pennsylvania, 1681–1726* (1968) and Edwin B. Bronner, *William Penn's "Holy Experiment": The Founding of Pennsylvania, 1681–1701* (1962, reprinted 1968). On religious liberty, two books that begin with Penn and continue the story through the colonial period are Sally Schwartz, *"A Mixed Multitude": The Struggle for Toleration in Colonial Pennsylvania* (1987) and J. William Frost, *A Perfect Freedom: Religious Liberty in Pennsylvania* (1990).

APPENDIX: PENN AND THE BIBLE

By 1679, within two years of his conversion, Penn had emerged as a minister and begun defending Friends' distinctive beliefs and practices in his preaching, writings, and debates with Anglicans, Independents, Presbyterians, and Baptists. The primary issue in many of his controversial writings was the authority of what Quakers saw as their experience of the Inward Light of Christ as opposed to the outward status of scripture. Quakerism was an attempt to make normative, and then institutionalize, this unmediated encounter with the divine, for which they used many terms: Light, Seed, Holy Spirit, Christ Within, Word/God. The seat of such experience was the conscience, but it was supernatural knowledge gained directly from God. However, Christ Within did not mean the fullness or omnipotence of God but was something received from God that was present within and available to all persons. Friends claimed that they encountered the same spirit that had inspired the writers of the Bible. Direct, immediate revelation had not ceased with the creation of the early church and scriptures but was available to any man or woman who stilled his or her will and allowed the Seed of God within to prevail. This experience, shared by members of the primitive church and still available to everyone, was the ultimate authority in religion and could yield new knowledge in situations not in the Bible. Revelation was not confined to biblical times; revelation in the present day could be confirmed by using the Bible because God was the same in all ages. For Quakers, the Bible was an authority, but it was a secondary witness to the Inward Light. Their many opponents considered the Quaker belief nonsensical, a confusion of their own earthly impulses or an effect of the devil's wiles. The terms of the debate over Quaker belief in the Inward Light and scriptural authority were established years before Penn converted, and while Penn added sources to buttress his claims, he did not seek or contribute new arguments.

Penn repeatedly insisted that Quakers valued the Bible. The scriptures contained "a Declaration of the Mind and Will of God . . . to the age they were written in given forth by the Holy Ghost moving in the Hearts of Holy Men. They contain Precepts, Prophecies, Threatnings, Promises, Providences, Rewards, Punishment, Deliverances, Doctrines, Examples, and Practices."[1] They were important "first, Historically, as giving us a true Narrative . . . in reference to the Church or State of both Jews and Christians, their Trials, Troubles, Temptations, Lapses, Recoveries, and perfect Victories. Second, Doctrinally, as presenting us with a true Account of the Principles and Doctrines of the People of God, their Holy Faith and Patience; I cannot praise it better than a Divine Glass, in which we see (I say WE SEE) opened by Inspiration and Revelation the States and Conditions of the Primitive Saints."[2]

For Penn, the Bible provided "Comfort and Confirmation" and "Good Example," but it was "only useful, as unfolded" by God's inspiration. Scholarship on the Bible was useful within its limits. One could get "Grammar and Critical Senses of the Words, and Allusions may be understood, but the Inside and Spiritual significance" would remain a "Riddle" unless the reader were illuminated by the spirit of God. "Humane Learning" was not necessary to understand the biblical "language of God."[3]

Penn insisted that the Bible was not the Word of God. Christ was the Word of God; the Bible consisted of words *about* God, a testimonial to an earlier experience. The Bible was not the Gospel, because the Gospel was preached before the Bible was written. There are four Gospels, but only one Gospel. The early church had no Bible, but it had the spirit of God, and this took precedent over the words in the Bible, which attested to what had already occurred. Salvation could not be bought from the bookseller, and even the devil could quote scripture.

Against the belief in the inerrant text of the Bible, Penn insisted that the original authors of the books of the Bible had been inspired by God and thus did not err, but that this could not be said of the many scribes who had copied the text over the centuries.[4] Surviving ancient texts contained many variations, and translators of the Hebrew and Greek often disagreed on punctuation and the meaning of words. In addition, Luke referred to many writings that had been lost. Were these divinely inspired? What would happen if these lost writings were discovered at some later date? Anyone who looked at the history of the creation of the canon by the various church councils could argue that politics had influenced its content. Given the different interpretations of Christ found in the New Testament (e.g., the Gospel of John, the letters of Paul, the letter to the Hebrews), how could one assume that the parties later condemned as heretical had not inserted their opinions into the text?[5] Penn noted that some commentators (though not Quakers) questioned whether the book of Revelation, the first and second letters of Peter, the second letter of John, the letters of James and Jude, and even the letter to the Hebrews belonged in the Bible. Roman Catholics added the Apocrypha to the list of questionable inclusions. If the Bible were the sole source of truth, then why were there so many different interpretations by scholars throughout the centuries? Why could Christians not agree on the date for Easter, free will versus predestination, or the nature of Christ? And not all parts of the Bible provided spiritual help to Christians: Satan talked in the book of Job, most of the kings of Israel and many in Judea were wicked, and there were many examples of evil men and woman. The Bible was complex and could be read as literal history or as typology, allegory, or poetry. Unfortunately for his readers, Penn did not provide examples of each kind of reading or discuss how to distinguish them.

For Penn and other Friends, the conclusion was clear. The only way a believer could be certain that he or she had the spiritual meaning of a verse was to have received knowledge from the Holy Ghost that had inspired the original writings. The scriptures were created by divine inspiration and must be read that way. This inspiration could come either via ordinary revelation, such as "daily and common Vision and Discovery to the Soul," including general knowledge of the status of God and man, or by "Extraordinary Revelation," which included foresight and divine projects. Both were useful in Bible study.[6]

The skepticism and historical caution in Penn's view of the formation of the canon, and his argument that errors had almost certainly crept into the text over centuries of transcriptions, drove his published debates with clergy on the authority of the Bible. Leading second-generation Quaker ministers shared his perspective, but most Friends, including Penn, stressed the secondary authority of the Bible regardless of the case for the probable corruption of the text over the centuries. Those who read Penn's devotional epistles, his defenses of Quaker customs on plain dress and speech, and his case for refusing to take oaths or pay tithes encountered an overwhelming number of biblical citations, often in paraphrase and out of context. Sometimes Penn distinguished between the Old and New Testament, the letter and the spirit, but these were the only hermeneutical perspectives he provided. He did insist that Christian doctrine and practice were reasonable, and on occasion he identified John's Logos as the Inward Light in the conscience. In his pursuit of religious peace and toleration in England in 1679, he wanted articles of religion for all denominations in the form of direct quotations from the Bible, because all agreed on its authority. "Who can express the will of God better than the holy spirit?"[7] Opinions were not authority but consisted of all beliefs "expressly laid down in Scriptures, or not so evidently Deduceable from Scripture; as to leave no doubt . . . or, lastly, such as have no new or Credible Revelation to vouch them." In other words, the Bible, reason, and the Inward Light established truth. Whatever ambiguities were in the Bible, Penn insisted that all essential beliefs and practices for salvation were clear. The scriptures contained the "Complete Declaration of the Will of God to Man."[8]

Before leaving England for Pennsylvania in 1699, Penn wrote *The Advice of William Penn to His Children*, in which he advised them to follow his example in daily readings of scripture. In waking, after a period of "pure silence" and getting dressed, they should read a chapter in the Bible and another in the evening so that God would be their "Alpha and Omega." The Old Testament should be studied for "History chiefly, the Psalms for Meditation and Devotion, the Prophets for Comfort and Hope, but especially the New Testament, for Doctrine, Faith, and Worship."[9] In his earliest and latest works, Penn quoted scripture extensively; for example, as a new convert, he defended his new faith to his father by citing fifty passages from nine books in the Old Testament and fifteen in the New; in his first published tract (1668) of seven folio pages, he had fifty-five citations and listed nine Old Testament and ten New Testament books.[10] In addition, he used metaphors and stories from the Bible. There are six hundred biblical citations in the 1682 edition of *No Cross, No Crown*.[11] In *Advice [. . .] to His Children* (ca. 1699), when discussing Quaker faith and the Light, he quoted extensively from the New Testament, primarily John, but when giving suggestions on conduct, the authority came from Proverbs.

Two modern sources are useful in attempting to discover what biblical passages Penn relied upon. The first two volumes of the *Papers of William Penn*, which cover his life before 1684, list many biblical citations and paraphrases in his letters. Esther Greenleaf Mürer itemized all Bible quotations and citations in Hugh Barbour's two volumes of excerpts of Penn's most important publications.[12] The conclusions in both sources should be understood as illustrative rather than definitive owing to the large number of metaphors and phrases that might or might not be scriptural; Penn read the Bible so often and so intently that he internalized its language. In the transcripts of his sermons, taken down by an outsider in 1693–94, he often quoted or paraphrased passages without providing the reference.[13] A listener would have difficulty in knowing their source and distinguishing what was a direct quotation from what sounded biblical but probably was not.

Mürer and the editors of the *Papers of William Penn* discovered twice as many New as Old Testament citations. Mürer listed the most frequent verses as coming from John, Matthew, Proverbs, and Isaiah. The Dunns and their co-editors found that Genesis, Isaiah, and Psalms are the most cited Old Testament books and Matthew and Luke the most cited in the New. There were more mentions of the anonymous letter to the Hebrews than of all of Paul's letters. In the brief period 1680–84 covered in volume 2 of *PWP*, the five-year span in which Penn gained, planned, and visited Pennsylvania, there were fewer direct citations and, most surprising, four mentions of a metaphor from the Song of Solomon ("the waters cannot quench," 8:7). In his early years, in which he was imprisoned four times and pronounced judgment on those who persecuted Quakers, Penn cited the judgment passages from Amos, Isaiah, Jeremiah, and Revelation. After limited toleration was won, first with James II and then in the Toleration Act of 1691, Penn placed more emphasis on personal sin and redemption than on national failings and judgment. The many citations from Proverbs in Mürer's "Quaker Bible Index" resulted from his using them in a manuscript that remained unpublished until it appeared in John Rhodes's 1726 edition of *Fruits of a Father's Love, Being the Advice of William Penn to His Children*. Because he used many of the same maxims in the 1693 *Fruits of Solitude* without mentioning the Bible, it may be that Penn concluded that his children needed to be instructed in religious authority rather than in reason and common sense.

Penn's published works omitted many Christians' favorite verses, including Psalm 23, "I know that my redeemer liveth," from Job, Jesus's feeding the multitudes, the story of Zacchaeus, the raising of Lazarus, and the widow's mite. In Mürer there are more citations to the short letter of James than to Joshua, Judges, 1 and 2 Samuel, 1 and 2 Kings, and 1 and 2 Chronicles. In the New Testament, neither the crucifixion, nor the resurrection stories, nor miracles were stressed. Even in *No Cross, No Crown* there is less emphasis upon the suffering Jesus in the crucifixion than on the denial of the world by true believers. Penn believed in the accuracy of the outward history of the events in ancient Israel and in Jesus's life as recorded in the Bible, but such ancient events lacked relevance for his readers unless experienced spiritually. The cosmic Jesus had saved men and women before he appeared in the flesh and established the possibility of salvation. Now Christ had returned for those who would repent, experience him inwardly, and follow his teachings. Salvation was also possible for those who had never heard of Jesus or read the Bible.[14] Fortunately for the English, in addition to the "Gentile Divinity," they had the Bible and gained knowledge of the history of the Jews, Jesus, and the early church.

The guiding principle in Penn's interpretation of the Bible was that true religion was spiritual, by which he meant knowledge of God found in the conscience. He remained suspicious of anything earthly or physical. If there was any question as to whether an outward practice of the early church was still valid, Penn's criterion was whether it was inward and spiritual. Reading the Psalms was useful, but singing them in church was not. True preaching under the immediate inspiration of God took place in meeting for worship, but using a written sermon or a prayer from the Book of Common Prayer was carnal. Penn came close to arguing that Quaker meeting was purer than the services of the early church because baptism was by water, and still Catholic and Anglican Communion used wine and bread. These were concessions to the Jewish influence or lack of clear thinking, but Christ's return in the hearts of believers allowed spiritual insights.

Penn's most frequent scriptural citations were those linked to Quaker testimonies, such as the beginning chapters of John's Gospel and John's first letter, or anywhere the word "Light" was used in either testament as a sign of revelation or as witness to the availability of the Inward Christ. The so-called scandal of particularity did not bother Penn because the Inward Christ could save good men and women even if they had no knowledge of Jesus or the Bible. He used as proof such examples in both Testaments as Job 32:8 ("But it is the spirit in a man, the breath of the Almighty, that makes him understand"), Jeremiah 31:33 ("I will write my Law in their Hearts, and place my fear in their Inward Parts"), and Romans 1:19 ("For what can be known about God is plain to them, because God has shown it to them").[15] In his epistles, tracts, and sermons, Penn relied on verses declaring God's judgment in this or the next life depending upon belief and behavior, exhortations to a life of moral rectitude and piety, and promises of salvation and eternal life. Because there were often differences among Quakers, Penn quoted frequently from the pastoral Epistles. For example, there are thirty-nine citations to Ephesians chapters 4 through 6 in Mürer's index, but few in the Dunns' edition of Penn's papers. When confronted by texts that seemingly contradicted Quaker beliefs, such as baptism by water or the use of wine in the Eucharist, Penn either found other verses that did not mention physical elements (Matt. 3:11: John will "baptize you with water," but Jesus will baptize you "with the Holy

Ghost and fire") or said that the early church had not yet emancipated itself from Jewish traditions and possessed only an uncertain understanding of Jesus's message. After all, revelation continued throughout history, and God could give new knowledge to those who hearkened to his inward guidance.

Penn internalized Bible stories as a guide to the Christian pilgrimage. The scriptures provided a picture of the trials and triumphs of Jews and Christians in the past that could inspire those in the present. The Bible facilitated self-evaluation and provided insight into correct doctrine and the religious experiences of good men. Bible stories were a guide to distinguishing between authentic and evil impulses, but they were not the ultimate authority. Only the Inward Light, known to individuals and shared in Quaker meeting, provided infallible authority. Critics charged Quakers with putting their writings on an equal footing with the Bible. Even if this was the logical conclusion of the expressed view of the early Friends, the mature Penn drew back from that conclusion by insisting that God had not changed. So authentic personal revelation, biblical authority, and right reason always agreed. Because Penn lived in a world in which he felt that God was eternally present, he used Bible passages to pass judgment on sinners, exhort his listeners to take up the cross, admonish them to keep the faith, console them when facing persecution or death, and assure them of salvation and eternal life.

NOTES

PREFACE

1. Video made by Anthony Fleet, "Abe Lincoln? Ben Franklin? Who Is on Top of City Hall?" January 23, 2015, https://www.youtube.com/watch?v=GhIvAO7D92s. I am grateful to Jordan Landes for sending me this video.

2. Elizabeth Milroy, "The Elusive Body of William Penn," and Catharine Dann Roeber, "Where William Penn Sept (and Why It Matters)," both in *The Worlds of William Penn*, edited by Andrew R. Murphy and John Smolenski (New Brunswick: Rutgers University Press, 2019), 13–48 and 49–67, respectively; Amelia Gummere, *The Quaker: A Study in Costume* (Philadelphia: Ferris and Leach, 1901).

3. The most commonly reproduced paintings are probably of his father, so we can at least infer a family resemblance. Penn lost most of his hair when he had smallpox as a child. If an image has a full head of hair and no scars, either the artist "gilded the lily" or it is not Penn. John Nickalls, *Some Quaker Portraits: Certain and Uncertain*, supplement 29 (London: Friends Historical Society, 1958), 9–18; William I. Hull, *William Penn: A Topical Biography* (Swarthmore: Swarthmore College Monographs, 1937), 294–309; Henry J. Cadbury, *Friendly Heritage: Letters from the Quaker Past* (Norwalk, CT: Silvermine, 1972), 85–86; Alison Hirsch, "A Tale of Two Wives: Mythmaking and the Lives of Gulielma and Hannah Penn," *Pennsylvania History* 61, no. 4 (1994): 438 (on the portraits of both wives); Harry Emerson Wildes, *William Penn* (New York: Macmillan, 1974), 427–29.

4. *PWP*, 2:22, 30–31, 35. The king and the Duke of York referred to "services" of the admiral and did not mention this debt, but other sources do. The editors of the *Papers of William Penn* could find no official record of any debt the Crown owed to Admiral Penn for feeding the sailors. Considering that King Charles gave the admiral a title, twelve thousand acres of Irish land, and profitable positions at a fort in Ireland and on the Naval Board, he might have concluded that the admiral's son deserved nothing more. Also, the admiral did not petition the king for payment before his death, and his son waited until 1680 to do so.

5. Thomas D. Hamm, *The Quakers in America* (New York: Columbia University Press, 2003) is the best introduction to the history and beliefs of past and present Friends.

6. See also Hugh Barbour, ed., *William Penn on Religion and Ethics: The Emergence of Liberal Quakerism*, 2 vols. (Lewiston, NY: Edwin Mellen Press, 1991), which contains excerpts from Penn's major publications with introductions by Barbour.

7. *PWP*, 2:460–61.

8. *PWP*, 3:336–43.

9. Hull, *Penn: A Topical Biography*; Catherine Owens Peare, *William Penn: A*

Biography (Ann Arbor: University of Michigan Press, 1956); Hans Fantel, *William Penn: Apostle of Dissent* (New York: William Morrow 1971); Wildes, *William Penn*; Bonamy Dobrée, *William Penn, Quaker and Pioneer* (New York: Houghton Mifflin, 1932); John Moretta, *William Penn and the Quaker Legacy* (New York: Pearsons, 2006); Mary Geiter, *William Penn* (New York: Longman, 2000).

10. Andrew R. Murphy, *William Penn: A Life* (New York: Oxford University Press, 2018), 48, 61–62, 152.

CHAPTER 1

1. *PWP*, 2:394–96; Shuichi Wanibuchi, "William Penn's Imperial Landscape: Improvement, Political Economy, and Colonial Agriculture in the Pennsylvania Project," in Murphy and Smolenski, *Worlds of William Penn*, 378–402.

2. In *The Christian Quaker and His Divine Testimony Vindicated* [. . .] (London, 1674) (which also contains a section by George Whitehead), 9, Penn mentioned a Baptist minister named "J. Binnion," by which he might have meant John Bunyan.

3. Leopold Damrosch Jr., *God's Plot and Man's Stories: Studies in the Fictional Imagination from Milton to Fielding* (Chicago: University of Chicago Press, 1985) has chapters on Bunyan, Milton, and Defoe that are useful for contrasting Penn with his contemporaries.

4. *PWP*, 4:66, 74, 228–29.

5. Defoe published *Robinson Crusoe* in 1719, a year after Penn's death; *Gulliver's Travels* appeared six years later, but both Defoe and Swift published satirical works much earlier. For excellent background on the literary world of the Restoration, see Leo Damrosch, *Jonathan Swift: His Life and His World* (New Haven: Yale University Press, 2013); James A. Winn, *John Dryden and His World* (New Haven: Yale University Press, 1987); and Paula Backscheider, *Daniel Defoe: His Life* (Baltimore: Johns Hopkins University Press, 1989).

6. Although it is often claimed that Penn met Locke, there is no certain evidence of this, but they were aware of each other's works. *PWP*, 2:137, 227, 3:447. Locke privately criticized Penn's Frame of Government; during James's reign, Penn sought a pardon so that Locke could return from exile, and Locke later returned the favor during William's reign.

7. Lisa Jardine, *On a Grand Scale: The Outstanding Life of Christopher Wren* (New York: Harper Collins, 2002).

8. David Turner, *Fashioning Adultery: Gender, Sex, and Civility in England, 1660–1740* (Cambridge: Cambridge University Press, 2002), 9. David Cressy estimates that illiteracy at the time of the English Civil War was 70 percent among men and 90 percent among women but had fallen to 55 percent in men and 75 percent in women by the accession of George I in 1714. Cressy, *Literacy and the Social Order: Reading and Writing in Tudor and Stuart England* (Cambridge: Cambridge University Press, 1980), 176–80. Literacy is not a test of intelligence, of course, and folk wisdom, traditional habits, and oral traditions of sermons and storytelling structured most people's lives. On the readership for dissenters' writings, see N. H. Keeble, *The Literary Culture of Nonconformity in Later Seventeenth-Century England* (Athens: University of Georgia Press, 1987), 130–37.

9. Because few in England had many gold or silver coins, people used barter rather than cash, and the poor obtained loans that were later forgiven as acts of charity or necessity. Craig Muldrew, "Debt, Credit, and Poverty in Early Modern England," in *A Debtor World: Interdisciplinary Perspectives on Debt*, edited by Ralph Brubaker, Robert M. Lawless, and Charles J. Tabb (Oxford: Oxford University Press, 2012), 30; Julian Hoppit, *A Land of Liberty? England, 1689–1727* (New York: Oxford University Press, 2000), 83. Sir William Petty, an acquaintance of Penn's, in attempting to calculate the wealth of Resto-

ration Ireland and England, divided the population into productive classes (farmers, artisans) and unproductive classes (clergy, lawyers) and concluded that two-thirds of the people were unproductive. Tony Aspromourgos, *On the Origins of Classical Economics: Distribution and Value from William Petty to Adam Smith* (London, Routledge, 1991), 45, 47, 50.

10. Hoppit, *Land of Liberty*, 56, 81.

11. W. A. Speck, *Reluctant Revolutionaries: Englishmen and the Revolution of 1688* (Oxford: Oxford University Press, 1988), 203. London had 10 percent of the population of England and was its only real city. Approximately a fourth of the city's population were dissenters.

12. Murphy, *Penn: A Life*, 41.

13. Swift sardonically labeled English history between 1626 and 1726 "a Heap of Conspiracies, Rebellions, Murders, Massacres, Revolutions, Banishments" caused by "Avarice, Factions, Hypocrisy, Perfidiousness, Cruelty, Rage, Madness, Hatred, Envy, Lust, Malice and Ambition." *Gulliver's Travels* (Oxford: Oxford University Press, 1998), 120.

14. Christopher Hill, *God's Englishman: Oliver Cromwell and the English Revolution* (New York: Dial Press, 1970), 145, 185–90.

15. Penn's 1701 will provided for freeing his slaves, but his final will did not mention them, either because he no longer owned any or was in debt. *PWP*, 4:113–14. When in Philadelphia, he advocated separate worship meetings for Native Americans and Negroes. Whether Penn knew of the antislavery sentiments expressed by a few Quakers is unknown.

16. Thomas Clarkson, *Memoirs of the Public and Private Life of William Penn* (Philadelphia: Bradford and Inskeep, 1813), 2 vols., 2:29; Hull, *Penn: A Topical Biography*, 267.

17. See N. H. Keeble, *The Restoration: England in the 1660s* (Oxford: Blackwell, 2002), on problems of Charles's government (77) and religious issues (91–93, 121–24). Charles publicly acknowledged six children by Lady Castlemain. *DSP*, July 27, 1667, 8:355.

18. Paul Seaward, *The Cavalier Parliament and the Reconstruction of the Old Regime, 1661–1667* (New York: Cambridge University Press, 1989), 60, 69–73, 173–81, 186–87, 191–95; John Spurr, *The Restoration Church of England, 1646–1689* (New Haven: Yale University Press, 2008), 47–52, 50, 123–27. An estimated ten thousand Quakers, or about a quarter of all Friends, were imprisoned during the Restoration.

19. See Tim Harris, Paul Seaward, and Mark Goldie, eds., *The Politics of Religion in Restoration England* (Oxford: Blackwell, 1990), particularly chapters by Harris on continuities between the 1660s and earlier, Goldie on Danby and the Whigs, and Jonathan Scott on the popish plot.

20. The most detailed account of Charles's motives is Mary Geiter, "The Restoration Crisis and the Launching of Pennsylvania, 1670–1681," *English Historical Review* 112 (1997): 300–318. Geiter's *William Penn* argues that Charles attempted to divide the Whigs by favoring Penn and shows how influential men helped Penn politically. See also *PWP*, 2:22. For the essential documents, see Jean Soderlund, ed., *William Penn and the Founding of Pennsylvania* (Philadelphia: University of Pennsylvania Press, 1983), 17–36. Also unknown is why Penn waited to apply to Charles until after the admiral's death and ten years after incurring the debt.

21. Speck, *Reluctant Revolutionaries*. Steve Pincus, *1688: The First Modern Revolution* (New Haven: Yale University Press, 2009) offers contrasting views of the causes of the revolution. See also George Southcombe and Grant Tapsell, *Restoration Politics, Religion, and Culture: Britain and Ireland, 1660–1714* (New York: Palgrave Macmillan, 2009), 79–93.

22. Craig Rose, *England in the 1690s: Revolution, Religion, and War* (Oxford: Blackwell, 1999), 26–29, 48.

23. *PWP*, 4:203, 224–27.

24. Murphy, *Penn: A Life*, 287–304. An indication of his lack of publications can be found in the MMM minutes on microfilm at Library of the Religious Society of Friends in London, which mention twenty items from 1692 to 1700 but contain only five references from 1700 to 1711.

25. In "Leaving Father or Mother for Christ's Sake: William Penn's Veiled Autobiography Through Scriptural References," *Quaker Studies* 25, no. 2 (2020): 169–88, Stephen W. Angell uses Penn's biblical references as an indication of his attitude toward his parents.

26. *DSP*, 6:78–79, 191, 246.

27. *PWP*, 1:160–61, 2:245.

28. William wrote a very laudatory account of the admiral's pious deathbed wishes in *NCNC* (1682), in *WWP*, 1:432.

29. Hill, *God's Englishman*, 161. There is no modern biography of Sir William Penn, but a good account is C. S. Knighton, "Sir William Penn," in the *Oxford Dictionary of National Biography* (Oxford: Oxford University Press, 2004), 1–10.

30. *DSP*, 1:241–42, 3:117, 126, 6:230. The admiral seems to have been an opponent of Pepys's patron, the Earl of Sandwich. It may not have helped that Penn earned his position and that Pepys was a placeman who got seasick when the commissioners took a short boat trip.

31. *PWP*, 1:173–74. There is no official record of the admiral's feeding the sailors, thereby creating an obligation that the Crown should pay. A judge during Bushel's case (see chapter 5) claimed that the admiral pocketed money designated for the sailors. There is no supporting evidence for this claim. "Truth Rescued from Importance," *WWP*, 2:496–99.

32. *DSP*, 10:131–37. In 1701 Penn claimed that the Crown owed him £20,000. When he accepted Pennsylvania, that colony was worth only £1,200. MPWP, reel 9, p. 488.

33. *DSP*, 2:65, 78, 3:99–100, 126, 132. "And in our way met with two country fellows upon one horse—which I did without much ado give way to, but Sir W. Penn would not but stroke them and they him—and so passed away; but they giving him some high words, he went back again and stroke them off of their horse in a simple fury, and without much honour in my mind." *DSP*, 8:241.

34. There were 160 secular lords; the Penn family should be ranked among the upper tiers of the sixteen thousand gentry families. Speck, *Reluctant Revolutionaries*, 192.

35. Knowledge of Latin was a requirement for attending Oxford. Penn attended school at Chigwell and probably studied with private tutors in Ireland. For summaries of what is known of his early education, see Peare, *Penn: A Biography*, 14–15, 28–34; and Murphy, *Penn: A Life*, 16–17, 23–28.

36. Thomas Clarkson says that Penn took part in a riot over the wearing of the surplice. *Public and Private Life of William Penn*, 1:9.

37. J. W. Frost, "William Penn: Quaker Humanist," *Quaker Studies* 16, no. 2 (2012): 174–89.

38. *DSP*, 5:257, 6:213, 225, 257, 270.

39. Nicolas Canny, "The Irish Background to Penn's Experiment," in *The World of William Penn*, edited by Richard S. Dunn and Mary Maples Dunn (Philadelphia: University of Pennsylvania Press, 1986), 136–56; the impact of Ireland is discussed in essays in Murphy and Smolenski, *Worlds of William Penn*, 101–52.

40. *PWP*, 1:41–43.

41. *PWP*, 1:49–50.

42. For standard interpretations of early Friends, see Rosemary Moore, *The Light in Their Consciences: Early Quakers in Britain, 1646–1666* (University Park: Penn State University Press, 2000); and H. Larry Ingle, *First Among Friends: George Fox and the Creation of Quakerism* (New York: Oxford University Press, 1994).

43. Penn frequently used the term "experimental" to describe a firsthand encounter with God but rarely in a scientific sense. He also called the Light "Word-God" and "Universal Principle." *Christian Quaker and His Divine Testimony*, 101. George Whitehead is also credited with being an author of this tract, but his sections were separate and all quotations here are from Penn.

44. Melvin B. Endy Jr., "William Penn's Political Pacifism as Seen in Pennsylvania and in His *Essay on the Present and Future Peace of Europe*," in *Keeping Us Honest, Stirring the Pot: A Festschrift in Honor of H. Larry Ingle*, edited by Chuck Fager (Fayetteville, NC: Kimo Press, 2011), 100–132.

45. Andres Finchman, "Faith in Numbers: Requantifying the English Quaker Population During the Long Eighteenth Century," *Religions* 10, no. 2 (2019): 13; Charles Leslie, *The Snake in the Grass* [. . .] (London: Charles Brome, 1697), 245.

46. *DSP*, 5:235. During the Commonwealth, 3,179 Friends were imprisoned; during the first year of Charles's reign, five thousand. Several leaders were so weakened that they died shortly after being released. Brooke Sylvia Palmieri, "Compelling Reading: The Circulation of Quaker Texts, 1650–1700" (PhD diss., University College, London, 2017), 92–93; Craig W. Horle, *The Quakers and the English Legal System 1660–1688* (Philadelphia: University of Pennsylvania Press, 1988), 46–55.

47. Mary Maples Dunn, "The Personality of William Penn," in Dunn and Dunn, *World of William Penn*, 5–9.

48. For essays on Quaker theology, politics, organizations, and customs in England and America during Penn's lifetime, see Richard C. Allen and Rosemary Moore, eds., *The Quakers, 1656–1723: The Evolution of an Alternative Community* (University Park: Penn State University Press, 2018).

49. Penn's view of George Fox's role and the significance of Quakers to Christianity was best summarized in his "Brief Account of the Rise and Progress of the People called Quakers," written as a preface to Fox's *Journal*. To Penn's mind, Fox's preaching, although "broken" and "uncouth," showed direct inspiration from God. In prayer, he had "the most Awful, Living, Reverent Frame I ever Felt or Beheld." *WWP*, 1:881, 883.

50. *DSP*, 9:327, 6:89.

51. *PWP*, 2:597, 3:432. Gulielma Penn's five surviving letters show that she was well educated and had better penmanship and spelling than most Quaker women. Hirsch, "Tale of Two Wives," 434–38; Thomas Ellwood, *The History of the Life of Thomas Ellwood* [. . .] (London: J. Sowle, 1714), 216. John Aubrey described her as "generous, wise, Humble, plaine, and generally beloved." *Aubrey's Brief Lives*, edited by Oliver Lawson Dicks (London: Secker and Warburg, 1949), 235. Her age at marriage was twenty-six, slightly older than most women; life expectancy in this period was thirty years, and 80 percent of babies did not survive their first year. Hoppit, *Land of Liberty*, 56–57.

52. *PWP*, 3:83–84.

53. *PWP*, 1:171–80, 5:119–23; Andrew R. Murphy, *Liberty, Conscience, and Toleration: The Political Thought of William Penn* (New York: Oxford University Press, 2016), 56–83; Horle, *Quakers and the English Legal System*, 116–18, 120–25.

54. Owen restricted liberty of conscience to those who accepted the rule of reason. Neither Quakers nor Roman Catholics qualified. John Owen, "Two Questions Concerning the Power of the Supreme Magistrate" (1659) and "A Brief Vindication of the Nonconformists from the Charge of Schism," both in *The Works of John Owen* (London: R. Baynes, 1826), 21 vols., 13:645–50, 481, 493. During the Restoration, Owen advocated toleration as a natural right and insisted that the magistrate had no power to restrict conscience or to demand subscription to articles of religion, but he also insisted that the supreme magistrate was to

further "true religion and right worship of God" in ways approved by God. W. K. Jordan, *The Development of Religious Toleration in England from the Convention of the Long Parliament to the Restoration, 1640–1660* (Cambridge: Harvard University Press, 1932), 430–34.

55. For letters to Fenwick and the "Concessions and Agreements of the Proprietors, Freeholders, and Inhabitants of the Province of New Jersey in America," see *PWP*, 1:383–416.

56. *PWP*, 1:384–410; Hoppit, *Land of Liberty*, 472. After the Glorious Revolution, England extended by fifty the number of crimes punishable by death, but "fewer people were actually hanged" (Hoppit, 481).

57. Jean Soderlund, *Lenape Country: Delaware Society Before William Penn* (Philadelphia: University of Pennsylvania Press, 2014).

58. Aubrey's *Brief Lives* mentions the debt owed to the admiral, which he probably learned from William Penn, with whom he mentions having conversations.

59. Geiter, "Restoration Crisis."

60. When Penn began the process, Spencer was a chief minister, but he lost favor before 1681 by favoring exclusion. *PWP*, 2:416–17, 3:52. Other prominent ministers who supported Penn were the Earl of Rochester, the Earl of Clarendon, and Sidney Godolphin. Penn managed throughout his life to retain the support of prominent politicians, even including Whigs and then Tories during the reign of Queen Anne.

61. Soderlund's *Penn and the Founding of Pennsylvania* reprints the original sources pertaining to Penn's obtaining a charter and the early settlers of Pennsylvania. Albert Cook Myers, ed., *Narratives of Early Pennsylvania, West New Jersey, and Delaware, 1630–1707* (New York: Scribner's, 1912), 177–460, includes Penn's publications during this time.

62. "A Summons or Call to Christendom" (1678), *WWP*, 1:187–98, and "To the Children of Light in This Generation" (1677), *WWP*, 1:223–25. Apocalyptic warnings had been a feature of Penn's writings since his convincement, and he could threaten judgment at almost the same time he made reasoned appeals to Parliament.

63. See chapter 8.

64. Gail McKnight Beckman, comp., *The Statutes at Large of Pennsylvania in the Time of William Penn*, vol. 1, *1680–1700* (New York: Vantage Press, 1976), 118; *PWP*, 2:213.

65. Soderlund, *Penn and the Founding of Pennsylvania*, 51–141; *PWP*, vol. 2 (1680–84).

66. Beckman, *Statutes at Large of Pennsylvania*, 117–18. On the Quaker origins of Penn's political thought, see Jane E. Calvert, *Quaker Constitutionalism and the Political Thought of John Dickinson* (Cambridge: Cambridge University Press, 2008), 77–99. Murphy, *Liberty, Conscience, and Toleration*, 125–57, stresses the relationship between political theory and practice in founding Pennsylvania.

67. Penn initially suggested four hundred and then three hundred men for the General Assembly, and finally proposed two hundred. Richard Ryerson has argued that by creating two small chambers, Penn created a distinction between authorities of similar status and thereby fostered the divisions that made Pennsylvania difficult to govern. Ryerson, "William Penn's Gentry Commonwealth: An Interpretation of the Constitutional History of Early Pennsylvania," *Pennsylvania History* 61 (1994): 393–428.

68. The best guide to the workings of the General Assembly is in Craig W. Horle, Marianne S. Wokeck, Jeffrey L. Scheib, David Haugaard, Joy Wiltenburg, Joseph S. Foster, and Rosalind J. Beiler, eds., *Lawmaking and Legislators in Pennsylvania: A Biographical Dictionary*, vol. 1, *1682–1709* (Philadelphia: University of Pennsylvania Press, 1991), 11–32.

69. *PWP*, 2:209.

70. William M. Offutt Jr. *Of "Good Laws" and "Good Men": Law and Society in the Delaware Valley, 1680–1710* (Urbana: University of Illinois Press, 1995), 261–65.

71. *PWP*, 2:304.

72. *PWP*, 2:435, 473.

73. "Letter from William Penn to the Committee of the Free Society of Traders," in Myers, *Narratives of Early Pennsylvania*, 230–37, 276. The map of Pennsylvania issued by Penn showed no Indian towns and assumed the king's right to give "vacant" lands. Emily Mann, "Beyond the Bounds: Exploitation and Empire in the First Map of Pennsylvania," in Murphy and Smolenski, *Worlds of William Penn*, 79–80.

74. Francis Jennings, "Brother Miquon: Good Lord!," in Dunn and Dunn, *World of William Penn*, 195–202.

75. *PWP*, 2:579–75.

76. *PWP*, 2:569.

77. *PWP*, 2:381–89.

78. *PWP*, 2:528.

79. James "loved him [Penn] as a singular [man] . . . and imparted to him many of his Secrets and Counsels"; the two men conferred privately "for many hours." The king said that "Penn talk'd Ingenously and he heard him willingly." Gerald Croese, *The General History of the Quakers* [. . .] (London: John Dunton, 1696), 106–7.

80. *PWP*, 3:77–80.

81. Scott Sowerby, *Making Toleration: The Repealers and the Glorious Revolution* (Cambridge: Harvard University Press, 2013), 34–35, 40–43.

82. See Penn's *Good Advice to the Church of England, Roman Catholic, and Protestant Dissenter* [. . .] (London: Andrew Sowle, 1687), which went through four printings, and *Mr. Penn's Advice in the Choice of Parliament-Men* [. . .] (London, 1688).

83. Geoffrey S. Holmes, *The Making of a Great Power: Late Stuart and Early Georgian Britain, 1660–1722* (London: Longman, 1993), 176–91.

84. Contrast *PWP*, 3:663–66, with Mary Geiger, "William Penn and Jacobitism: A Smoking Gun?" *Historical Research* 73, no. 181 (2000): 213–18. My conclusion is that it is impossible to prove that Penn plotted James's return but that he remained sympathetic to the exiled king. For a similar case, see Stephen Saunders Webb, *Lord Churchill's Coup: The Anglo-American Empire and the Glorious Revolution Reconsidered* (New York: Knopf, 1995), 146–48, 165–68, 245.

85. John Smolenski, *Friends and Strangers: The Making of a Creole Culture in Colonial Pennsylvania* (Philadelphia: University of Pennsylvania Press, 2010), part 2, is the most recent history of the colony, but still useful are Edwin B. Bronner, *William Penn's "Holy Experiment": The Founding of Pennsylvania, 1681–1701* (Philadelphia: Temple University Press, 1962); and Gary B. Nash, *Quakers and Politics: Pennsylvania, 1681–1726* (Princeton: Princeton University Press, 1968).

86. *PWP*, 3:44.

87. *PWP*, 3:50, 199.

88. *PWP*, 3:27, 74, 129.

89. *PWP*, 2:243, 3:131.

90. J. William Frost, "Adjusting to New Conditions in Britain and America, 1690–1700," in Allen and Moore, *Quakers, 1656–1723*, 200–213. The best theological account is Madeleine Ward, *The Christian Quaker: George Keith and the Keithian Controversy* (Leiden: Brill, 2019).

91. *PWP*, 3:328.

92. *PWP*, 3:411–13, 422–36. Prominent London Friends did journey to Bristol for the marriage of George Fox and Margaret Fell.

93. Hirsch, "Tale of Two Wives," 129; *PWP*, 4:245.

94. Mary Geiter, "Affirmation, Assassination, and Association: The Quakers, Parliament, and the Court in 1696," *Parliamentary History* 16, no. 3 (1997): 271–88; J. W. Frost, "The Affirmation Controversy and Religious Liberty," in Dunn and Dunn, *World of William Penn*, 322–23.

95. *PWP*, 3:541–42.

96. Murphy, *Penn: A Life*, 235–41, 243–45.

97. Horle et al., *Lawmaking and Legislatures in Pennsylvania*, 1:490–500.

98. *PWP*, 3:608–10, 614. For an inventory of goods and a drawing of Pennsbury, see 4:36, 132–35.

99. *PWP*, 3:583–87, 600–601, 618–19, 4:49–55.

100. *PWP*, 4:42–46.

101. *PWP*, 4:91, 98, 104–11.

102. Richard S. Dunn, "Penny Wise and Pound Foolish: Penn as a Businessman," in Dunn and Dunn, *World of William Penn*, 37–54.

103. William Jr. was left his mother's Irish and English lands; Hannah and her children received Pennsylvania. With the aid of trustees, Hannah managed Pennsylvania after her husband's stroke and death, and the proprietorship went to their sons, none of whom remained Friends.

104. *PWP*, 1:348.

105. Hannah Penn began managing his affairs and, with the assistance of trustees after his death, paid off the mortgage on Pennsylvania by 1726. Alison Hirsch, "'Instructions from a Woman': Hannah Penn and the Pennsylvania Proprietorship" (PhD diss., Columbia University, 1991), 10.

106. Besse, "To the Reader," *WWP*, vol. 1, preface; Peare, *Penn: A Biography*, 414.

CHAPTER 2

1. *PWP*, 1:460–61, 598. Penn referred to himself (and also to Princess Elizabeth) as a person of "quality." William I. Hull, *William Penn and the Dutch Quaker Migration to Pennsylvania* (Swarthmore: Swarthmore College, 1935), 153. With respect to the title of this chapter, Quakers normally used the term "convinced" rather than converted, because it was a process rather than a singular dramatic event. Penn used both terms.

2. *WWP*, 1:2; "Fragments of an Apology for Himself," *Memoirs of the Historical Society of Pennsylvania* 3 (1836): 236–42.

3. *PWP*, 1:444. The visit to the princess occupied several days and included long periods of worship. One day Penn preached to the servants while Barclay spoke with the princess. The company had divided so that Fox was not present then. Note that Penn and Barclay dined with the princess, but when Fox visited Cromwell, he was invited to dine with the servants.

4. "To the Princess and Countess of Herford," *WWP*, 1:186.

5. Penn and Burnet both supported toleration for dissenters and Catholics but did not wish to allow them any political offices, as security against a king of a different religion. When Penn argued that King James would use the dispensing power but also wanted a law that would guarantee freedom of religion forever, Burnet replied that the recently voided Edict of Nantes had been supposed to last "forever." Gilbert Burnet, *History of His Own Time* (Oxford: Clarendon Press, 1823) 3:128–33. Jonathan Swift described Burnet as "the worst qualified for an historian that I ever met." *Gulliver's Travels*, 344.

6. Against Burnet's opinion of Penn are comments from King James II, the Duke of Buckingham, the Earl of Romney, and Jonathan Swift, all of them welcoming Penn's company and conversation. MPWP, reel 5, documents 626, 635, 838.

7. *PWP*, 1:459.

8. It should be remembered that, for Friends, silence is a theological term and that a "silent meeting" could include extensive preaching.

9. Pepys described young William as playing cards, going to the theater, dancing, and attending fireworks displays. *DSP*, 2:236, 239–41, 3:1, 5, 5:205–57, 6:213.

10. *DSP*, 2:143, 6:78, 8:166, 9:166, 194.

11. *DSP*, 3:99–100, 126, 132, 6:230, 8:595. Charles II named Sir William a commissioner because of his talent and with the support of the Duke of York, but Pepys was there because of a wealthy noble relative, the Earl of Sandwich. Pepys, whether

because of jealousy or greed, soon began listing Sir William's bad characteristics. His discussion of Admiral Penn's and his family's character traits must thus be read with caution.

12. "An Account of the Convincement of William Penn," *Journal of the Friends' Historical Society* 32 (1935): 22. Historians frequently call this the Harvey manuscript, after the name of the man who told the story.

13. Melvin B. Endy Jr., *William Penn and Early Quakerism* (Princeton: Princeton University Press, 1973), 97, cites John Oldmixon, *The British Empire in North America* [. . .] (London: J. Nicholson, 1708), 296, and R. W. Blencowe, *Diary of the Times of Charles the Second* [. . .] (London: Henry Colburn, 1843), 2 vols., 1:xxxviii–xxxix, as early sources saying that Penn sought out Loe at Cork, Ireland.

14. *PWP*, 1:264–65, 303; *WWP*, 2:198; *DSP*, 2:206, 3:17. Two sources suggest that Penn may have later dated his conversion to his hearing Loe as a child. Describing Penn's confrontation with his father, the Harvey manuscript says, "how he observed his Father in tears at that time and that he believe[d] him to be convinced of the truth of ye Doctrine of ye Quakers *as well as himself* only ye Grandure of ye World was to Great for him to Give up." "Convincement of William Penn," 24 (emphasis added). Samuel Pepys called Penn's conversion in Ireland "sad news," adding that young Penn "is Quaker *again*, or some melancholy thing, that he cares for no company." *DSP*, 8:595 (emphasis added). At least the Pepys account occurred at the time of Penn's conversion.

15. *PWP*, 1:303, 460, 476.

16. *Aubrey's Brief Lives*, lxxxiv, 234. Aubrey's is the first account of the distinction between Penn's spiritual awakenings and his later convincement in Ireland after hearing Loe. Aubrey must have known Penn well because Penn gifted him six hundred acres in Pennsylvania. Aubrey's account was not published before those of Besse and Harvey. *WWP*, 2:394–95.

17. *PWP*, 1:437. The closest to a contemporary account is that of George Bishop, who, on November 30, 1667, justified Penn's convincement to the admiral: "The Lord hath Visited this thy Son, to give him the true sence and Conviction of that, wch all along since his Childhood, he had sought to Understand. . . . He is come to know that wch gives to Escape the Pollution of the World." *PWP*, 1:54.

18. Besse, "Introduction," *WWP*, 1:2.

19. "Convincement of William Penn," 22–26. William I. Hull notes that this manuscript claims that Penn was expelled from Oxford for writing and publishing a pamphlet or for leading a riot against wearing the surplice. There is no contemporary evidence for either of these stories. Hull, *Penn: A Topical Biography*, 77.

20. In 1658 Sarah Blackbarrow described several childhood experiences of God that resemble those of the young Penn. Mary Garman, Judith Applegate, Margaret Benefiel, and Dortha Meredith, eds., *Hidden in Plain Sight: Quaker Women's Writings, 1650–1700* (Wallingford, PA: Pendle Hill Publications, 1996), 49–50.

21. "Convincement of William Penn," 23. In a religious context, crying was socially acceptable, but even there it was expected to be kept under control. It was observed to be more common among Puritans and sectarians than among gentlemen. Bernard Capp, "'Jesus Wept' but Did the Englishman? Masculinity and Emotion in Early Modern England," *Past and Present* 224, no. 1 (2014): 87–88.

22. Among gentlemen, weeping could be seen as a sign of compassion and morality, but it was frowned upon as unmanly for those who believed in Stoicism and humanist civility. Capp, "'Jesus Wept,'" 81.

23. "Quakers lay down, as a main fundamental in religion, That God, through Christ, hath placed a Principle in every man, to inform him of his *Duty*, and to

enable him to do it, and that those who live up to this Principle, are the people of God, those that live." "Primitive Christianity Revived" (1696), *WWP*, 2:855. Penn calls this an "ancient and most general" "standing Testimony."

24. Mal. 3:2. The closest Penn came to this emphasis was in the preface to the 1682 edition of *NCNC*, where he wrote, "as one knowing the Terrors of the Lord."

25. In *DSP*, 5:270, Pepys mentioned a romance in Ireland and worried that young William would seduce his wife. It may be that Pepys was projecting his own constant attempts at seduction onto the young Penn. The admiral thought that a romance in Ireland might be behind his son's delay in coming home. In *Penn: A Life*, 48, Andrew Murphy discusses a charge made fifteen years later that Penn had carried on an affair with a married woman. Penn's later assertion that he had always been outwardly moral before his conversion makes it unlikely that there was any serious early romantic attachment.

26. John Tomkins, comp., *Piety Promoted in a Collection of Dying Sayings of Many of the People Called Quakers*, 3rd ed. (London: T. Sowle, 1723), 86; *PWP*, 1:68–71.

27. *WWP*, 1:3–4; *PWP*, 1:272.

28. See Kenneth Carroll, "Thomas Loe, Friend of William Penn and Apostle to Ireland," in *Seeking the Light: Essays in Quaker History*, edited by John M. Moore and J. W. Frost (Wallingford, PA: Pendle Hill Publications and Friends Historical Association, 1986), 61–72.

29. *PWP*, 1:264–65.

30. "The Guide Mistaken" (1668), *WWP*, 2:3. Mornay DuPlessy was a founder of the Protestant Academy in Saumur and a defender of religious toleration in France, where Penn studied; like Hugo Grotius, he presented rationalist defenses of Christianity. Penn also often cited the early Christian theologians Origen and Tertullian. On Amyraldus (Amyraut)'s influence on Penn,

see Frost, "William Penn, Quaker Humanist," 177–82.

31. Endy, *William Penn and Early Quakerism*, 99.

32. *Christian Quaker and His Divine Testimony*, in *WWP*, 1:564. Penn mentioned Amyraldus once and the Puritan John Owen three times, and he quoted and praised Blondel in his "General Discourse of the General Rule of Faith and Practice." *WWP*, 1:592, 600, 603, 605; *PWP*, 1:272.

33. Stephen W. Angell, "William Penn's Debts to John Owen and Moses Amyraut on Questions of Truth, Grace, and Religious Toleration," *Quaker Studies* 16, no. 2 (2012): 157–73. Penn referred to Owen as a leader of the Independents. Given his opinion of that party, this was at best a qualified endorsement.

34. *PWP*, 1:199.

35. *PWP*, 1:60–61.

36. We know from Pepys that Admiral Penn occasionally got drunk, and it is hard to imagine a battle-hardened seventeenth-century sailor who did not swear.

37. For example, "flee fornication"; "let us walk honestly as in the day, not in rioting and drunkenness, not in Chambring & Wantonness"; "neither filthiness, nor foolish talking." *PWP*, 1:67.

38. *PWP*, 1:476. See also 1:264, 303, 460; *WWP*, 1:198.

39. *PWP*, 1:263.

40. *WWP*, 1:574, 873, 2:38, 326, 329. Penn used many metaphors to describe the states of becoming a Christian and insisted that theological distinctions between different states were of little use.

41. "A Summons or Call to Christendom" (1677), *WWP*, 1:192–93, 188.

42. "Tender Counsel and Advice" (n.d.), *WWP*, 1:206.

43. "To those Professors of Christianity" (n.d.), *WWP*, 1:212.

44. "Guide Mistaken," *WWP*, 2:20–21.

45. Not until the fall of James II would Penn experience the disillusioning effect that the Puritans and many Quakers felt

after the fall of the Commonwealth and the Restoration.

46. The effect of receiving Christ was "an inward Force and Ability to do whatever he requires; Strength to mortifie their Lusts, Control their Affections, resist Evil Motions, deny themselves, and overcome the World in its most inticing Appearances." *NCNC* (1682), in *WWP*, 1:280.

47. See chapter 7.

48. Alexandra Shepard, *Meanings of Manhood in Early Modern England* (Oxford: Oxford University Press, 2006), 30, 37–38; Isabel Karremann, "Augustan Manliness and Its Anxieties: Shaftesbury and Swift," in *Constructions of Masculinity in British Literature from the Middle Ages to the Present*, ed. Stefan Horlacher (New York: Palgrave Macmillan, 2011), 109–11. Robert Barclay, like Penn, a gentleman, provided no details of his conversion except that it had occurred in a meeting for worship.

49. See William James, *The Varieties of Religious Experience* (New York: New American Library, 1958), chap. 16. Penn's religious experiences conform to James's very Protestant definitions of ineffability, noetic quality, transiency, and passivity.

50. "Primitive Christianity Revived," *WWP*, 2:864 (sec. 6).

CHAPTER 3

1. For analysis of the three disputes, see Clare J. L. Martin, "Controversy and Division in Post-Restoration Quakerism: The Hat, Wilkinson-Story, and Keithian Controversies [. . .]" (PhD diss., Open University, 2003). For Penn's role in the Keithian controversy, see chapter 4.

2. If not before convincement then soon thereafter, Penn began to read Quaker authors, and in 1672 he defended passages from George Fox, James Nayler, William Smith, Isaac Penington, William Dewsbury, James Parnel, Edward Burrough, Francis Howgill, William Smith, Thomas Story, George Fox the Younger, Richard Farnsworth, and George Whitehead. "Quakerism a New Nick Name for Old Christianity," *WWP*, 1:258.

3. *PWP*, 1:51–53.

4. *PWP*, 1:54–55. Bishop, like the young Penn, mixed appeals to reason and nature with warnings of the coming day of judgment. George Bishop, *A Few Words in Season* [. . .] (London: Robert Wilson, 1660), 4, and *The Warnings of the Lord to the King of England and His Parliament* [. . .] (London, 1667), 7.

5. *WWP*, 1:3–4.

6. *PWP*, 1:72–80, 5:94–95.

7. Penn and his wife, Gulielma, met with Fox and his wife upon Fox's return from North America; the two couples journeyed to Penn's house. It is tempting to speculate that discussions about flourishing Quaker meetings there prompted Penn's later interest in colonization, but there is no evidence either way. See Edwin B. Bronner, "George Fox and William Penn: Unlikely Yokefellows and Friends," *Journal of the Friends' Historical Society* 56, no. 2 (1991); Melvin B. Endy Jr., "George Fox and William Penn: Their Relationship and Their Roles Within the Quaker Movement," in *George Fox's Legacy: Friends for 350 Years*, edited by Charles L. Cherry, Caroline L. Cherry, and J. William Frost (Haverford: Friends Historical Association, 2006), 1–39.

8. *PWP*, 1:208.

9. Rosemary Moore, "Gospel Order: The Development of Quaker Organization," in Allen and Moore, *Quakers, 1656–1723*, 54–75.

10. *PWP*, 1:249–59. As to the latter, in *First Among Friends*, H. Larry Ingle argues that the dispute originated with George Rogers and Bristol Friends, not with Wilkinson and Story, who were obscure northern England ministers (348n11).

11. *Judas and the Jews, Combined Against Christ and his Followers* (n.p., 1673), 11, 13, 18.

12. *WWP*, 2:208. In this, Penn cited Fox's *True Honour Amongst the Jewes*.

13. Kenneth Carroll, *John Perrot: Early Quaker Schismatic* (London: Friends Historical Society, 1971); Carla Gardina Pestana, "The Conventionality of the Notorious John Perrot," in *Early Quakers and Their Theological Thought, 1647–1723*, edited by Stephen W. Angell and Pink Dandelion (Cambridge: Cambridge University Press, 2015), 173–89; William Charles Braithwaite, *The Second Period of Quakerism*, 2nd ed., edited by Henry Cadbury (Cambridge: Cambridge University Press, 1961), 228–49.

14. The titles of the tracts by Penn are *The Spirit of Alexander the Copper-Smith Justly Rebuked: or An Answer to a late Pamphlet, Intituled The Spirit of the Hat, or the Government of the Quakers* (n.p., 1673); *A Brief Examination, and the State of Liberty Spiritual, both with Respect to Persons in their Private Capacity, and in their Church-Society & Communion* (London: Andrew Sowle, 1681); *Just Measures, in an Epistle of Peace and Love, to such Professors of Truth, as are under any Dissatisfaction, about the present Order practis'd in the Church of Christ* (London: Northcott, 1692).

15. Penn's "Discourse of the General rule of Faith and Practice" (1673) is a defense of the authority of the Inward Light and is addressed to opponents of Friends. *WWP*, 1:550–608.

16. Ingle, *First Among Friends*, 197–206, 259–60.

17. "For old time I have broken thy yoke, and burst thy bands; and thou saidst, I will not transgress; when upon every high hill and under every green tree thou wanderest, playing the harlot." Jer. 2:20 (on the apostacy of Israel).

18. *PWP*, 1:251.

19. "Ceremonies Typical," or typology, meant the prefiguring of a Christian custom by an earlier Jewish one: for example, baptism was a type of circumcision. Mystical meant cloudy or unclear, like a mist, and referred to the uncertain meaning of a prophecy.

20. *PWP*, 1:251–52.

21. *PWP*, 1:253.

22. *PWP*, 1:254–55.

23. William Mucklow, *The Spirit of the Hat, or the Government of the Quakers Among Themselves, As it hath been Exercised of late years by George Fox, and other Leading-Men, in their Monday, or Second dayes Meeting at Devonshire-House, brought to Light in a Bemoaning Letter of a Certain ingenious Quaker to another his Friend; Wherein their Tyrannical and Persecuting Practises are detected and reargued* (London: F. Smith, 1673), 20.

24. Mucklow, *Spirit of the Hat*, 38.

25. *Alexander the Copper-Smith*, 4.

26. *Alexander the Copper-Smith*, 8–9, 13; *Judas and the Jews*, 11–12, 15–16, 19.

27. Wilkinson and Story claimed liberty of conscience, accused Fox of innovations, disliked the assertion of spiritual power by London ministers, and insisted that they should not be forced to engage in outward customs for which they had received no inward revelation. They were willing for women to preach and have separate meetings to deal with women's issues, but not to have men appear before the women's meeting seeking approval for marriages, at least not in country meetings. William Rogers, *The Christian-Quaker Distinguished from the Apostate & Innovator in Five Parts* (London, 1680), part 1, 58–66; part 3, 8, 15; part 4, 11–12, 20–21.

28. *PWP*, 1:327–32, 520–32, 556; Braithwaite, *Second Period of Quakerism*, 290–323, 360–66, 469–82.

29. William Rogers's *Christian-Quaker Distinguished* comprises five tracts totaling more than five hundred pages, includes the essential documents of the schism, and attacks Barclay's *Anarchy* from the dissenters' perspective. Rogers does not mention Penn. Penn, when writing against opponents, normally referred to them by name and analyzed their errors paragraph by

paragraph. Penn's irenic style here is far removed from his normal way of responding to apostate Quakers. Hugh Barbour, "The Young Controversialist," in Dunn and Dunn, *World of William Penn*, 28.

30. *Brief Examination*, preface, 1–2, 11. Penn wrote this tract in November 1681, and it was submitted to the MMM and published before March. The main Quaker migration to Pennsylvania began in the spring of 1682. Only once did Penn mention the issues involved in the separation, in a short section that follows a defense of the authority and unity of the meeting. William Rogers responded with *The Eighth Part of the Christian Quaker the Apostate* (1682), attacking Penn's 1679 *Address to Protestants upon the Present Conjuncture* [. . .] (London: Andrew Sowle, 1679), without saying anything new.

31. *Brief Examination*, 4–5.
32. *Judas and the Jews*, 17.
33. *Brief Examination*, 5.
34. *Brief Examination*, 5, 10.
35. *Brief Examination*, 11.
36. *Brief Examination*, 2, 7.
37. *Just Measures*, 1, 2.
38. *Just Measures*, 4–5, 10–11.
39. *Just Measures*, 8–9, 12. Men and women alike took care of the poor, aged, sick, orphans, marriages, and burials.
40. *Just Measures*, 1–2.
41. *Christian Quaker and His Divine Testimony*, 155–56, 109.
42. *PWP*, 1:85.
43. "Guide Mistaken," *WWP*, 2:42.

CHAPTER 4

1. Chapter 7 contains an analysis of all extant messages by Penn during worship.
2. See Penn's preface to *The Journal of George Fox*, edited by John L. Nickalls (London: London Yearly Meeting, 1975), xlii–xlviii.
3. LYM, minutes, 23/3/1702, 23.
4. LYM, minutes, 12/4/1677, 52–55.
5. It is printed as the frontispiece of Arnold Lloyd's *Quaker Social History, 1669–1738* (New York: Longmans, Green, 1950), with no indication that it is satire.
6. For example, Hookes notes that a letter from George Fox to William Penn was "read and the chief heads of it debated." MFS, minutes, 24/5/1679, 113. The topic could have been the Wilkinson-Story controversy, lobbying for Parliament, or dealing with the king.
7. Russell Mortimer, ed., *Men's Meeting of the Society of Friends of Bristol, 1686–1704* (Bristol: Bristol Record Society, 1977), 92–93, 118, 127; Beatrice Saxon Snell, ed., *The Minute Book of the Monthly Meeting of the Society of Friends for the Upperside of Buckinghamshire, 1669–1690* (High Wycombe: Hague and Gill, 1937). The sermons discussed in chapter 7 all took place in London, when Penn's primary residence was in Sussex.
8. Dunn, "Personality of William Penn," 11; Penn, "The Blessed End of Gulielma Maria Penn and Springet [*sic*: printer's error] Penn," *WWP*, 1:231.
9. LYM, minutes, 29/3/1672, 3; 27/3/1675, 18–20; 17/3/1676, 33–34. Women attended the worship sessions of LYM, but only men served as delegates and made all decisions.
10. Craig W. Horle, "Changing Quaker Attitudes Toward Legal Defense: The George Fox Case, 1673–76, and the Creation of Meeting for Sufferings," in Moore and Frost, *Seeking the Light*, 17–40.
11. MMM, minutes, 31/3/1675, 7; 2/2/1684, 79.
12. MFS, minutes, 15/9/1677, 39; 4/12/1680, 7; 22/11/1680, 12. The MFS met so often that few people were present at every meeting and there is no mention of who took the minutes. In the minutes of the 22/11/1680 meeting, the order of names was Fox, Penn, Mead, and Whitehead; Penn is in the middle rank on 29/2/1680, 154; and first on 9/2/1680; but on 9/2/1681, 79, Fox and Whitehead are first and Penn is in the second column. Whitehead is

above Fox on 18/9/1681, 72; Penn is in second row on 17/1/1681/82, 100.

13. MMM, minutes, 10/6/1699, 299; 4/1/1699, 326; 2/1/1701/2, 65.

14. Penn to John Tillotson, January 29, 1686, *PWP*, 3:78–80; Henry Sydney to Penn, January 19, 1680/81, MPWP, reel 5, document 635; Duke of Buckingham to Penn, December 4, 1686, MPWP, reel 5, document 626.

15. Seeking advice on whether Friends would be affected by a bill prohibiting Roman Catholics from sitting in Parliament, MFS told William Mead and Jobe Boulton to "confer with Penn about it and give an account to Friends next meeting." MFS, minutes, 21/9/1678, 23; 8/1/1678/79, 88.

16. MFS, minutes, 23/3/1678, 55; 6/4/1678, 61; 20/1/1679, 20; MMM, minutes, 18/8/1675, 8–9; 20/1/1679, 20.

17. MFS, minutes, 23/3/1678, 55; 6/4/1678, 61; 20/1/1679, 20.

18. *PWP*, 3:73, 83–84; MFS, minutes, 17/11/1677, 43–44; 7/1/1677, 49; 16/3/1678; 30/3/1678, 61; 17/4/1680, 167; 29/2/1684; 20/3/1681; 4/10/1685. The fine would have been £20 per month for missing church.

19. *PWP*, 3:135–37; MFS, minutes, 14/2/1687, 23.

20. Sowerby, *Making Toleration*, 40–44, 143–44; *PWP*, 3:175–77.

21. MFS, minutes, 20/11/1684, 20/2/1686, 10/4/1686, 17/4/1687, 11/9/1687, 13/2/1687.

22. LYM, minutes, 5/8/1687, 178.

23. MFS, minutes, 30/1/1687/88, 169; 13/2/1688, 173.

24. LYM, minutes, 6/4/1688, 199.

25. LYM, minutes, 6/4/1688, 201.

26. LYM, minutes, 20/3/1689, 219–20.

27. LYM, minutes, 7/4/1694, 31–57. For the most complete theological study, see Ward, *Christian Quaker: George Keith*.

28. Penn to Phineas Pemberton, February 8, 1687, MPWP, reel 5, document 701; *PWP*, 3:56; MMM, minutes, 20/1/1693, 23; 19/11/1693, 45; 29/11/1693, 46; 9/2/1694, 51–52; 19/1/1694, 52. In 1679, Algernon Sidney, a man of strong opinions, called Mead "niggling, shifting, cavilling, and indeed [guilty of] downright lying and knavery" and of "casting unjust reproaches on Will. Penn." Jonathan Scott, *Algernon Sidney and the Restoration Crisis, 1677–1683* (Cambridge: Cambridge University Press, 2002), 131.

29. LYM, minutes, 13/3/1694, 39–40, 43–44.

30. LYM, minutes, 13/3/1694, 85, 91.

31. MFS, minutes, 2/17/1696, 206. Even before the Peers insisted on adding the "witness" phrase, which the MFS said was an "addition of some words somewhat immaterial," Friends began gathering materials for a pamphlet, intended for members only, to justify accepting a compromise in the wording of the oath.

32. Frost, "Affirmation Controversy and Religious Liberty," 303–22.

33. *A Treatise of Oaths* [. . .] (London: Andrew Sowle, 1675), *WWP*, 1:614–17; "To the Commons of England" (1678), *WWP*, 1:117.

34. "To the Commons of England," *WWP*, 1:117. "We shall engage, by God's assistance, to lead peaceable, just, and industrious Lives." *WWP*, 1:464.

35. "The New Athenians," *WWP*, 2:794–95.

36. "So help me God" meant not only "help me tell the truth" but also that God should in the future deal with one according to one's truthfulness.

37. *An Epistle from the Meeting for Sufferings*, Ordered/17/ 2nd month/1696, MFS, minutes, 17/2/1696, 205.

38. *PWP*, 3:450–51; MPWP, reel 7, p. 170. The MFS drew up its epistle, sent it to the MMM, and wished it printed as fast as possible in early May. Penn's letter was read without comment. MFS, minutes, 8/4/1696; 3/1/1695, 215, and 8/3/1696, 220, 215, 220.

39. LYM, minutes, 4/4/1696. Friends "will walk Charitably and tenderly towards one another, and not Judge nor think

hardly one of another for either using or not using the liberty granted."

40. MMM, minutes, 30/9/1696, 149–54.

41. MMM, minutes, 8/5/1700, 10/1/1700, 17. In his autobiography, Ellwood said there was already a sufficient answer to Keith, but that is not what he told the MMM.

42. *WWP*, 1:589. Endy, in *William Penn and Early Quakerism*, summarizes Penn's theology: "On most issues, he had his more or less orthodox moments" (98).

43. MMM, minutes, 10/5/1699, 291; 28/5/1701, 35; 1/1/1702/3, 106.

44. MMM, minutes, 4/1/702, 71–72; 4/21/1702, 74.

45. James Jenkins, *Records and Recollections of James Jenkins*, edited by J. W. Frost (New York: Edwin Mellen Press, 1984), 292.

46. MMM warned women Friends not to talk too long when "several publick & serviceable men friends are present and are by them prevented in their service." MMM, minutes, 1/7/1700, 10.

47. For essays describing the transformation of Quakerism in this period, see Allen and Moore, *Quakers, 1656–1723*.

CHAPTER 5

1. In 1993, President Bill Clinton proclaimed January 16 National Religious Freedom Day in honor of the Virginia Statute for Religious Freedom, and appreciation of it is included in public school curricula.

2. Alexandra Walsham, *Charitable Hatred: Tolerance and Intolerance in England, 1500–1700* (Manchester: Manchester University Press, 2006), 7–13, 80–91, 117, 127, 135, 231, 236, 257–67, 309.

3. A. H. Woolrych, "The Good Old Cause and the Protectorate," *Cambridge Historical Journal* 8, no. 2 (1957): 133–61; George Bishop, *Warning of the Lord to Men of this Generation* [. . .] (London: M. Innis, 1659), 12. Bishop's tract contains eight epistles written over several years by Bishop to Oliver Cromwell, Richard Cromwell, and the army.

4. In *Meme Tekel, or the Council of Officers of the Army* [. . .] (London: Thomas Brewster, 1659), 9, 14–16, Bishop compares the army's declarations of 1648–49 with its more recent demands. See Maryann S. Feola, *George Bishop: Seventeenth-Century Soldier Turned Quaker* (York: Sessions, 1996), 49–50.

5. The earliest public reference seeking religious freedom for all is in George Bishop, *Jesus Christ, the same to day, as Yesterday* [. . .] (London: Giles Calvert, 1655): "Nor do we deny the same liberty to others which we ought to have" (4). The Burrough tract of 1659 is reprinted in Barry Reay, "The Quakers and 1659: Two Newly Discovered Broadsides by Edward Burrough," *Journal of the Friends' Historical Society* 54, no. 2 (1977): 107. It could be argued that because Friends insisted from the beginning that no legislation address religion, they had implicitly extended liberty of conscience to all.

6. William Charles Braithwaite, *The Beginnings of Quakerism*, 2nd ed. (Cambridge: Cambridge University Press, 1962), 156, 179, 435, 438.

7. Samuel Fisher, *The Scorned Quakers True and Honest Account . . . before the Protector and Parliament* [. . .] (1652), in *The Testimony of Truth Exalted, by the Collected Labours of the Worthy Man . . . Samuel Fisher* (n.p., 1679), 3–9, Digital Quaker Collection, Earlham School of Religion, Richmond, IN, http://dqc.esr.earlham.edu.

8. *PWP*, 1:533–41.

9. George Fox, *This for each Parliament-Man That they May see the Wisdom By Which All Things were Created with It, To Order All Things to His Glory* [. . .] (London: Thomas Simmons, 1656); James Nayler, "A Warning to the Rulers, in the Year 1659, wherein a Just Liberty of Conscience is Pleaded," in *The Works of James Nayler*, 4 vols. (Farmington, ME: Quaker Heritage

Press, n.d.), 4:244, available online at http://www.qhpress.org/texts/nayler/index.html. See also Edward Burrough, *Antichrist's Government Justly Detected of Unrighteousness, Injustice, Unreasonableness, Oppression, and Cruelty* (London: Wilson, 1661); Isaac Penington, "Concerning Persecution [. . .]," in *The Works of the Long Mournful and Sorely Distressed Isaac Penington* (London: Clark, 1681), 372–80 (reprint, Glenside, PA: Quaker Heritage Press, 1995–97, 2 vols., 2:459–77). The unsigned work *Several Reasons Rendered by . . . Quakers Why no Outward Force, or Imposition on the Conscience* [. . .] (n.p., 1668) lists twenty-nine reasons for toleration, using the Bible, early church writings, and common sense, but not reason or natural law.

10. Michael P. Graves, *Preaching the Inward Light: Early Quaker Rhetoric* (Waco: Baylor University Press, 2009), 208–16. For an example of this prophetic style, see Morgan Watkins, *A Lamentation over England* [. . .] (1664).

11. "First Publishers of Truth" is the name given to early converts who spread the Quaker message. John Crook, *Sixteen Reasons Drawn from the Law of God, the Law of England, and Right Reason, to Shew Why diverse true Christians (called Quakers) refuse to Swear at All* [. . .] (London: Robert Wilson, n.d.); John Crook, Samuel Fisher, Francis Howgill, and Richard Hubberthorne, *Liberty of Conscience Asserted and Several Reasons Rendred, Why no Outward Force, nor Imposition, ought to be used in Matters of Faith and Religion* [. . .] (London: Robert Wilson, 1661); Edward Burrough, *The Case of Free Liberty of Conscience in the Exercise of Faith and Religion* [. . .] (London: Simmons, 1661).

12. See Richard Farnsworth, *The Liberty of the Subject by Magna Charta or Several weighty things to be considered* [. . .] (1664).

13. Gervase Benson, *The Cry of the Oppressed* [. . .] *Concerning Tythes and Oathes* (London: Giles Calvert, 1656), 37; and Anthony Pearson, *The Great Case of Tythes Truly Stated and Fully Resolved* [. . .] (London: Giles Calvert, 1657), 4, 5, 15, 21, which argued that Old Testament precedents did not apply and cited Origin, Chrysostom, church councils, Ambrose, Augustine, and Wycliffe. Both Benson and Pearson insisted that because by English law only ecclesiastical courts could collect tithes and now were abolished, any enforcement was illegal.

14. Farnsworth, in *Liberty of the Subject*, 8, 10, 16–19, also cited the statutes of Edward IV, Coke's *Institutes*, the early Christians Tertullian and Eusebius, and Roman emperors.

15. Bishop, Penn, and Crisp confused opponents then (and scholars later) by using vague terminology to distinguish the divine light, divine reason, and human reason as arguments for toleration and the Inward Light. For example, here is Crisp: "the light would often shine through all this, and quell my reasonings, and showed me, when I was but a child, that in the pure reason that is from God, there is no reason for any evil . . . and so I often stripped naked from all my reasonings and coverings." *A Memorable Account of the Christian Experiences* [. . .] *of Stephen Crisp* (London: T. Sowle, 1694), 19, 20, 27, 28, available at the Digital Quaker Collection, http://dqc.esr.earlham.edu.

16. George Fox, *The Law of God, the rule for Law and Makers, the Ground of all just Laws, and the corruption of English Laws and Lawyers Discovered* (London: Giles Calvert, 1658), 8, 10. "Reason and equity and the Law of God" "written in the heart" are Fox's standards. He mentions reason or unreason eighteen times. One section and a few scattered phrases sound like Fox, but most of this pamphlet (like Fox's *Primer*) was written by someone else who had experience in equity courts—e.g., "if the Plantiff file his bill, then ten Groats to an Attorney, twelve pense a sheet, ten shillings to a Counsellor doth this smell like a Court of Equity, doth this savour of equity" (22).

17. See especially Mary Maples Dunn, *William Penn: Politics and Conscience* (Princeton: Princeton University Press, 1967); Murphy, *Liberty, Conscience, and Toleration*, 10. Murphy's many articles, listed in the bibliographies of his books, provide an accurate account of, and the political context for, Penn's ideas. Murphy devotes little space to the possible origins of Penn's ideas or their similarity to those found in Huguenot and Quaker sources, noting only that Penn's ideas were "far from original when viewed in the context of seventeenth-century discourses of toleration and liberty of conscience." Murphy, "The Emergence of William Penn, 1668–1671," *Journal of Church and State* 57, no. 2 (2014): 334. All of Penn's main arguments can be found in the Restoration tracts of John Owen and Charles Wolseley. However, there are differences: only Penn is anticlerical, and, unlike Owen and Wolseley, he definitely extended toleration to Roman Catholics as early as 1671, in Pennsylvania, and during James's reign, but he was less clear during the exclusion crisis in 1679. Penn feared Catholicism as a political movement and disliked its religious emphases. *PWP*, 1:209–11. Owen did not oppose paying tithes to the Church of England; Penn did not mention tithes or oaths in his major works on toleration, but in his early tracts he did insist that forcing Quakers to pay tithes to Anglicans and penalizing them for refusing to swear oaths went against the religion of the early church as well as traditional English practices and natural law. Wolseley and Owen restricted the king's power over conscience but, unlike Penn, seemed to allow the king a limited role in the outward affairs of the church. One must wonder whether Wolseley was joking when he suggested that the king (Charles, of course) should lead by example. Only Penn opposed a comprehensive Church of England with a limited role for bishops and tithes. A logical conclusion of the premises of all three writers would be to end the political role of bishops in the House of Lords, but they do not make this argument. Charles Wolseley, *Liberty of Conscience upon its true and proper Ground, Asserted and Vindicated* [. . .], 2nd ed. (London, 1668), 20–25, 46, 60–62; John Owen, *Indulgence and Toleration Considered* [. . .] (London, 1667), 5, 14, 26; John Owen, *A Peace-Offering in an Apology and Humble Plea for Indulgence and Liberty of Conscience* [. . .] (London, 1669), 13, 31–32.

18. Winifred Lady Burghclere, *George Villiers, Second Duke of Buckingham, 1628–1687: A Study in the History of the Restoration* (Port Washington, NY: Kennikat Press, 1903), 128, 198, 307–9.

19. *The People's Ancient and Just Liberties in the Trial of William Penn and William Mead*, in *WWP*, 1:13–62. Penn denied that he kept shorthand notes of the trial proceedings, and it seems unlikely that he could have, but he may have edited the final version. See his "Truth Rescued from Imposture" (1670), *WWP*, 1:487; Thomas Rudyard, Penn's lawyer, has an appendix in this work. Sir Samuel Sterling, in *An Answer to the Seditious and Scandalous Pamphlet* [. . .] (London: G. W., 1671), presents the judge's perspective, calling Penn a "Youngster," a "Wild Rambling Colt," and a "Novice at Law," while opposing empowering "twelve Jury-men, eleven of which its possible can neither write nor read, to be the Judges of both of Law and Fact" (2–3).

20. When Penn asked the judges to cite the specific common law, they accused him of being unfair. "In its early modern form, the English common law system differed markedly from a statute-based system: the authority of the law not said to derive from the power of the legislature but from its already being the law of the peoples from time immemorial. . . . In that setting, the doctrine of precedent was more or less fundamental to the whole law-finding undertaking. It committed judges (in theory) to doing what they had always done. And what made the law into law today corre-

sponded to what had always been the law in the past." Noah Feldman, "Why Precedent Won't Protect Roe," *New York Review of Books*, July 2, 2020, 29–30.

21. John D. Walter, "Body Politics in the English Revolution," in *The Nature of the English Revolution Revisited: Essays in Honour of John Morrill*, edited by Stephen Taylor and Grant Tapsell (Woodbridge, UK: Boydell Press, 2012), 81–102, discusses how the refusal to remove one's hat became a political symbol of disrespect during the Civil War and Commonwealth. I am indebted to Stephen Angell for sending me a copy of this essay.

22. *The Great Case of Liberty of Conscience Once more Briefly Debated and Defended* [. . .] (London, 1670), 11, 44.

23. *Great Case of Liberty of Conscience*, 12, 44.

24. *Great Case of Liberty of Conscience*, 12–13.

25. Penn ignored stories in Hebrew scripture in which prophets and kings called down the wrath of God and slew opponents of the Yahweh cult, because in the New Testament Jesus had provided a new spiritual revelation. *Great Case of Liberty of Conscience*, 19.

26. *Great Case of Liberty of Conscience*, 14–19, 23.

27. Readers, then and now, might be confused by Penn's varying senses of reason. Reason could be the Logos, as described in the first chapters of the Gospel of John, but it could also be a human faculty best described as intelligence or common sense, and the conclusions derived from using reason. Something could be reasonable because it came from the Inward Light of Christ, or unreasonable because it did not cohere logically. Conscience, a human faculty and the site of the Inward Logos, could give certain truth or be mistaken. Morality could be a human endeavor, or it could mean following the universal love of God. See n. 15 for similar language in Bishop and Crisp, and Sara Partridge, "For Conscience' Sake: Dissent and the Divine in Early American Literature" (PhD diss., New York University, 2020), 4–17, on seventeenth-century debates on certainty and the authority of conscience. See also Endy, *William Penn and Early Quakerism*, 249–52.

28. *Great Case of Liberty of Conscience*, 20, 22–23.

29. Perhaps because Penn realized that religious reasons would not sway an intolerant Anglican and royalist Parliament, he used arguments based on the nature of law and interest dominate his tract *England's Present Interest Considered* [. . .] (London: Andrew Sowle, 1675), 6 (my citations are to the 1676 edition). This tract used the arguments of the government against itself. It was written in response to Charles's opening speech to Parliament, in which he presented himself as a defender of Protestants and property, and the speaker for the government, Lord Keeper, Heneage Finch, Earl of Nottingham, defended persecution as compatible with freedom of conscience. "For, when we consider Religion in Parliament, we are supposed to consider as Parliament should do . . . as it is Part of our Laws, A Part and a necessary Part of our Government. For, as it works upon the Conscience, as it is an inward Principle of the Divine Life by which good Men do govern all their Actions, that State hath nothing to do with it, it is a Thing which belongs to another kind of Commission than that by which we seat here." Penn quoted this passage twice to show that persecution contradicted true faith, which was "an INWARD Principle of Divine Life." *Journal of the House of Lords* (London: His Majesty's Stationary Office, 1767–1830), 12:652–61. I am indebted to Jordan Landes for finding these speeches.

30. "Municipal laws of countries . . . are only as far right as they are founded upon the laws of nature." John Locke, *Second Treatise of Government*, chap. 2, sec. 12.

31. See George Bishop, *A Tender Visitation of Love, to both the Universities of Oxford and Cambridge, and the Inns of Court and Chancery* (London: Robert Wilson, 1660), 8–14. "Law is a beam of Divine Light," Penn wrote, "and the right Reason of the Sovereign God. Now who is the Divine Light, but Christ the Light of the World." The "law of Nature is the law Eternal and who is the law eternal, but the King immortal." *Great Case of Liberty of Conscience*, 6.

32. *England's Present Interest Considered*, 6, 22, 24; *Great Case of Liberty of Conscience*, chap. 5. "For the Reasonable Part in Man, is his Spiritual Part, and that guided by the Divine Logos, or Word, which Tertullian interprets as Reason in the most Excellent Sense, makes Man truly reasonable; and then it is that man comes to offer up himself to God a Reasonable Sacrifice. Then is Man indeed a Complete Man; such a man as GOD made, when he made Man in His Own Image." "Primitive Christianity Revived," *WWP*, 2:283 (part 1), 863. Penn goes on to say that the Light of Reason is the Holy Spirit.

33. *England's Present Interest Considered*, 6, 21, 22, 24.

34. *England's Present Interest Considered*, 14.

35. *England's Present Interest Considered*, 33–34.

36. *England's Present Interest Considered*, 38, 48.

37. *England's Present Interest Considered*, 51.

38. *England's Present Interest Considered*, 42.

39. *England's Present Interest Considered*, 42–47. Hammond (1605–1660) and Taylor (1613–1667) were prominent high church Anglicans committed to Charles I during the Civil War. Even today, Taylor is esteemed as one of the masters of English prose and is celebrated as a saint by the Church of England. Algernon Sidney and John Locke also cited these men.

40. *Great Case of Liberty of Conscience*, 6; see also his *Address to Protestants*, preface, 2.

41. *Great Case of Liberty of Conscience*, Irish edition, preface, 6; see also his *Address to Protestants*.

42. No "pretense of Conscience" or Christian freedom allowed a person to "be drunk, Whore, be Voluptuous, to Game, to Swear, Curse, Blaspheme and Prophane." These were sins against "Nature, and against Government, as well as God's Written Law." *Address to Protestants*, 7, 33. In this 248-page book, Penn began as a hellfire preacher condemning immorality and threatening the final judgment, evolved into a fundamentalist-literalist on the Bible, changed into a rationalist (almost a deist) on the essence of Christianity, added a pietist perspective based on his personal religious experience, and ended as a pragmatist defending religious liberty. The book, written in the middle of the so-called popish plot, went through four printings in 1679 and reflects Penn's view of society just before he sought a charter for Pennsylvania.

43. *Address to Protestants*, 76. The same year, Penn praised Samuel Fisher's *Rusticus ad Academicos [. . .] the Rustics Alarm to the Rabbies* (London: Robert Wilson, 1660), 129, 194–99, available at the Digital Quaker Collection, http://dqc.esr.earlham.edu. Fisher argued for the "fallibility of the bare naked letter of the Scriptures, and of its liableness to [be] corrupted and falsified by mistranslations, so as to have various Lections in the Original Copyes of it." The original writers had been divinely inspired, but that could not be said of all who copied it, and we cannot know how much is missing or falsified.

44. *A Perswasive to Moderation to Church-Dissenters, in Prudence and Conscience: Humbly submitted to the King and His Great Council* (London: Andrew Sowle, 1685), and *Good Advice to the Church of England, Roman Catholick, and Protestant Dissenter in Which it is endeavoured to made appear, that it is their Duty, Principle, and*

Interest, to abolish the Penal Laws and Tests (London: T. Sowle, 1687). The first tract was issued before the king had suspended the laws; it exhorted James to keep his promise and dissenters to approve. The second sought to gain public support for a new law ensuring religious toleration.

45. Latitudinarians were Anglicans who favored toleration, the Whig party, and an emphasis on morality as the essence of religion. Penn, like John Owen and Charles Wolseley, insisted that all agreed on essential doctrines. A crucial issue was the definition of "essential." For political purposes, Penn simplified Christianity into a few beliefs and ignored practices in a way that Roman Catholics, Protestants, and even Quakers would have opposed. Opponents argued that if everything else was nonessential, why did dissenters, including Quakers, not join the Church of England? Andrew R. Murphy and Sarah A. Morgan Smith, "Law and Civil Interest: William Penn's Tolerationism," in *Religious Tolerance in the Atlantic World: Early Modern and Contemporary Perspectives*, edited by Eliane Glaser (New York: Palgrave Macmillan, 2013), 119.

46. David Wykes, "Friends, Parliament, and the Toleration Act," *Journal of Ecclesiastical History* 45, no. 1 (1994): 45–51, 61.

47. Beckman, *Statutes at Large of Pennsylvania*, 124. Penn wrote no tracts on religious liberty from the time he received his charter until James became king. This could have been because he was busy with Pennsylvania but also did not wish to irritate Charles, who had been so generous, or jeopardize his new colony.

48. The Duke of York's laws that applied to Pennsylvania before Penn's charter did not list moral offenses but gave constables the power to arrest "such as are overtaken with Drinke, Swearing, Sabbath Breaking, Vagrant Persons and Night Walkers." Beckman, *Statutes at Large of Pennsylvania*, 85. "The Concessions and Agreements for New Jersey" issued by Carteret and Berkeley and "The Concessions and Agreements for East and West Jersey" promised liberty of conscience and included no moral legislation.

49. Beckman, *Statutes at Large of Pennsylvania*, 117, 128.

50. The Crown's instructions to Fletcher insisted that officeholders take an anti-Catholic oath, but there is no evidence of any such oath or affirmation after 1696 until 1705, when the Crown vetoed Penn's section I and the Assembly required an anti-Catholic abjuration. J. William Frost, *A Perfect Freedom: Religious Liberty in Pennsylvania* (New York: Cambridge University Press, 1990), 21–24.

51. These seven principles had prevailed at the time of Noah and were discoverable by reason because they were self-evident.

52. Disturbing the peace was a serious offense that carried a potential fine of twenty shillings.

53. Governor Fletcher insisted upon an anti-Catholic oath when he was governor, but it is uncertain whether that policy continued under his successor, William Markham. In 1705 Penn protested the infringement on his charter rights when the Board of Trade required an anti-Catholic loyalty oath, but it became standard policy until the American Revolution.

54. Beckman, *Statutes at Large of Pennsylvania*, 128–31. "Pennsylvania's effort at enforcing moral standards was brief and arguably faint." Enforcement of laws on victimless moral crimes decreased after 1700 and virtually ceased after 1720. Jack Marietta and G. S. Rowe, *Troubled Experiment: Crime and Punishment in Pennsylvania, 1682–1800* (Philadelphia: University of Pennsylvania Press, 2006), 40.

55. Marietta and Rowe, *Troubled Experiment*, 12–14.

56. Marietta and Rowe, *Troubled Experiment*, 14, 17–19.

57. Marietta and Rowe, *Troubled Experiment*, 50; Offutt, *"Good Laws" and "Good Men,"* 14, 152–53, 264–65.

CHAPTER 6

1. There was one exception: when advertising Pennsylvania in 1683, Penn praised the "lovely flowers" in the woods and the "beauty" of the gardens, though arguably these were more God's handiwork than man's. Jay David Miller, "Willian Penn's Imperial Georgic and the Vernacular Landscapes of Pennsylvania in Eighteenth-Century Quaker Journals," *Pennsylvania Magazine of History and Biography* 145, no. 3 (2021): 194. See also *WWP*, 2:701.

2. Penn's guides included "experiences," "reasoning, the scriptures, natural law, the teachings of tradition, the lessons of history, the views of great and wise men through the ages, the appeal to miracles, and an analysis of the expected results of action." Jay Thomas Allen, "The Guide for Ethics in the Thought of William Penn" (PhD diss., University of Syracuse, 1967), 23.

3. Quakers' decision to have weighty Friends review all publications came in 1674; *Some Fruits of Solitude* was one of many Penn works not directed at Friends and not formally approved by any meeting. In "Compelling Reading," 188, Brooke Palmieri shows that two-thirds of Friends' publications were not submitted to the MMM.

4. Carroll, "Thomas Loe, Friend of William Penn," 67.

5. Since the Quaker salutation for everyone was "Friend," the term "ancient Friends" could refer simply to old men Penn knew who were not Quakers. After all, a seventeen-year-old movement hardly deserves to be called "ancient." See Hugh Barbour's preface to *No Cross, No Crown* in *Penn on Religion and Ethics*, 1:39n1; Braithwaite, *Second Period of Quakerism*, 61–62.

6. *NCNC* (1669), preface, A2. Early Friends regarded spoken and written messages as interchangeable ways to reach potential converts. Palmieri, "Compelling Reading," 43–46.

7. Friends allowed titles that functioned as descriptions of one's occupation (such as king, magistrate, or doctor), but not those that merely expressed respect by a subordinate.

8. *NCNC* (1669), 11–12.

9. *NCNC* (1669), 6–7.

10. George Fox, John Stubs, and Benjamin Furly, *A Battle-Door for Teachers & Professors to Learn Singular & Plural* (London: Robert Wilson, 1660); see also Penn, *Treatise of Oaths*, 17, 19.

11. *NCNC* (1669), 17; see also 24, 37, 41, 45.

12. *NCNC* (1669), 27, 47. In *Christian Quaker and His Divine Testimony* (1674), Penn condemned the "Infamous Plays" of Shakespeare and Ben Jonson (8).

13. *NCNC* (1669), 50.

14. Barbour, *Penn on Religion and Ethics*, 1:80.

15. Penn's descriptions of "Romances" shows that he must have read many early in life: "Some strange Adventures, some passionate Amours, unkind Refuses, grand Impediments, tedious Addresses, miserable Disappointments, wonderful Surprizes, unexpected Rencounters, and meeting of supposed dead Lovers, bloody Duels . . . then are dead People alive, enemies Friends, despair turn'd to Enjoyment, and all their Impossibilities reconcil'd." *NCNC* (1669), 41–42; *WWP*, 1:362.

16. *PWP*, 2:106–9. See also his "Some Account of the Province of Pennsylvania" (1681) and "A Further Account of Pennsylvania" (1685), both in Myers, *Narratives of Early Pennsylvania*.

17. "Penn certainly did not compartmentalize his activities into 'religious' and 'political' categories. Each one represented a particular aspect of the larger aim that animated all of his political theorizing and activism: the articulation of a social and political vision that would enable individuals and groups to build a common life together." Murphy, *Liberty, Conscience, and Toleration*, 85.

18. *NCNC* (1682), in *WWP*, 1:395, 441. Unless otherwise noted, all subsequent quotations of *NCNC* are from the 1682 edition reprinted in Joseph Besse's 1726 collection of Penn's works.
19. *NCNC*, in *WWP*, 1:273.
20. *NCNC*, in *WWP*, 1:376, 382, 384.
21. *NCNC*, in *WWP*, 1:273, 275.
22. *NCNC*, in *WWP*, 1:284, 285.
23. *NCNC*, in *WWP*, 1:297–98.
24. *NCNC*, in *WWP*, 1:282, 286, 289.
25. *NCNC*, in *WWP*, 1:306, 331.
26. *NCNC*, in *WWP*, 1:336.
27. *NCNC*, in *WWP*, 1:310, 336.
28. *NCNC* (1682), 256, 274; see also *WWP*, 1:341.
29. *NCNC*, in *WWP*, 1:373.
30. *NCNC*, in *WWP*, 1:296.
31. *PWP*, 5:228; *NCNC*, in *WWP*, 1:135, 414.
32. Rochester does not appear in the 1682 edition but first appeared in a 1705 edition and is included in *WWP*, 1:430. Penn admired Crowley because he retired to and praised the secluded country life. Elizabeth Gray Vining has analyzed how Penn was very selective in his use of Cowley. See her essay "Penn and the Poets," in *Then and Now: Quaker Essays, Historical and Contemporary*, edited by Anna Brinton (Philadelphia: University of Pennsylvania Press, 1960), 113–18. Vining suggests that Penn's preface to the Frame of Government was influenced by Cowley's statement "The liberty of a people consisted in being governed by laws which they have made themselves, under whatsoever form it be of government."
33. *NCNC*, in *WWP*, 1:430–432, 363, 404.
34. *NCNC*, in *WWP*, 1:404, 430.
35. *NCNC*, in *WWP*, 1:355. Both of Penn's wives were capable women who at times managed his affairs. Traveling male ministers relied upon their wives in their absence, and the daughters of Margaret Fell and the printer Tace Sowle illustrate the economic roles that Penn ignored.

36. Penn contrasted "Wantonness, Idleness, Effeminacy" with "Wisdom, Knowledge, Manhood, Temperance, Industry," and "Duty, Reason, and true Pleasure of Man," writing, "Luxury brings Effeminacy, Laziness, Poverty and Misery." *NCNC*, in *WWP*, 1:372, 395, 399.
37. Erin Bell, "The Early Quakers, the Peace Testimony, and Masculinity in England, 1660–1730," *Gender and History* 32, no. 2 (2001): 283–303.
38. *NCNC*, in *WWP*, 1:436.
39. Quakers had long been suspicious of "politeness" as being untruthful. By providing counsel on how to succeed in society, Penn softened the distinction between sectarian isolation and adjusting to English norms, and this ran counter to earlier Quaker principles. Keith Thomas, *In Pursuit of Civility: Manners and Civilization in Early Modern England* (New Haven: Yale University Press, 2018), 24–28, 112, 306–7, 313.
40. Penn followed up *Some Fruits of Solitude in Reflections and Maxims* (London: Thomas Northcott, 1693) with *More Fruits of Solitude: Being the Second Part of Reflections and Maxims* (London: T. Sowle, 1702). A modern edition is *Some Fruits of Solitude: Wise Sayings on the Conduct of Human Life*, edited by Eric Taylor (Scottdale, PA: Herald Press, 2003), 161–66. Taylor argues that most of the biblical influence in *FOS* came from the New Testament, and none from Proverbs.
41. Even when he offered the same advice he had given in *NCNC*, the context made it seem different.
42. E. H. Blackmore and A. M. Blackmore, introduction to *La Rochefoucauld: Collected Maxims and Other Reflections*, edited and translated by E. H. Blackmore, A. M. Blackmore, and Francine Giguère (New York: Oxford University Press, 2007), xx–xxi.
43. Penn cited Machiavelli's *Discourses* and histories favorably and had probably read *The Prince*. Although he agreed with

Algernon Sidney about toleration and disliked the political power of the clergy, his sayings have no similarity to Sidney's maxims, which promoted republicanism and attacked monarchy. See Sidney, *Court Maxims*, edited by Hans W. Blom, Eco Haitsma Mulier, and Ronald Janse (Cambridge: Cambridge University Press, 1996).

44. *PWP*, 3:365–74, 377–78.

45. For example, Penn wrote, "Men are generally more careful of the Breed of their Horses and Dogs, than of their children." *FOS*, no. 79, p. 28. Stanley quoted Pythagoras, who wrote, "They who love dogs, are very careful of their breed," "yet men have no respect to their own Offspring, but beget inconsiderately and bring them up negligently," and "Comprehend not few things in many Words, but many things in few words." Sir Thomas Stanley, *The History of Philosophy: Containing the lives, opinions, actions and discourses of the philosophers of every sect*, 3rd ed. (1701) (Eighteenth Century Collections Online, n.d.), part 9, 395, 397. Stanley also quoted the Macedonian sophist Brion, who wrote, "Of a rich Man covetous: He hath no money, but money him" (part 4, 143).

46. Esther Greenleaf Mürer, comp., Quaker Bible Index (1993, 1996), manuscript at Friends Historical Library, Swarthmore College. Mürer provides lists of Bible quotations from selected works by Fox, Barclay, Penn, and Woolman.

47. *FOS*, preface, unpaginated.

48. *NCNC*, in *WWP*, 1:370.

49. The one exception in Plutarch was the statement "the love we feel for such very young children . . . is an absolutely pure pleasure undisturbed by anything like anger or blame." *Plutarch: Moral Essays*, edited and translated by Rex Warner (London: Penguin, 1971), 176–77.

50. See Desiderius Erasmus, *Proverbs or Adages, Englished 1659 by Richard Taverner* (Gainesville, FL: Scholars Facsimile and Reprints, 1951), 30; Erasmus, *Prolegomena to the Adages*, in *The Collected Works of Erasmus*, trans. Margaret Mann Phillips, vol. 30 (Toronto: University of Toronto Press, 1982), 567, 764; George Herbert, *Jacula Prudentum, or Outlandish Proverbs, Sentences & etc.* (1651), in *The Complete Works of George Herbert*, edited by Alexander B. Grosart, 3 vols. (London: T. Maxey, 1874), 1:322, 149, 326, 232, 246; Rochefoucauld, *Collected Maxims and Other Reflections*, 23; *Plutarch: Moral Essays*; *Epictetus: Discourses*, edited by Robert Dobbin (Oxford: Clarendon Press, 1998); Francis Bacon, *Apothegms: New and Old* (London, 1625; reprint, New York: Da Capo Press, 1972).

51. J. W. Frost, *The Quaker Family in Colonial America* (New York: St. Martin's Press, 1973), 96. Penn referred not to schools but to education. In Ireland as a child, he probably had a tutor, and the same was true for his own children.

52. *FOS*, nos. 6, 8, 9, 11, 12, 13, pp. 3–6.

53. In his posthumous tribute to Gulielma, he described her as an "Excellent Wife and Mother, but an entire and constant Friend of a more than common Capacity, and greater Modesty and Humility; yet most equal and undaunted in Danger, Religious as well as Ingenuous, without Affection. An easie Mistress, and good Neighbour, especially for the Poor. Neither lavish, nor penurious, but an Example of Industry, as well as other Virtues." *WWP*, 1:232. Notice that modesty seems more important than capacity.

54. *FOS*, nos. 83, 76, 78, 86, pp. 27, 28, 32.

55. Penn argued in an unpublished essay on marriage (ca. 1671) that "natural Affection that is commendable in its place, & necessary in the natural relation," must immediately receive validation from the Inward Light of God. *PWP*, 1:232, 234. There should be a "visible Harmony" between husband and wife in "Education, manner of Life, Temper and Disposition."

56. *FOS*, nos. 86, 93, 94, pp. 32, 33, 35–36.

57. In 1699, before sailing to Pennsylvania with his pregnant wife, Hannah, and daughter Letitia, Penn wrote a letter of instruction to his children. John Rhodes published it in 1726 as *Fruits of a Father's Love, Being the Advice of William Penn to His Children*, and it was included in *PWP*, 1:893–911. To whom was it directed—to his wayward son Billy, who opposed his father's second marriage and later was jealous of Penn's second family? Billy's situation might explain why Penn advised that in the case of a child gone astray, "make not his folly an excuse to be strange" (advice no. 26). Several of the maxims echo the advice in *More Fruits of Solitude* but were not included in his childrearing suggestions; for example, "Love them with Wisdom, Correct them with Affection; Never strike in passion, and suit the Correction to their Age as well as Fault. Convince them of Error before you chastise them. Never use that but in case of obstinacy or impenitency. Punish them more by their Understanding than the rod." *WWP*, 1:901. Why Penn did not include his eloquent maxims on family in *More Fruits of Solitude* I can't explain.

58. *FOS*, 33–38. In *More Fruits of Solitude*, he says, "Children can't well be too hardy bred: for besides that it fits them [to] bear the roughest providences, it is more masculine, active, and healthy" (no. 141). Notice the omission of female children, though Penn also followed the biblical precept that souls had no sex.

59. *FOS*, nos. 158, 161, 164, pp. 53–55, 57–59.

60. *FOS*, nos. 100, 102, 108, pp. 38–40.

61. *FOS*, nos. 21, 24, 66, 123, 125, 141, 258, pp. 24, 44–45, 49, 56–57, 65, 71, 75, 79.

62. *FOS*, nos. 86, 93, 94, pp. 81–82, 84, 90.

63. *FOS*, nos. 299, 324, 326, 330, 333, pp. 86, 87, 93, 94, 95.

64. As noted above, Penn published a sequel to *FOS*, called *More Fruits of Solitude*, in 1702. It had no section on government and only one maxim on magistrates, but it contained a long section on "Great Men."

65. *FOS*, no. 520, pp. 107–8, 110.

66. These statements first appeared in an edition of *FOS* published in 1705 and were repeated in Besse's 1726 edition of *WWP*, 1:843, nos. 519, 545.

67. *FOS*, nos. 419, 439, 440, 447, pp. 117–19, 126.

68. *WWP*, 1:237. By contrast, in *Good Advice to the Church of England* (1687), he wrote, "Christianity is the Sole Religion of the World, that is built upon the Principles of Love." *WWP*, 2:750.

69. *FOS*, nos. 465, 466, pp. 133–34. In *More Fruits of Solitude*, "charity" replaced "love" as a governing principle.

70. Worminghurst Manor was "large, but ugly, & yet has convenient, room for 12 or 20 people more than our & your family." Penn to Hannah Callowhill, *PWP*, 3:432.

71. *PWP*, 3:425.

72. Dunn, "Personality of William Penn," 11. When Penn referred to acquaintances as friends, he meant aristocrats like Henry Sydney.

73. *PWP*, 4:100–102, 753.

CHAPTER 7

1. In 1696, Gerald Croese described the power of Quaker preaching as "not placed in words, or bodily motions (unless the compass of his Voice and Countenance) be suitably managed by simplicity and gravity," but in "plain and obvious words." Croese, *General History of the Quakers*, 54–55.

2. Robert Barclay, *An Apology for the True Christian Divinity* [. . .] (1st English ed., 1676), prop. 11, viii. Thomas Story expressed a similar sentiment. See *A Journal of the Life of Thomas Story* (Newcastle upon Tyne: Isaac Thompson, 1747), 32–33.

3. Graves, *Preaching the Inward Light*, appendix B; for a complete list, see 318–20.

4. MMM, minutes, 15/7/1673, 1.

5. The editors of the *Papers of William Penn* suggest that a manuscript (*PWP*,

1:184–90), perhaps written while Penn was in prison, was typical of his preaching. But this document was written, not given in meeting, and its stern tone and apocalyptic images present a striking contrast to the sermons discussed here.

6. *PWP*, 1:425–507. This version of his account of his trip to Holland is based on the manuscript, which was published in 1694.

7. George Fox to Henry Sidon, May 25, 1677, published in *Journal of the Friends' Historical Society* 6 (1909): 187. In 1698 Penn was instructed by the MFS to add a statement on wigs to Ambrose Rigge's "Testimony against Extravagant Wigs," MFS, minutes, 11/10/1698, 248. When he left Pennsylvania in 1702, Penn gave James Logan his periwigs. Pierre Eugene Du Simitiere's portrait of an older Penn shows a very elaborate curled wig. Either Penn had different kinds of wigs for meeting and court, or the painting and sculptures are misleading.

8. Penn summarized Bushel's case in *Great Case of Liberty of Conscience*; see *WWP*, 1:7–35.

9. John Whiting, quoted in Hull, *Penn: A Topical Biography*, 126. Hull discusses the only two accounts of Penn's preaching, the first from *WWP*, 1:4, and the second from *Journal of the Life of Thomas Story*, 128.

10. *The Quakers Quibbles in Three Parts [. . .] An Expository Epistle to William Penn* (London: W. Smith, 1675), 5–7, 10–11, 24. David Crystal argues that there was no received pronunciation (what we might call an Oxbridge accent) until around 1800. "If you wanted to show you were educated, i.e., literate, that means you would know how to spell and your pronunciation could be influenced by it." David Crystal, "Original Pronunciation," *English Language Texts in Printed Speech*, May 3, 2017, https://originalpronunciation.com/GBR/Home.

11. *Aubrey's Brief Lives*, lxx, lxxxiv. Penn spoke in meetings "with much eloquence and fervency of spirit" (234). Penn gave Aubrey, who showed sympathy to Friends, six hundred acres in Pennsylvania.

12. MMM, minutes, 8/16/1688, 6/12/1688, 93, 103. The MMM made sure that ministers attended different meetings for worship in London so that too many would not be at one and not enough at another. They also told ministers not to go to the country on Sunday without telling them. Whitehead addressed a congregation at this meeting in 1694 as "Friends and friendly people." *Concurrence and Unanimity of the People called Quakers: In Owning and Asserting the Principal Doctrines of the Christian Religion* (London: Nath. Crouch, 1694), 120.

13. These sermons appear in the following compilations: *Concurrence and Unanimity*; Penn, *Harmony of Divine and Heavenly Doctrines: Demonstrated as Sundry Declarations on Variety of Subjects* (London: Jane Sowle, 1696); *Several Sermons or Declarations of Mr. Stephen Crisp, late of Colchester, in Essex, Deceased* (London: Nath. Crouch, 1693; London: Thomas Northcott, 1696). *Concurrence and Unanimity* was frequently sent abroad by eighteenth-century London Friends.

14. Besse was right to call this an "epistle" in that the audience is the Society of Friends everywhere. Its tone is different from the tone of Penn's sermons. *WWP*, 1:236–38. "A Farewell Sermon, preached by Mr. William Penn, on Sunday last, the 13th Instant, at the Quakers' Monthly Meeting House at Westminster," *Friend*, 1st ser., 7 (1847): 23–25. It was reprinted in Barbour, *Penn on Religion and Ethics*, 2:652–54.

15. *PWP*, 5:431.

16. Jenkins, *Records and Recollections*, 242.

17. Preface to *Scriptural Truths Demonstrated*, unpaginated.

18. In 1711 the actual printer would have been Tace Sowle, using her mother's name. I am indebted to Jordan Landes for this information.

19. Preface to *Scriptural Truths Demonstrated*, unpaginated. Note that the editor

says that only the "sense" has been maintained.

20. The MMM decided not to reprint Fox's sermon "Gospel Family Order" in 1703, ostensibly because part of it was a "declaration taken in a Meeting." MMM, minutes, 12/6/1703, 154. That the subject was slavery might also have been a factor. Robert Mayer, "Nathaniel Crouch, Bookseller and Historian: Popular Historiography and Cultural Power in Late Seventeenth-Century England," *Eighteenth-Century Studies* 27, no. 3 (1994): 391–419.

21. Ethyn Kirby, *George Keith (1638–1716)* (New York: American Historical Association, 1942). See also Frost, "New Conditions in Britain and America." For the best theological analysis, see Ward, *Christian Quaker: George Keith*.

22. MFS, minutes, 28/9/1692, 175–78.

23. LYM, minutes, 2–7/4/1694, 23–61; 15/3/1695, 91–92.

24. *PWP*, 2:77–80.

25. Penn, after twice being summoned by the Privy Council, in December 1688 and again in 1689, went into hiding in 1691 after being accused of treason; he was exonerated by King William in November 1693. He lost control of Pennsylvania over defense issues in 1692 and regained the colony in July 1694. Joseph E. Illick, *William Penn the Politician: His Relations with the English Government* (Ithaca: Cornell University Press, 1965), 103–22.

26. During LYM, when members were selected to write epistles or to answer the chaplain of the bishop of London, Whitehead and Penn headed the lists. LYM, minutes, 3/17/1695, 130.

27. Graves, *Preaching the Inward Light*, chap. 7.

28. Barbour, *Penn on Religion and Ethics*, 2:651, reprints Penn's only long prayer. It also appears in *Harmony of Divine and Heavenly Doctrines*, 23–42, consisting of nine pages of sermon and seven of prayer.

29. The sermons average twenty-nine lines per page and seven to eight words per line. Barbour says they averaged 6,006 words and would have taken one hour to deliver. *Penn on Religion and Ethics*, 2:60. Whitehead's sermon frequently used phrases like "My Friends" as a way of shifting gears and moving to a new topic. Penn rarely did this.

30. *Quaker Post-Bag*, cited in Frost, *Quaker Family in Colonial America*, 35–39.

31. MMM, minutes, 6/11/1700, 10; 10/1/1700, 17.

32. *Harmony of Divine and Heavenly Doctrines*, 88–89. "O You YOUNG ONES! I have a travel [*sic*: travail] in my soul for you." There was no distinctive advice to youths, who were compared to "unblotted white paper" even though they, like all people, lived in the realm of sin.

33. *Harmony of Divine and Heavenly Doctrines*, 135.

34. *Harmony of Divine and Heavenly Doctrines*, 96, 109, 113.

35. "God hath made man Reasonable, and his Judgment shall be most Righteous and Reasonable"; men who denied God "live in a contradiction to their own reason." *Harmony of Divine and Heavenly Doctrines*, 163. Penn also appealed to "interest" as a means to persuade.

36. *Concurrence and Unanimity*, 13.

37. *Harmony of Divine and Heavenly Doctrines*, 73.

38. *Harmony of Divine and Heavenly Doctrines*, 59, 85, 1. Penn's reticence in discussing his own personal experience is the more striking because he did publish an account of the deaths of his wife and son and asked for a hundred copies that he would give to his family. MMM, minutes, 8/6/1699, 298.

39. *Harmony of Divine and Heavenly Doctrines*, 12, 98–99, 111.

40. *Harmony of Divine and Heavenly Doctrines*, 122, 123; *Concurrence and Unanimity*, 98, 99 (Marshall), 130 (Bingly).

41. *Sermons or Declarations of Mr. Stephen Crisp* (1696 ed.), 8–10, 18–19, 25, 51.

42. *Harmony of Divine and Heavenly Doctrines*, 123. In his "Brief Account of the Rise and Progress of the People called Quakers," Penn asserted that the Quakers preached not "in their own Time or Will, but in the *Will of God*; and spoke not their own studied Matter, but as they were opened and moved of his Spirit." *WWP*, 1:873.

43. *Harmony of Divine and Heavenly Doctrines*, 153, 161, 164, 166, 167.

44. *Unanimity and Concurrence*, 73, 74, 76, 77. Here is his only reference to Travers: our "Deceased Friend, who received the Truth in early Days . . . the Remembrance of it was sweet to her soul."

45. *Harmony of Divine and Heavenly Doctrines*, 81, 104. Penn sometimes mixed biblical metaphors, e.g., "Our Lord Jesus will feed us with the Heavenly Manna and with Honey out of the Rock will he Satisfie us, who is himself the Rock of our Salvation, and the true and living Bread, that came down from Heaven: He will make a Feast of Fat Things, and with Wine on the Lees well refined."

46. *Harmony of Divine and Heavenly Doctrines*, 87–90, 81.

47. "Primitive Christianity Revived," *WWP*, 2:873. Michael Graves argues that by the 1680s an earlier form of incantatory preaching had been replaced by a catechetical style. Graves, *Preaching the Inward Light*, 208–16.

48. *Harmony of Divine and Heavenly Doctrines*, 87, 88, 101, 105. "During this Apostacy, the Devil has sat as God, and therefore is called the God of this World, and Prince of Power of the Air, that Rules, Where? In the Saints; in the Sanctified; no such Matter, Where then? In the Hearts of the Children of Disobedience." "To the Princess and Countess of Herford" (1676), *WWP*, 1:181, 216. Penn seems to be saying here that the devil is like Jesus, having a bodily existence elsewhere but, in the reign of the Antichrist on earth, dwelling within sinful peoples as a kind of evil seed in some ways analogous to the good seed, which can receive God.

49. *Harmony of Divine and Heavenly Doctrines*, 32, 33, 127, 134.

50. *Harmony of Divine and Heavenly Doctrines*, 58.

51. *Harmony of Divine and Heavenly Doctrines*, 12, 60. "Therefore lay hold on Christ now, believe in him, Lay hold of his Power and Spirit in this Day of your Visitation."

52. *Harmony of Divine and Heavenly Doctrines*, 71–72; see also 11–12, 76.

53. MMM, minutes, 14/3/1675, 6.

54. Jenkins, *Records and Recollections*, 203 (on doffing the hat), 67, 87–89, 96, 157–58, 172–74 (on the pace of speaking and musical tone).

CHAPTER 8

1. Nancy Black Sagafi-Nejad, *Friends at the Bar: A Quaker View of Law, Conflict Resolution, and Legal Reform* (Albany: State University of New York Press, 2012), 89.

2. Samuel M. Janney, *The Life of William Penn: With Selections from His Correspondence and Auto-Biography*, 2nd ed. (Philadelphia: Lippincott, 1852), 51.

3. William Sewel, *History of the Rise, Increase, and Progress of the Christian People, called Quakers* (London: J. Sowle, 1722), 609.

4. Sewel, *History of the Rise*; Croese, *General History of the Quakers*, 105. See also William Hepworth Dixon, *William Penn: An Historical Biography of William Penn* (London: Hall, 1851), 228.

5. Clarkson, *Public and Private Life of William Penn*, 1:185. In his *History of England from the Accession of James II* (Philadelphia: Lippincott, 1861), 2:229, Thomas Macaulay says that James first heard Penn preach on a tennis court while on a royal procession.

6. *WWP*, 1:6.

7. "Convincement of William Penn," 23.

8. Thomas Harvey, a minister from Taunton Monthly Meeting, appears the most likely source. Harvey, who died in 1733, married in 1690 and had children by 1694. Penn would have been in the Bristol area often, as this was where Hannah Callowhill lived, and he may have moved there in 1697 because his father-in-law fell ill. It is possible that Thomas Harvey was not a Friend, but the careful wording of the manuscript as to the reliability of his memory seems congruent with Friends' testimony on truth telling. LYM, "Testimonies Concerning 1728–1758," manuscript, Library of the Religious Society of Friends, London, 73; LYM, minutes, 1734, 87; Tyeth A. T. Spencer, *Quakerism at Hogstye End, Buckinghamshire* (Leighton Buzzard: H. Jackson, 1939). I am indebted to Malcolm Thomas for help in trying to identify Thomas Harvey.

9. Three parts of the Harvey manuscript suggest that it contains at least some reliable information. First, Penn's account of first hearing Thomas Loe in Ireland, around 1657, mentions his father's Black slave, and Pepys's diary says that the admiral brought an enslaved person back from Jamaica. Second, when Penn hears Loe for the second time, he is so moved that he begins to weep, and he stands up so that Friends can see his tears. This sounds like the act of a self-important rich young gentleman. Third, when Penn surrenders his sword, he gives it to his manservant. The offhand way in which Penn refers to the servant is typical of a gentleman. DSP, 2:60.

10. WWP, 1:4.

11. There are only a few references to Penn's relationship with his mother. Penn's biographer Sydney George Fisher speculated that Lady Penn must have been "a plain, mediocre person; or we would know more about her." Parson Weems, best known for his account of George Washington and the cherry tree, created an imaginary dialogue between Penn and his mother to concoct a tender domestic scene. Weems used Clarkson and other sources, but he also created dialogue between Penn and King Charles, King James, and prominent Friends. A reader would have no way of separating fact from fiction. Sydney George Fisher, *The True William Penn* (Philadelphia: J. B. Lippincott, 1900), 39; M. L. Weems, *The Life of William Penn* (Philadelphia: Carey and Lea, 1833), 2.

12. In a comment delivered at a conference of Quaker historians in Guilford County, North Carolina, in 1998, Rosemary Moore noted that Friends tolerated many deviations from Isaac Penington, who was, like Penn, a prominent member of the gentry. See also Ingle, *First Among Friends*, 140–41; the quotation is from a personal communication from Ingle, July 1, 1998.

13. Robert Sutcliff, *Travels in Some Parts of North America* (York: Sutcliff, 1811), 110, 111. Sutcliff could have heard both of these anecdotes from Owen Jones's sister. Jones's grandmother was Gainer Owen, whose brother was married to Ann Wood of Darby. There were Wood families with children in Darby at the time of Penn's visit, but Rebecca Wood's name is not mentioned in meeting minutes. There is no record of Penn's visit to a Haverford meeting. Living in Philadelphia, Penn would have had no reason to go to Darby en route to Haverford. Thanks to Patricia O'Donnell for this information.

14. Clarkson, *Public and Private Life of William Penn*, 2:83.

15. Clyde A. Milner II, *With Good Intentions: Quaker Work Among the Pawnees, Otos, and Omahas in the 1870s* (Lincoln: University of Nebraska Press, 1982), 2.

16. Soderlund, *Lenape Country*, 111, 202, shows that Native Americans and New Jersey settlers had worked out a pattern of accommodation and peace before the settlement of Pennsylvania.

17. Nicholas B. Wainwright, *One Hundred and Fifty Years of Collecting by the Historical Society of Pennsylvania, 1824–1974* (Philadelphia: Historical Society of Pennsylvania, 1974), 3.

18. "C'est le seul traite entre ces peuples et les Chretiens qui n'ait point ete rompu." M. de Voltaire, *Letters Concerning the English Nation* (London: C. Davis and A. Lyon, 1733), 25. See also "Essays in Literature, Philosophy, Art, History," in *The Works of Voltaire: A Contemporary Version*, translated by William F. Fleming, 21 vols. (New York: Dingwall-Roch, 1927), vol. 19, *Philosophical Letters*, part 1, 209. A variant of this saying appears in Clarkson, *Public and Private Life of William Penn*, 1:131.

19. For a more accurate text than the first published version, see *PWP*, 2:127.

20. Oldmixon, *British Empire in North America*, 21.

21. Henry J. Cadbury, ed., "Caleb Pusey's Account of Pennsylvania," *Quaker History* 64, no. 1 (1975): 49–51.

22. Samuel Smith, *History of the Province of Pennsylvania*, edited by William M. Mervine (Philadelphia: J. B. Lippincott, 1913); Robert Proud, *The History of Pennsylvania, in North America* [. . .] (Philadelphia: Zacharia Poulson Jr., 1797), 2 vols.

23. *WWP*, 1:121, 124.

24. *Presentation to the Historical Society of Pennsylvania of the Belt of Wampum Delivered by the Indians to William Penn, at the "Great Treaty" Under the Elm Tree, in 1682* (Philadelphia: Historical Society of Pennsylvania, 1857), 236; see also Albert Cook Myers, *William Penn: His Own Account of the Lenni Lenape or Delaware Indians* (Moylan, PA: Myers, 1937), 95.

25. Charles Keyser, *Penn's Treaty with the Indians* (Philadelphia: David McKay, 1882), 39, 43, 47.

26. The best account of the painting and its reproductions is Ellen Starr Brinton, "Benjamin West's Painting of Penn's Treaty with the Indians," *Bulletin of Friends Historical Association* 30, no. 2 (1941): 99–189.

27. Clarkson, *Public and Private Life of William Penn*, 1:129–31; Kett received the sash from Mrs. Mary Penn, daughter-in-law of the founder. Another sash, pink with blue stripes, which Penn is also alleged to have worn at the signing, was inherited by Hudson Gurney, Esq., MP, of the Barclay family. *Records and Proceedings of the Outiani Society* (London: Nicol, 1822), 36 (pamphlet at the Library of the Religious Society of Friends, London).

28. John F. Watson, *Annals of Philadelphia and Pennsylvania, in the Olden Time* (1842), 2 vols. (Philadelphia: Elijah Thomas, 1857), 55–56; John Frost, *The Life of William Penn, the Founder of Pennsylvania* [. . .] (Philadelphia: Lindsay and Blakiston, 1849), 98–100, 117.

29. Roberts Vaux, *A Memoir on the Locality of the Great Treaty Between William Penn and the Indian Natives in 1682* (Philadelphia: Historical Society of Pennsylvania, 1826; reprint, 1864), 87.

30. *Presentation to the Historical Society of Pennsylvania of the Belt of Wampum*, 205–82. Horatio Hale concluded after conferring with Iroquois chiefs that the design on the treaty belts was of Iroquois origin. Frank Speck later argued that the belt could have been from the Iroquois, the Lenni Lenape, or another northern tribe. The Penn family owned several wampum belts that, when sold at auction, were all labeled as coming from Penn's treaty with the Indians. Horatio Hale, *Four Huron Wampum Records: A Study of Aboriginal American History and Mnemonic Symbols* (London: Harrison and Sons, 1897), 251; Frank G. Speck, "The Penn Wampum Belts," *Leaflets of the Museum of the American Indian* 4 (March 22, 1925): 11–15. The belts were auctioned as lot 139 at a Christie's sale on July 10, 1916.

31. In 1728, Governor Patrick Gordon told the Native Americans that "you, you[r] Father William Penn, & with his Governours are in Writing on Record" in oral traditions of the Indians, adding, "& I desire

that you may repeat them over and over Children, & to all your People." Gordon then listed the nine links in the covenant of perpetual peace. *Minutes of the Provincial Council of Pennsylvania from the Organization to the Termination of the Proprietary Government*, 10 vols. (Philadelphia: Severns, 1838–52), 3:329–30 (see also 3:88); John Watson, *The Indian Treaty for the Lands Now the Site of Philadelphia and the Adjacent Country* (Philadelphia: J. B. Lippincott, 1836), 132; and Peter S. du Ponceau and Joshua F. Fisher, *A Memoir on the History of the Celebrated Treaty Made by William Penn with the Indians Under the Elm Tree at Shackamaxon, in the Year 1682* (Philadelphia: M'Carty and Davis, 1836), part 3, 192, 200–202; Marsillac quoted in Hull, *Penn: A Topical Biography*, 85.

32. Captain Black Beaver, a Delaware Indian, claimed to have a "Great Treaty" on parchment that the tribe had kept intact until it was destroyed during the Civil War. Thomas C. Battey, "The Penn Parchment," *Friend*, January 30, 1897. Henry Cadbury evaluated this story in "Letter from the Past 62," *Friends Intelligencer*, January 20, 1945, 43. Charles Keyser was skeptical about both the treaty and the "precious story" of the "Divine Master" and insisted that this oral tradition, which endured for many generations, put the story into the "secure treasure-house of Earths most valuable possession—the credence of our common humanity." Keyser, *Penn's Treaty with the Indians*, 14.

33. Fisher, *True William Penn*, 212–14, 234.

34. Brinton, "Benjamin West's Painting," 129–32. Pictures of these artifacts are in two exhibition catalogues: Charles Coleman Sellers, *Symbols of Peace: William Penn's Treaty with the Indians* (Philadelphia: Pennsylvania Academy of the Fine Arts, 1976), and *An Image of Peace: The Penn Treaty Collection of Mr. and Mrs. Meyer P. Potamkin* (Harrisburg: Pennsylvania History and Museum Commission, 1996).

35. In 1893, Penn Treaty Park was dedicated at the alleged original site. A recent proposal wanted the site renamed to include the Lenape leader Chief Tamanend, who also allegedly signed the treaty. An attempt by the National Park Service to remove the statue of William Penn was abandoned after popular outcry and intervention by the governor of Pennsylvania. Michael Clemmons, "Penn's Treaty Park Should Be Renamed to Honor Chief Tamanend," op-ed, *Philadelphia Inquirer*, November 24, 2022.

36. For example, one can see Hicks's *Peaceable Kingdom* on the wall in a scene from the television sitcom *Three's Company*.

37. In 1805, West said, "The great object I had in forming that composition, savages brought into harmony and peace by justice and benevolence, by not withholding them what was their right, and giving them what they were in want of, and as well as by that art that a conquest that was made over native people without sward or Dadger." Quoted in Brinton, "Benjamin West's Painting," 114.

38. James O'Neil Spady, "Colonialism and the Discursive Antecedents of Penn's Treaty with the Indians," in *Friends and Enemies in Penn's Woods: Indians, Colonists, and the Racial Construction of Pennsylvania*, edited by William A. Pencak and Daniel K. Richter (University Park: Penn State University Press, 2004), 18–40. Recent studies of Native Americans in Pennsylvania include Jane T. Merritt, *At the Crossroads: Indians and Empires on a Mid-Atlantic Frontier, 1700–1763* (Chapel Hill: University of North Carolina Press, 2003); and Kevin Kenny, *Peaceable Kingdom Lost: The Paxton Boys and the Destruction of William Penn's Holy Experiment* (New York: Oxford University Press, 2009).

39. *PWP*, 2:108.

40. In *Penn: A Life*, 363–64, Andrew Murphy argues that Penn used the phrase once and that historians have overemphasized it. But Murphy does not mention

that Penn used the concepts behind the phrase on several occasions, including in his prayer for Philadelphia.

41. The text of Trueblood's speech appears in Benjamin F. Trueblood, *William Penn's Experiment in Civil Government* (Boston: American Peace Society, 1895). See also Violet Oakley, *The Holy Experiment: A Message to the World* (Philadelphia: privately printed, ca. 1922); Maxwell Burt, *Philadelphia: Holy Experiment* (New York: Doubleday, Doran, 1945); Bronner, *Penn's "Holy Experiment"*; Paul Cromwell, "The 'Holy Experiment': An Examination of the Influence of the Society of Friends upon the Development and Evolution of Correctional Philosophy" (PhD diss., Florida State University, 1986); Robert Grant Crist, ed., *Penn's Example to the Nations: 300 Years of the Holy Experiment* (Harrisburg: Pennsylvania Council of Churches for the Pennsylvania Religious Tercentenary Committee, 1987); J. Jason Browne II, *A Holy Experiment II: The Resurrection of the Spirit of America* (Scottsdale, AZ: Visionary Press, 1995); William Kashautus III, *The Making of William Penn's Holy Experiment in Education* (Philadelphia: Committee on Education, Philadelphia Yearly Meeting, 1992).

42. Proud, *History of Pennsylvania*, 1:40, 41, 44; Clarkson, *Public and Private Life of William Penn*, 2:109; WWP, 2:535, 587, 590, 873. As a member of the Royal Society, Penn knew about scientific experiments, but he rarely used the word in this sense.

43. PWP, 2:110.

44. PWP, 2:106.

45. Fisher, *True William Penn*, 213.

46. PWP, 2:591. Penn is using the millennial vision differently here than he did in the letters he wrote before first visiting Pennsylvania. In the earlier references, he seems to be saying that Friends will create the conditions for the millennium to begin in Pennsylvania and that it will then spread to the rest of the world. Ever since the second century and the eschatological teachings of Montanus, who believed that the New Jerusalem would be created somewhere in Asia Minor, where he was living, it was common to believe that the millennium would begin in one area and then expand to others. By contrast, the prayer for Philadelphia is more of an exhortation upon common themes. Penn now recognized the problems facing his new colony but was still holding on to his millennial hopes.

47. PWP, 2:523, 503. For other migrants who shared Penn's vision, see J. William Frost, "Penn's Experiment in the Wilderness: Promise and Legend," *Pennsylvania Magazine of History and Biography* 107, no. 4 (1983): 591–95.

48. Penn's purpose, Proud wrote, was "to render men as free and happy as the nature of their existence could bear, in their civil state, and in a religious state, to restore to them those lost rights and privileges, with which God and nature had originally blessed the human race." Proud, *History of Philadelphia*, 1:168–69.

49. Endy, *William Penn and Early Quakerism*.

50. Frost, *Perfect Freedom*, 34.

51. Jonathan Marsden, "William Penn and Sir Francis Dashwood's Sawmill," *Georgian Group Journal* 8 (1988): 147–48; *Aubrey's Brief Lives*, 234–36; Proud, *History of Philadelphia*, 1:148.

52. Jane Calvert argues that there was such a thing as Quaker constitutionalism even before Penn, that it continued through the eighteenth century, and that it influenced the Articles of Confederation and the US Constitution, primarily through John Dickinson. *Quaker Constitutionalism*, 10, 17–21, 314.

53. Calvert, *Quaker Constitutionalism*, 89.

54. Montesquieu and Jefferson quoted in Weems, *Life of William Penn*, preface, and again in the 1944 University of Pennsylvania commencement address by Charles Francis Jenkins; see Jenkins, "The Founding of Pennsylvania," *General Magazine and*

Historical Chronicle 47, no. 11 (1945): 67–68; Lord Acton quoted in J. Carroll Hayes, "Penn vs. Lord Baltimore: A Brief for the Penns, in re Mason and Dixon Line," *Pennsylvania History* 8, no. 4 (1941): 279.

55. Dixon, *Historical Biography of William Penn*, 43, 54.

56. Fisher, *True William Penn*, 70–71, 91, 94, 100–101.

57. John W. Graham, *William Penn, Founder of Pennsylvania* (London: George Allen & Unwin, 1917), 133, 142.

58. Thomas Macaulay, *History of England from the Accession of James Second* [. . .] (London: Longman, Brown, 1858), 6 vols., 2:80–83, 483. See also W. E. Forster, *William Penn and Thomas B. Macaulay; Being Brief Observations on the Charges* [. . .] (London: Gilpin, 1849), proving that some of Macaulay's charges involving the Monmouth Rebellion and Magdalen College lack documentary evidence. But Forster ignores the charge that Penn avoided tithes on the Worminghurst estate by including them in the purchase price. There is no record that Penn paid tithes on his estates and no one has investigated how he managed this.

59. Vincent Buranelli, *The King and the Quaker: A Study of William Penn and James II* (Philadelphia: University of Pennsylvania Press, 1962), 14–15, 209–13. Buranelli insists that Penn was right to support James.

60. Illick, *William Penn the Politician*, 79–80, 86–95.

61. Dunn, *Penn: Politics and Conscience*, ix, 150–51; Dunn, "Penny Wise and Pound Foolish."

62. Geiter, *William Penn*, vii, 1, 6, 33–34, 68–70.

63. *PWP*, 3:62n8; Trudy Bayer, "Rethinking William Penn," *Friends Journal*, January 1, 2022, https://www.friendsjournal.org/rethinking-william-penn/; Kathleen Bell, "Flawed Quaker Heroes," *Friends Journal*, January 1, 2022, https://www.friendsjournal.org/flawed-quaker-heroes; Adlai Amor,

"William Penn House: What's in a Name?," Friends Committee on National Legislation, December 1, 2020, https://www.fcnl.org/updates/2020-12/william-penn-house-whats-name. Bayer notes that Quakers have engaged in many discussions about whether contemporary moral standards can be applied to the past.

64. "History: William Penn Has 300th Anniversary," *Life*, October 16, 1944, 67–75.

65. William Wistar Comfort, *William Penn and Our Liberties* (Philadelphia: Lippincott, 1947), 112, 131.

66. "Penn and Religious Liberty: Interpreted by Representatives of Sixteen Denominations," *Founder's Week* (Philadelphia: Ketterlinus, 1908) (print at Friends Historical Library, Swarthmore College); Stanley Yarnall, "Lest We Forget: A William Penn Tercentenary Recollection on Religious Liberty," *Friend*, September 14, 1944, 6.

67. Daniel Hoffman's *Brotherly Love* (New York: Vintage Books, 1981) was used as the libretto for Ezra Laderman's music in the oratorio *Brotherly Love*, performed by the Philadelphia Singers in 2000.

68. R. D. Littleboy, "To the Editor of the Times," 1984, clipping at Friends House, London; Pub. L. No. 98–516, S. J. Res. 80, 98th Cong., 98 Stat. 2433 (1984).

69. Margaret Bacon, "Our Continuing Holy Experiment: What Love Can Do in '82," *Friends Journal* 28, no. 15 (1982): 1–12.

70. Philadelphia Yearly Meeting, *Faith and Practice* (Philadelphia: Philadelphia Yearly Meeting, 2017); LYM, *Quaker Faith and Practice*, 5th ed. (London: Yearly Meeting of the Religious Society of Friends, 2014).

71. Scott Turow, "Order in the Court: The Jurors Were Starved, Jailed—and Victorious," *New York Times Magazine*, April 18, 1999, 109; Murray Dubin, "Predecessor to MOVE in Unruliness: Billy Penn," *Philadelphia Inquirer*, January 18, 2020. In *A Virtuous Education: Penn's Vision for Philadelphia Schools* (Wallingford, PA: Pendle

Hill Publications, 1997), William C. Kashatus examines how the themes in Penn's writing remained important in private and public Pennsylvania schools until the mid-nineteenth century.

72. Thomas Budd, *Good Order Established in Pennsylvania and New Jersey in America* (London[?], 1685), 29; Proud, *History of Philadelphia*, 1:148.

CHAPTER 9

1. Alison Olson, "William Penn, Parliament, and Proprietary Government," *William and Mary Quarterly* 18 (April 1961): 176–95, shows how Penn relied upon support from noble Whig and Tory acquaintances to preserve Pennsylvania.
2. Mann, "Beyond the Bounds," 70–71.
3. *PWP*, 3:267–71. The document is undated but was probably written in 1689.
4. Dunn, "Personality of William Penn," 11. The original conference was sponsored by the William Penn Foundation and sought to create a plan to publicize Penn as a forgotten founding father; it failed in its purpose.
5. *PWP*, 3:411–13, 419, 422, 425.
6. An exception (and even then not an unqualified endorsement) is "Love thy neighbor as thyself" (Matt. 19:19, 22:39). In *NCNC*, Penn distinguished between the lawful and unlawful self in terms of morality.
7. Garman et al., *Hidden in Plain Sight*.
8. Leo Damrosch, *The Sorrows of the Quaker Jesus: James Nayler and the Puritan Crackdown on the Free Spirit* (Cambridge: Harvard University Press, 1996), 267–69.
9. Angell and Dandelion, *Early Quakers and Their Theological Thought* contains essays on the most significant Quaker thinkers. See also R. Melvin Keiser and Rosemary Moore, eds., *Knowing the Mystery of Life Within: Selected Writings of Isaac Penington in Their Historical and Theological Context* (London: Quaker Books, 2005), 213–19.

APPENDIX

1. "The Invalidity of John Faldo's Vindication" (1673), *WWP*, 2:377.
2. "A Serious Apology for the People called Quakers" (1671), *WWP*, 2:37.
3. "A Defense of a Paper called Gospel Truth" (1692), *WWP*, 2:912.
4. Penn had read and praised Samuel Fisher's *Rusticus ad Academicos*, 129, 194–95, which made an argument about the "fallibility of the bare naked letter of the Scriptures, and of its liableness to [be] corrupted and falsified by mistranslations, so as to have various Lections in the Original Copyes of it" (available at the Digital Quaker Collection, http://dqc.esr.earlham.edu). He had also read a history of the Council of Trent by the "Learned and Judicious Pietro Soane Polano" and echoed Roman Catholic critiques of Protestant reliance on the Bible. Endy, *William Penn and Early Quakerism*, 191–93.
5. "Invalidity of John Faldo's Vindication," *WWP*, 2:325–27, 338–40.
6. "Invalidity of John Faldo's Vindication," *WWP*, 2:363; "Urim and Thummim" (1674), *WWP*, 2:623–24.
7. *Address to Protestants*, in *WWP*, 1:745–47. The essentials in "the Language of the Holy Scripture" included "Belief of God, Christ, Spirit, Man's Lapse or Fall, Justification, Repentance, Sanctification, Resurrection, and Eternal Recompense."
8. *Address to Protestants*, in *WWP*, 1:748.
9. *The Advice of William Penn to His Children, Relating to Their Civil and Religious Conduct*, ca. 1699, *WWP*, 1:896–97.
10. *PWP*, 1:60–67; *Sandy Foundation Shaken*, *WWP*, 1:248–65.
11. Edwin B. Bronner, "William Penn and the Scriptures," in *Truth's Bright Embrace: Essays and Poems in Honor of Arthur O. Roberts*, edited by Paul N. Anderson and Howard R. Macy (Newberg: George Fox University Press, 1996), 58.
12. Mürer, "Quaker Bible Index" (1993); *PWP*, 1:668, 2:683. Volumes 3 and 4 of *PWP* do not index Bible citations, perhaps

because there was such a large quantity of nonreligious materials. The compilers of these two sources had very different interests. Mürer sought to compare citations of the Bible by George Fox, Robert Barclay, Penn, and John Woolman. The focus of the editors of *PWP* is less on Penn's religion than on his history and role in early Pennsylvania.

13. See, for example, his *Harmony of Divine and Heavenly Doctrines*, 81, 104.

14. "General Rule of Faith and Practice" (1673), *WWP*, 1:597. God created scripture so that men would have an "Outward" as well as an "Inward Witness." He "condescended" to provide an "external medium."

15. "General Rule of Faith and Practice," *WWP*, 1:597.

INDEX

Page numbers in italics refer to illustrations.

advocacy for religious liberty
   ancient authorities and, 92–93, 207nn13–14
   at business meetings, 69–71
   consistency of, xii, 50, 87, 102
   contrast with restricted liberty in meetings, 52
   extension to additional faiths, xvi, 2
   ideas put into practice, 82
   inability to coerce conscience and, 180
   influences on, xv–xvi
   reason in, 86, 87, 90, 209n27
   tactics used in, 14–17, 85–94
affirmations of loyalty
   Anglicans on, 33
   for citizenship or naturalization, 21
   debate regarding, xv, 72, 74–77, 81
   law on allowance of, 30, 64, 75, 139
   oaths vs., xv, 30, 33, 75, 85, 105, 120
   in Pennsylvania, 102
Amyraut (Amyraldus), Moses, 41, 42, 45, 201n30, 201n32
anarchy, xii, 52, 99, 162
Anglicans
   Defoe's satire of, 2
   on Inward Light, 179–80
   Latitudinarians, 96, 211n45
   No Cross, No Crown on, 113
   pamphlet war with, 139
   in Pennsylvania, 27, 30, 33
   Quaker debates with, 50, 185
   religious authority of, 62
   See also Church of England
Anne (queen of England), 4, 6, 30, 33, 127, 197n60

antislavery movement, 137, 158, 168, 176, 194n15
Aubrey, John, 37–39, 169, 196n51, 197n58, 200n16, 216n11

Bacon, Francis, 122, 123
Baltimore, Lord (Charles Calvert), 19, 23–24, 69, 94, 98, 103, 169, 171
Bancroft, George, 170
Baptists
   persecution of, 4, 17
   Quaker debates with, 12, 50, 52, 134, 185
   on Westminster Confession, 83
Barbour, Hugh, 112, 188, 217nn28–29
Barclay, Robert
   on affirmations of loyalty, 76
   Anarchy of the Ranters, 57, 203n29
   Apology for the True Christian Divinity, 120, 132
   conversion to Quakerism, 202n48
   Frame of Government and, 99
   lack of self-doubt in writings of, 179
   land purchases by, 18
   on paradoxical nature of Christian belief, 146
   Penn's preface to collected works of, 28
   on Quaker preaching, 132, 215n2
   sermons from, 133, 134, 138
   spiritual sensitivity of, 61
   traveling ministry of, 35, 199n3
   Wilkinson-Story dispute and, 59
Batt, Jasper, 33
Baxter, Richard, 15
Bayer, Trudy, 223n63
Beard, Charles, 132
Benson, Gervase, 86
Berkeley, John, 18, 211n48

Besse, Joseph
Collection of the Works of William Penn, xiii, 35, 38, 135
editorial processes used by, 166–67
on farewell sermon as epistle, 132, 216n14
on Native American relations with, 155–56
on Penn's conversion to Quakerism, 35, 38, 39, 41, 50, 151
Bettle, Samuel, 170
Billings, Edward, 18
Bingly, William, 140
Bishop, George, 50, 84, 86, 90–91, 200n17, 202n4, 206nn3–5, 207n15
Blackbarrow, Sarah, 200n20
Black Beaver (Delaware captain), 221n32
Blackwell, William, 27
Blondel, David, 41, 201n32
Boulton, Jobe, 205n15
Boyle, Robert, 1
Bradford, William, 57
Bronner, Edwin, xiii, 135, 173
Budd, Thomas, 136, 174
Bugg, Francis, 81, *100*, 136
Bunyan, John, 1, 193nn2–3
Buranelli, Vincent, 171, 223n59
Burnet, Gilbert, 2, 36, 96, 171, 199nn5–6
Burnyeat, John, 28
Burrough, Edward, 79, 84, 85, 133, 206n5
Bushel's case, 28, 88–89, 133, 170, 195n31, 208–9nn19–20, 216n8
business meetings, 64–81
affirmation debate and, 74–77
attendance records, 67, 68
by dissidents, 57, 74
omission in Penn scholarship, 64
on political engagement, 71–72
power structure in, 65–66
on religious liberty, 69–72, 80
spiritual guidance in, 13, 65
women and, 56–57, 59–62, 203n27, 204n39
See also London Yearly Meeting; Meeting for Sufferings; Second Day Morning Meeting of Ministers

Calder, Alexander Milne, 174
Callowhill, Hannah. *See* Penn, Hannah Callowhill
Calvert, Charles. *See* Baltimore, Lord
Calvert, Jane, 222n52
Calvinists, 5, 8–10, 25, 41–42, 45–47, 51, 120, 180
Camm, John, 84
Carteret, Phillip, 18, 211n48
Catholics
Inquisition and, 3, 8, 51, 96
Penn on, 96–97, 208n17
Protestant alliance against, 5, 92
religious liberty and, xvi, 2, 16, 25, 62, 70, 98, 101, 199n5
as threat to Church of England, 92
Cato, 109, 119
Charles I (king of England), 3, 39, 93, 96, 210n39
Charles II (king of England)
assassination plot against, 210n42
death of, 17, 24
debts owed by, x, 18
Fifth Monarchist revolt against, 11
illegitimate children of, 4, 25, 194n17
land grants by, x, 5, 9, 18–19, 23, 192n4, 194n20
as patron of Royal Society, 1
Penn and, xvii, 15, 62, 69, 199n11
religious persecution under, 5, 24, 70, 82, 94
restoration to throne, 3, 7, 45, 82, 83
Whig opposition and, 18, 19, 94
Christianity
authentic, 60, 62, 63, 86, 162
paradoxical nature of beliefs in, 146
primitive, 10, 52, 102, 171
reasonableness of, 8, 140
triumph over paganism, 16
See also specific denominations
Church of England
Articles of Religion, 83, 85, 96
Catholics as threat to, 92
enforcement of conformity with, 51, 82, 83
Glorious Revolution and, 5
hierarchical organization of, 62
Penn family and, 6, 25
persecution initiated by, 84
Puritan views of, 83
tithes to, xii, 4, 98, 104, 208n17
See also Anglicans
Clapham, Thomas, 50

Clarkson, Thomas, 35, 148, 150, 152, 154, 157, 161, 195n36
Clinton, Bill, 206n1
Coale, Benjamin, 134, 139
Coale, Josiah, 50
Coke, Edward, 86, 90, 207n14
Comfort, William Wistar, 172
Commonwealth of England
    creation of, 3
    fall of, 202n45
    Quakers during, 11, 82, 86, 196n46, 209n21
    religious liberty and, xvi, 91
    See also Cromwell, Oliver
Connecticut, 23, 69, 103
conversion to Quakerism, 34–48
    Aubrey's account of, 37–39, 200n16
    Besse's account of, 35, 38, 39, 41, 50
    childhood experiences and, 37–40, 47
    Harvey's account of, 37–39, 41, 43, 150–51, 200n14
    justification of, 42, 200n17
    life trajectory altered by, xv, 34
    Loe's influence on, 9, 37–43, 47–48, 200nn13–14, 200n16
    Penn's writings on, 35–36, 42–45
    reactions of Penn family, 34, 43, 50, 151
    stages of, 40, 44, 46, 47, 201n40
    terminology for, 199n1
    visible transformation following, 106
Cowley, Abraham, 118, 213n32
Craven, Avery, 132
Cressy, David, 193n8
Crisp, Stephen, 72, 134, 135, 139, 140, 207n15
Croese, Gerald, 150, 215n1
Cromwell, Oliver
    Fox's visit to, 199n3
    land grants by, 7, 37
    New Model Army and, 83
    as public weeper, 39
    purging of Quakers from army, 11
    religious liberty and, 4, 9, 83–85
    See also Commonwealth of England
Crouch, Nathaniel, 135, 136
crying, 39, 200nn21–22
Crystal, David, 216n10

Danson, Thomas, 50
Dashwood, Francis, 169
Defoe, Daniel, 2, 193n3, 193n5

Delaware
    Act of Union with Pennsylvania, 21
    militia and fort supported by, 27, 31, 32
    population demographics, 26–27
    religious liberty in, 101, 104, 105
    title granted to Penn, 20, 24
Dewsbury, William, 133, 134, 140
Dickinson, Jonathan, 170
Dixon, William, 170
Dobrée, Bonamy, xiv
Donne, John, 2
Dryden, John, 2
Dunn, Mary, xiii–xiv, 12, 66, 87, 129–30, 149, 171, 178
Dunn, Richard S., xiii–xiv, 149, 171, 178
DuPlessy, Mornay, 41, 119–20, 201n30
Du Simitiere, Pierre Eugene, 216n7

East New Jersey, 18, 98, 211n48
Edict of Nantes (1598), 5, 8, 96, 120, 199n5
Edmundson, William, 74
Edward VI (king of England), 83, 91, 207n14
Elizabeth (princess of Bohemia), 35–36, 38, 47, 118–19, 199n1, 199n3
Elizabeth I (queen of England), 1, 83, 91, 148
Ellwood, Thomas, 2, 13–14, 76–78, 206n41
England
    Dutch wars with, 3, 7, 9, 18, 95
    French wars with, 3, 6, 28, 30, 139
    justice system in, 197n56
    literacy rates in, 2, 193n8
    Penn's support of monarchy, ix, xvii, 4–5, 15, 24–26, 29–30
    Quaker traveling ministry in, xv, 29, 134
    religious liberty in, 4–5, 9, 24–25, 28, 83–84, 95–98, 104–5, 120
    See also Church of England; Commonwealth of England; Glorious Revolution; London; Restoration England; *specific rulers*
English Civil War
    causes of, 15, 89
    literacy rates during, 193n8
    Quaker refusal to remove hats during, 209n21
    religious freedom debate and, 83, 84
    sectarian group emergence during, 9, 45
Erasmus, Desiderius, 16, 112, 122, 123
ethics. *See* morality

Evans, Harold, 149
Evans, John, 32, 33

Faldo, John, 55
Fantel, Hans, xiv
Farnsworth, Richard, 86
Fell, John, 45
Fell, Margaret, 50, 84, 198n92, 213n35
females. *See* women
Fenwick, John, 18
Finch, Heneage, 209n29
Fisher, Samuel, 84–85, 210n43, 224n4
Fisher, Sydney George, 158–59, 164, 171, 219n11
Fletcher, Benjamin, 30, 101, 102, 211n50, 211n53
Ford, Philip, 6, 32
Forster, W. E., 223n58
Fox, George
    on affirmations of loyalty, 76
    authentic Christianity discovered by, 62, 63
    business meetings and, 65, 68, 204–5n12
    conversion narrative of, 44
    depression experienced by, 179
    efforts to convert Cromwell, 84
    on experimental knowledge, 10, 162
    funeral of, 26, 73, 137
    imprisonment of, 6, 50, 67
    Journal, 28, 66, 73, 77, 121, 162
    leadership of, 12–13, 61, 62, 65
    marriage of, 50, 198n92
    meeting with Penn, 151, 202n7
    Penn on, 52, 62, 65, 196n49
    Perrot dispute and, 54, 55, 62
    on political engagement, 72
    on reason and unreason, 86, 207n16
    on religious liberty, 16, 59, 60, 85, 86, 104
    sermons from, 217n20
    traveling ministry of, 35
    visit to Cromwell, 199n3
Frame of Government (1701)
    drafts of, 20, 22, 99
    Liberty Bell and, xi, 166
    Locke's criticism of, 193n6
    preface to, 213n32
    on religious liberty, ix, 101, 102
    revisions to, 30, 31
France
    English wars with, 3, 6, 28, 30, 139
    religious liberty in, 5, 8, 25, 92, 201n30
Franklin, Benjamin, 116, 158, 169
Fraser, David, xiii, 135
freedom of conscience. *See* religious liberty
Fry, Elizabeth, 148
Furly, Benjamin, 99, 110

Geiter, Mary, xiv, 171, 194n20
George I (king of England), 4, 193n8
Glorious Revolution (1688)
    Catholics following, 102, 104
    causes of, 194n21
    James II deposed during, xiii, 5, 26
    justice system after, 197n56
    Penn in hiding after, 67
Gordon, Patrick, 158, 220–21n31
Graham, John W., 171
Grant, Ulysses S., 153, 161
Gratten, John, 77
Graves, Michael, 132, 138, 218n47
Grotius, Hugo, 41, 92, 201n30
Gurney, Hudson, 220n27

Haas, Otto and Phoebe, 173
Hale, Horatio, 220n30
Hall, David, *154*, 157
Hammond, Henry, 93, 96, 210n39
Harrison, James, 161, 163
Harvey, Thomas, 37–39, 41, 43, 150–51, 167, 200n14, 219nn8–9
Henry VIII (king of England), 91, 96, 148
Herbert, George, 122–24
heresy, 10, 28, 45, 50, 73–74, 85, 92, 136–37
Hicks, Edward: *The Peaceable Kingdom*, 159–60, *160*, 221n36
Hicksites, 152, 153, 159, 168
Historical Society of Pennsylvania, xiii, 155, 157, 158, 169, 170, 172, 173
Hoffman, Daniel, 223n67
Holmes, Geoffrey, 25
Holmes, Thomas, 27
Hookes, Elias, 66, 204n6
Howgill, Francis, 84
Hubberthorne, Richard, 84
Huguenots, 25, 92, 96, 98, 208n17
Hull, William I., xiv, 200n19, 216n9
humanism, 8, 121, 124, 129, 146, 180, 200n22

imperialism, xii, 2, 160, 171
incantatory style, 85, 218n47

Independents
   Glorious Revolution and, 5
   hat removal during prayer, 55
   Owen as leader of, 201n33
   persecution of, 4, 17
   Quaker debates with, 12, 50, 52, 185
   theological differences with Anglicans, 96
   on Westminster Confession, 83
Ingle, H. Larry, 152, 202n10
Inward Light
   authority of, 46, 80, 84–85, 101, 108, 185, 191, 203n15
   biblical citations and, 190
   clearness from, 99
   in the conscience, 187
   cross as metaphor for, 115
   direct guidance of, 60, 65
   dissident Quakers and, 51, 52, 55
   experimental knowledge and, 10, 162
   as intellectual basis for democracy, 170
   Puritans and Anglicans on, 179–80
   reasonableness and, 209n27
   religious liberty and, 15
   transformations due to, 106
   truth established through, 188
   vague terminology regarding, 207n15
Ireland
   land seizures in, 9
   Penn family land in, 7, 37, 199n103
   Quaker traveling ministry in, xiii, 7, 29, 37, 47, 134
   Restoration and, 193–94n9
   uprising in (1941), 3
Iroquois, 220n30

James, William, 47, 202n49
James I (king of England), 35, 39, 93, 96, 118
James II (king of England)
   accession of, 95
   deposition of, xiii, 3, 5, 26, 97
   Dutch wars and, 3, 7, 95
   oral traditions surrounding, 150
   Penn and, xvii, 4–5, 15, 24–29, 62, 69–71, 94–98, 176–77, 198n79, 198n84, 199n6
   religious liberty under, 5, 9, 24–25, 36, 70, 80, 95–97
   Whitehead and, 68, 70
Janney, Samuel, 149, 151–53, 167
Janney, Thomas, 163

Jefferson, Thomas, 82, 170
Jones, Owen, Jr., 152, 219n13

Kashatus, William C., 224n71
Keith, George
   accusations against Penn, 33
   business meetings on, 73–74
   disciplinary action against, 74, 136
   efforts to repeal Pennsylvania charter, 30
   lack of self-doubt in writings of, 179
   LYM on, 59, 73–74, 80–81, 137
   pamphlet war with, 137, 139
   in religious debates, 134
   theological dispute with, 27–28, 59, 136–37, 145
   traveling ministry of, 35
Keith, William, 156
Kett, Joseph, 157, 220n27
Keyser, Charles, 221n32

La Rochefoucauld, François de, 122, 124
Latitudinarians, 96, 211n45
Lay, Benjamin, 158
Lenape, ix, 18, 20, 22–23, 155–61, 174, 176, 221n35
Leslie, Charles, 81, 136
Liberty Bell, xi, 166
liberty of conscience. *See* religious liberty
literacy, 2, 27, 193n8, 216n10
Lloyd, David, 31
Lloyd, Thomas, 27, 73
Locke, John, 2, 20, 99, 170, 193n6, 209n30, 210n39
Loe, Thomas
   death of, 29, 40, 50
   Penn's conversion to Quakerism and, 9, 37–43, 47–48, 200nn13–14, 200n16
   traveling ministry of, 7, 37
Logan, James, 31–32, 66, 216n7
London
   Great Fire (1666), 2, 3
   pamphlet war in, 137, 139
   plague in, 2–3, 9, 43
   population of, 2–3, 194n11
   Royal Society in, 1, 222n42
   Tower of, 7, 13–14, 62, 66, 96, 106, 108
London Yearly Meeting (LYM)
   on faith and practice, 12, 67
   hierarchical organization of, 57, 65
   on Keith, 59, 73–74, 80–81, 137

Penn's attendance at, 33, 51, 67, 77, 137
  on political engagement, 71–72
  recording of minutes for, 66
  on religious liberty, 70, 71, 87
  satirical portrait of, 100
  secret worship condemned by, 99
Louis XIV (king of France), 5, 8, 18, 25, 94, 96–97
LYM. *See* London Yearly Meeting

Macaulay, Thomas, 171, 218n5, 223n58
Machiavelli, Niccolò, 213n43
Markham, William, 30, 211n53
Marshall, Charles, 140
Marsillac, Jean de, 158
Marvell, Andrew, 2
Maryland
  border dispute with Pennsylvania, 23–24, 31, 94–95
  overthrow of charter government, 26
  religious liberty in, 98, 101–2, 105
  restrictions on Quakers in, 69
Mary (queen of England), 4–6, 26, 75, 91, 96–97, 120, 126
Massachusetts
  justice system in, 103
  overthrow of charter government, 26
  persecution of Quakers in, 50, 69
  Puritans in, x
Mather, Cotton, 180
Mead, William, 14, 73, 87–88, 174, 204n12, 205n15, 205n28
Meeting for Sufferings (MFS)
  on affirmations of loyalty, 30, 75, 76
  as executive body, 12, 57
  hierarchical organization of, 65
  manuscript submission to, 113, 166
  Penn's attendance at, 33, 67, 204–5n12
  on persecution, 14–15, 67
  recording of minutes for, 66, 204n12
  on religious liberty, 15, 69–72, 80, 87
  standing of individuals in, 68, 204–5n12
meetings. *See* business meetings; worship meetings
MFS. *See* Meeting for Sufferings
Milton, John, 1–2, 193n3
MMM. *See* Second Day Morning Meeting of Ministers
Montaigne, Michel de, 118, 122–24
Montesquieu, 170

Moore, Rosemary, 151–52, 219n12
morality
  guides to, 107, 121, 212n2
  Latitudinarians on, 211n45
  of Lenape, 22
  religious liberty and, 102–3
  self-denial as essence of, 13, 128
  standards for, xii, 104, 176, 211n54, 223n63
  state's role in fostering, 8, 17, 59
  weeping as sign of, 200n22
  See also *No Cross, No Crown*; *Some Fruits of Solitude in Reflections and Maxims*
Moretta, John, xiv
Mott, Lucretia, 152
Mucklow, William, 52–53, 55–57
Muldrew, Craig, 2
Mürer, Esther Greenleaf, 188–90, 214n46, 224–25n12
Murphy, Andrew, xiv, 87, 201n25, 208n17, 221–22n40
mysticism, 47, 53, 93, 203n19

Nash, Gary, 178
Native Americans
  assimilation strategies for, 161
  land purchases from, 9, 20, 22, 176
  peace treaty with Penn, ix, 153–61, 168, 172
  relations with colonists, xii, 153, 155–60, 168, 219n16
  wampum belts of, 155, 158, 169, 220n30
  worship meetings and, 194n15
Nayler, James, 79, 84–86, 133, 179
Newton, Isaac, 1
New York
  justice system in, 103
  overthrow of charter government, 26
  Penn's relationship with governor of, 23
  religious liberty in, 98, 105
No Cross, No Crown (Penn), 106–20
  1669 edition, 106–12, 116, 119, 130
  1682 edition, 42, 57, 60, 107, 112–20, 129, 130, 201n24
  ancient sources in, 109, 114, 117–18, 139
  audience for, 108, 109, 113, 115
  biblical citations in, 188
  on effect of receiving Christ, 202n46
  as exemplar of Quaker beliefs, 78
  on lawful and unlawful self, 117, 224n6
  moral instruction in, 20, 114, 130

No Cross, No Crown (Penn)(*continued*)
   on pride, 109–11, 115–17
   on recreations and frivolity, 110–12
   on rejection of outward deference, 108–10
   on second-person singular, 108–10
   on self-denial as essence of morality, 13, 128
   style and tone of writing, 108–10, 112
   on suffering as signal of working for truth, 178
   women in, 111, 112, 117–19
Norris, Isaac, II, 166

Oakley, Violet, 161
Oates, Titus, 3, 18
oaths of loyalty
   affirmations vs., xv, 30, 33, 75, 85, 105, 120
   anti-Catholic, 105, 211n50, 211n53
   exemption from, 15, 51, 71
   Quaker refusal of, 11, 16, 69, 70, 208n17
Offutt, William, Jr., 22
Oldmixon, John, 155
Owen, John, 8, 15, 41–42, 44–45, 196–97n54, 201nn32–33, 208n17, 211n45

pacifism, xii, 6, 139, 156–57, 162, 169–70, 172, 176
Palmieri, Brooke, 212n3
Peare, Catherine Owens, xiv
Pearson, Anthony, 86
Penington, Isaac, 13, 50, 76–77, 86, 133, 152, 179, 219n12
Penington, Mary, 77
Penn, Billy (son), 31–32, 121, 125, 215n57
Penn, Granville (great-grandson), 155, 169
Penn, Gulielma Maria Springett (first wife)
   death of, 28, 29, 120, 137, 217n38
   descriptions of, 14, 196n51
   meeting with Fox, 202n7
   Penn's correspondence with, xiii, 14, 20
   posthumous tribute by Penn, 14, 214n53
   on traveling ministry, 66
   wealth and social status, 13
Penn, Hannah Callowhill (second wife)
   complaints regarding Penn's absences, 29, 32, 66
   Penn's correspondence with, 29, 31, 129
   as proprietor of Pennsylvania, 29, 199n103, 199n105
   Quaker opposition of Penn's marriage to, 29, 178
Penn, Letetia (daughter), 121, 215n57
Penn, Margaret (sister), 6
Penn, Margaret Jasper (mother), 3, 6, 34, 36, 137, 219n11
Penn, Mary (daughter-in-law), 220n27
Penn, Richard (brother), 6
Penn, Richard (son), 168–69
Penn, Springett (son), 29, 121
Penn, Thomas (son), 156–57, 168–69
Penn, William, Jr.
   on affirmations of loyalty, 75–77
   apocalyptic warnings from, 13, 87, 111, 130, 146, 180, 197n62, 216n5
   authoritarian stance of, xiv, 49, 59, 61, 62
   Bible as viewed by, 185–91
   birth of (1644), 6
   Bushel's case and, 88–89, 133, 170, 208–9nn19–20, 216n8
   conservatism of, xvii, 49, 78, 146, 168
   contemporaries of, 1–6, 193n3
   contradictions of, xvi–xvii, 52, 59, 146
   death of (1718), 33, 176, 199n103
   debts owed by, 5–6, 27, 28, 32, 120, 176
   on dissident Quakers, xvii, 46, 49, 51–63
   education of, 8, 9, 37–38, 41–42, 195n35, 214n51
   as enigma, xvi, 35, 181
   failures of, 24, 33, 62, 171–73, 175–77
   as founding father, ix, xvii, 148, 172, 224n4
   in historical memory, 148–49, 166–74
   images of, ix–x, *xi*, 148, 169, 192n3, 216n7
   imprisonment of, xiii, xvii, 6, 13–14, 24, 26, 28, 50, 62, 66, 106, 133
   land grant given to, x, 5, 18–19, 194n20
   leadership of, xv, 12, 70, 71, 81, 134, 137
   monarchy supported by, ix, xvii, 4–5, 15, 24–26, 29–30
   as moralist, xvi, 20, 129, 181
   oral traditions surrounding, 149–53, 156, 158–59, 166, 168
   peace treaty with Native Americans, ix, 153–61, 168, 172
   radicalism of, xvii, 14, 49, 146
   reputation of, x, xiii, 146, 175
   slavery and, 3, 171, 176, 194n15
   smallpox experienced by, 133, 158, 192n3
   status of, xiv, xv, 8, 13, 34, 41, 50, 68–69, 134, 146

stroke suffered by, xii, 29, 31–33, 35, 47, 78, 199n103
sword anecdote and, 149–53, 219n9
traveling ministry of, xiii, xv, 29, 35, 47, 50, 66, 134
treason accusations against, 3, 26, 59, 72, 106, 120, 137, 217n25
See also advocacy for religious liberty; conversion to Quakerism; Pennsylvania; preaching; Quakers and Quakerism

Penn, William, Jr., writings by
Address to Protestants, xvi, 94, 210n42
The Advice of William Penn to His Children, 188, 189, 215n57
"Brief Account of the Rise and Progress of the People called Quakers," 28, 65, 73, 77, 121, 167, 196n49, 218n42
A Brief Examination, and the State of Liberty Spiritual, 57–59, 99, 204n30
The Christian Quaker and His Divine Testimony Vindicated, 78, 193n2, 212n12
"Discourse of the General rule of Faith and Practice," 203n15
England's Present Interest Considered, 209n29
Essay on the Present and Future Peace in Europe, 28, 67, 121, 139, 168
Fruits of a Father's Love, 167
"Fundamentals of Government," 99
General Rules, 60
The Great Case of Liberty of Conscience, 89–94, 210n32
"The Guide Mistaken," 49
Innocency with her Open Face, 13
Judas and the Jews, 52
A Key Opening the Way, 28
A Key to the Scriptures, 73, 78, 121, 167
"Letter to the Free Society of Traders," 155, 156, 166
More Fruits of Solitude, 107, 215nn57–58, 215n64, 215n69
The Sandy Foundation Shaken, 13, 14, 66, 150
The Spirit of Alexander the Copper-Smith, 52
A Treatise of Oaths, 42, 75, 139
Truth Exalted in a Testimony against all those Faiths, Worships, and Religions that have been formed in the Darkness of Apostacy, 46
See also No Cross, No Crown; *Some Fruits of Solitude in Reflections and Maxims*

Penn, William, Sr. (father)
authoritarianism of, 62
on conversion to Quakerism, 34, 43, 50, 151
deathbed wishes of, 195n28
debt owed to, x, 7–8, 18
during Dutch wars, 3, 7, 18, 95
land grants given to, 7, 9, 37, 192n4
marriage and family life, 6
Pepys and, 7, 8, 36–37, 195n30, 200n11, 201n36
social status of, 8, 195nn33–34
theft accusations against, 7, 195n31

Pennsbury estate, 31, 129, 172, 199n98

Pennsylvania
Act of Union with Delaware, 21
affirmation requirement in, 102
border dispute with Maryland, 23–24, 31, 94–95
charter for, 19, 20, 24, 30, 98, 175, 197n61
citizenship and naturalization in, xvi, 21, 175
as "holy experiment," 33, 148, 160–66, 173, 221–22n40
justice system in, 21–22, 103–4
land distribution in, 23, 198n73
legislative process in, 22, 30, 31
moral laws in, 102–3, 211n54
recruitment of colonists for, 57, 98–99, 113, 212n1
religious liberty in, xii, 20, 21, 27, 98–105
See also Frame of Government; Philadelphia; Quakers and Quakerism

Pennsylvania General Assembly, ix, 5, 21, 30–31, 101, 166, 197n67
Penn Treaty Park, 155, 221n35
Pennyman, Mary, 41
Pepys, Samuel
Diary of Samuel Pepys, 36, 201n25
patron of, 195n30, 199n11
on Penn family, 6–9, 36–37, 199n9, 200n11, 201n36
on Quakers, 11–13, 200n14
Perrot, John, 51–56, 58, 62
persecution. *See* religious persecution
Peters, Richard, Jr., 158

Petty, William, 193–94n9
Philadelphia
    as city of "brotherly love," xii, 148, 163
    Liberty Bell in, xi, 166
    moral behavior in, 103
    Penn's design for, xii, 2, 23
    Penn's prayer for, 164–65, 181, 222n40, 222n46
    Penn statue in, ix, 161, 172, 174, 175, 181
    religious liberty in, 101
Place, Francis: *Portrait of William Penn*, xi
Plutarch, 122–24, 214n49
Polano, Pietro Soane, 224n4
preaching, 132–47
    assessments of, 132, 215nn1–2
    biblical metaphors in, 138, 141–42, 218n45
    content of sermons, 138–42, 145–47
    criticisms of, 132, 134
    farewell sermons, 20, 135, 216n14
    funeral sermons, 26, 73, 134, 137, 138, 141
    hats worn during, 51, 54, 55, 147
    incantatory style of, 218n47
    Keith dispute and, 27–28
    leadership and, xv, 12
    length of sermons, 138–39, 216nn28–29
    level of personal detail in, 47, 140, 217n38
    marriage sermons, 141
    Penn's basic sermon, 142–45, 177
    preservation of sermons, 133–38
    on public streets, 14, 133
    speaking ability and, 133–34, 216n11
    traveling ministry and, 29, 134
predestination, 10, 13, 45, 139, 187
Presbyterians
    Glorious Revolution and, 5
    hat removal during prayer, 55
    in Pennsylvania, 26, 27
    persecution of, 4, 17
    Quaker debates with, 12, 13, 50, 52, 185
    religious authority of, 62
    theological differences with Anglicans, 96
    on Westminster Confession, 83
Preston, Mary, 157–58
proprietary government, ix, 18, 19, 29–31, 98, 127, 157
Protestants
    alliance against Catholics, 5, 92
    religious liberty for, 5, 8, 25, 28, 59, 92
    See also specific denominations
Proud, Robert, 155, 161, 166, 222n48

Puritans
    on Church of England, 83
    crying among, 200n21
    on Inward Light, 179–80
    preaching style of, 138
    in Restoration England, 46, 201–2n45
    spiritual autobiographies of, 40
    stages of conversion for, 44, 46
Pusey, Caleb, 155
Pyott, Edward, 84

Quakers and Quakerism
    antislavery movement and, 137, 158, 168, 194n15
    in Commonwealth of England, 11, 82, 86, 196n46, 209n21
    dissident, xvii, 27–28, 46, 49–63, 74, 136–37, 168
    duty in, 40, 200–201n23
    experimental knowledge and, 10, 38, 46, 143, 162, 196n43
    hierarchical organization of, 12–13, 55, 57, 65
    imprisonment of, 12, 51, 63, 70, 75, 83, 194n18, 196n46
    literacy among, 27
    meeting houses of, x, 14, 24, 68, 88, 133–35, 146, 172
    origins and growth of, 9, 11
    pacifism of, xii, 6, 139, 156–57, 162, 169–70, 172, 176
    peace testimony and, xii, 151, 168, 171
    persecution of, 4, 12, 14–17, 50, 56, 67, 69, 82–85
    plain style of, ix, 42, 84, 108, 114–15, 120, 139, 146, 150, 187
    in popular culture, x–xi, 159
    reputation of, 80, 159
    in Restoration England, 12, 51, 64, 82–83, 86, 194n18
    suspicion regarding politeness, 121, 213n39
    traveling ministry of, xiii, xv, 7, 11, 29, 35, 37, 47, 50, 66, 134
    unity of, xv, 74
    See also affirmations of loyalty; business meetings; conversion to Quakerism; Inward Light; preaching; religious experience; religious liberty; worship meetings

religious experience
  authenticity of, 46, 128
  biblical norms compared to, 179
  institutionalization of, 10, 185
  moral standards learned through, xii
  necessity of, 40, 127
  Penn's basic sermon on, 177
  subjectivity of, xv, 42
religious liberty, 82–105
  allies in fight for, 87
  business meetings on, 69–72, 80
  Cromwell and, 4, 9, 83–85
  defenses of, 17, 49, 85–86, 89–94
  as defined by Penn, 89, 95
  in Delaware, 101
  dissident Quakers and, 51, 53–55, 60, 62
  early Quaker efforts for, 84–86, 206n5
  Edict of Nantes and, 5, 8, 96, 120, 199n5
  in England, 4–5, 9, 24–25, 28, 83–84, 95–98, 104–5, 120
  Frame of Government on, ix, 101, 102
  in France, 5, 8, 25, 92, 201n30
  morality and, 102–3
  National Religious Freedom Day, 206n1
  as natural right, 59, 84, 89, 196n54
  in Pennsylvania, xii, 20, 21, 27, 98–105
  as public good, 177
  theological motivations for, 101
  in West Jersey, xii, 18
  See also advocacy for religious liberty
religious persecution
  Bishop's defense against, 86
  Charles II and, 5, 24, 70, 82, 94
  Finch on, 209n29
  migration as escape from, 99
  Penn on, xvi, 2, 16–17, 89–93, 96
  of Quakers, 4, 12, 14–17, 50, 56, 67, 69, 82–85
Religious Society of Friends. See Quakers and Quakerism
religious tolerance. See religious liberty
Restoration England
  immorality in, 45
  literary world of, 193n5
  Puritans in, 46, 201–2n45
  Quakers in, 12, 51, 64, 82–83, 86, 194n18
  wealth of, 7–8, 193–94n9
Rhode Island, 74, 98, 105
Rhodes, John, 122, 189, 215n57
Rigge, Ambrose, 68, 78, 216n7

Rogers, George, 202n10
Rogers, William, 203
Roman Catholics. See Catholics
Royal Society (London), 1, 222n42
Rudyard, Thomas, 69, 208n19
Ryerson, Richard, 197n67

Second Day Morning Meeting of Ministers (MMM)
  Mucklow on, 52, 55
  organizational structure of, 65
  Penn's attendance at, 33, 67, 77–79
  on political engagement, 68
  publication supervision by, 12, 67, 76–78, 113, 133, 135, 166, 204n30
  recording of minutes for, 66
  women rebuked by, 120, 139, 206n46
sermons. See preaching
Sewel, William, 149–50
Sidney, Algernon
  Anglicans cited by, 210n39
  arrest and execution for treason, 3
  Frame of Government and, 99
  maxims of, 214n43
  Mead and, 73, 205n28
  Penn's support of, 3, 15, 57, 170
  religious liberty and, 15, 87
slavery
  justifications for, 2
  Penn and, 3, 171, 176, 194n15
  sermons on, 217n20
  slave trade, 3, 176
  See also antislavery movement
Smith, Samuel, 155
Society of Friends. See Quakers and Quakerism
Soderlund, Jean, 197n61, 219n16
Some Fruits of Solitude in Reflections and Maxims (Penn), 120–29
  audience for, 121, 123
  biblical influences on, 123, 213n40
  on children, 123–25, 214n45
  on Christian love, 128–29
  on education, 123–24, 214n51
  as guidance for ethical life, 28–29, 139
  on marriage, 124–25
  on personal conduct, 126
  political advice in, 126–27
  preface to, 120–22, 129
  on religion, 127–28, 130–31

Index | 235

Some Fruits of Solitude in Reflections and Maxims (Penn)(*continued*)
  revisions to, 33, 106–7
  style and tone of writing, 122
Sowerby, Scott, 25
Sowle, Jane, 135
Sowle, Tace, 213n35, 216n18
Speck, Frank, 220n30
Spencer, Robert, 19, 197n60
Springett, Gulielma. *See* Penn, Gulielma Maria Springett
Springett, William, 13
Stanley, Thomas, 112, 122, 214n45
Sterling, Samuel, 208n19
Stillingfleet, Edward, 13, 96
Stoicism, 47, 90, 110, 117, 121–23, 129, 200n22
Story, Thomas, 51, 53, 56–62, 69, 77, 99, 202n10, 203n27
Stubs, John, 110
Sutcliff, Robert, 152–53, 219n13
Swift, Jonathan, 2, 176, 193n5, 194n13, 199nn5–6
Sydney, Henry, 69, 215n72
synteresis, 90–91, 93, 101

Tamanend (Lenape chief), 221n35
Taylor, Eric, 213n40
Taylor, Jeremy, 93, 96, 122, 210n39
Tillotson, John, 96
Tories, 197n60, 224n1
Travers, Rebecca, 134, 141, 218n44
Trueblood, Benjamin, 161, 222n41
Turner, Robert, 163

Urban, P. Linwood, 142
US Constitution, 170, 222n52

Vaux, Roberts, 158, 170
Villiers, George, 69
Vincent, Thomas, 50
Vining, Elizabeth Gray, 213n32
Voltaire, 155, 156, 159

Waldenfield, Samuel, 134, 139
Waldo, Peter and Waldensians, 118
wampum belts, 155, 158, 169, 220n30
Watson, John, 157, 158
Weems, Parson, 170, 219n11
weeping, 39, 200nn21–22

West, Benjamin: *William Penn's Treaty with the Indians*, xi, 148, 153–60, *154*, 221n37
Westminster Confession, 83
West New Jersey
  dispute mediation in, 57
  justice system in, 18, 21
  religious liberty in, xii, 18, 98, 104, 211n48
Whigs
  Charles II and, 18, 19, 94
  Latitudinarians and, 211n45
  Penn and, 2, 5, 57, 170, 176, 197n60, 224n1
  on religious liberty, 5
Whitehead, George
  business meetings and, 65, 68, 73, 74, 77, 204–5n12
  lack of self-doubt in writings of, 179
  leadership of, 68, 137–38
  opposition to Penn's marriage to Hannah, 178
  in religious debates, 50, 134
  sermons from, 134–35, 139, 140, 216n12, 217n29
  spiritual sensitivity of, 61
Whitehead, John, 84
Wildes, Harry Emerson, xiv
Wilkinson, John, 51, 53, 56–62, 69, 77, 99, 202n10, 203n27
William III (king of England)
  affirmation of loyalty to, 75, 120
  Glorious Revolution and, 5, 26
  military stoicism of, 4
  Penn and, 5–6, 25, 29, 217n25
  political advice for, 126–27
  religious liberty under, 36, 80, 97–98, 104–5
Williams, Roger, 22, 82, 98
Wolseley, Charles, 208n17
women
  age at first marriage, 196n51
  business meetings and, 56–57, 59–62, 203n27, 204n39
  literacy among, 2, 27, 193n8
  misogyny and, 118, 124
  MMM rebuke of, 120, 139, 206n46
  in *No Cross, No Crown*, 111, 112, 117–19
  worship meetings and, 12–13, 101, 194n15, 204n9
Wood, Rebecca, 152, 153, 219n13
Woolman, John, 179

Worminghurst estate, 129, 215n70, 223n58
worship meetings
    by dissidents, 28, 49, 59
    encounters with God in, xv, 20
    hat removal during prayer, 51–56, 62
    Native Americans and, 194n15
    silent meetings, 10–11, 36, 42, 51, 133, 178, 180, 199n8
    spiritual authority and, 50, 52–56
    women and, 12–13, 101, 194n15, 204n9
    See also preaching
Wren, Christopher, 2

Printed in the USA
CPSIA information can be obtained
at www.ICGtesting.com
LVHW092238210924
791583LV00002B/7